MYSTICAL DISCOURSE IN WORDSWORTH AND WHITMAN

A Transatlantic Bridge

Studies in Spirituality Supplements
Edited by Titus Brandsma Institute – Nijmegen – The Netherlands

2. **Franco Imoda**, *Human Development. Psychology and Mystery*, 1998, 397 p., ISBN: 90-429-0028-8.

3. **Marieke van Baest**, *Poetry of Hadewijch*, 1998, VIII-330 p., ISBN: 90-429-0668-7.

4. **Hildegard Elisabeth Keller**, *My Secret is Mine. Studies on Religion and Eros in the German Middle Ages*, 2000, VIII-294 p., ISBN: 90-429-0871-8.

5. **Franco Imoda**, *A Journey to Freedom. An Interdisciplinary Approach to the Anthropology of Formation*, 2000, XIV-482 p., ISBN: 90-429-0894-7.

6. **Albrecht Classen**, *'Mein Seel fang an zu singen'. Religiöse Frauenlieder des 15.-16. Jahrhunderts. Kritische Studien und Textedition*, 2002, 395 p., ISBN: 90-429-1098-4.

7. **Marie L. Baird**, *On the Side of the Angels. Ethics and Post-Holocaust Spirituality*, 2002, 143 p., ISBN: 90-429-1156-5.

8. **Kees Waaijman**, *Spirituality. Forms, Foundations, Methods*, 2002, VIII-968 p., ISBN: 90-429-1183-2.

9. **John D. Green**, *'A Strange Tongue'. Tradition, Language and the Appropriation of Mystical Experiences in the Late Fourteenth-Century England and Sixteenth-Century Spain*, 2002, VII-227 p., ISBN: 90-429-1236-7.

10. **Hein Blommestijn, Charles Caspers and Rijcklof Hofman (Eds.)**, *Spirituality Renewed. Studies on Significant Representatives of the Modern Devotion*, 2003, VI-276 p., ISBN: 90-429-1327-4.

STUDIES IN SPIRITUALITY
Supplement 11

MYSTICAL DISCOURSE IN WORDSWORTH AND WHITMAN

A Transatlantic Bridge

by

D.J. Moores, Ph.D.
Sacred Heart University

PEETERS
LEUVEN - PARIS - DUDLEY, MA
2006

Library of Congress Cataloging-in-Publication Data

Moores, D.J.
Mystical discourse in Wordsworth and Whitman : a transatlantic bridge : D.J. Moores.
p. cm. -- (Studies in spirituality. Supplements ; 11)
Includes bibliographical references.
ISBN 90-429-1809-8 (alk. paper)
1. Wordsworth, William, 1770-1850--Criticism and interpretation. 2. Whitman, Walt, 1819-1892--Criticism and interpretation. 3. Mysticism in literature. 4. Romanticism. I. Title. II. Series: Studies in spirituality. Supplements ; 11.

PR5892.M95M66 2006
821'.7--dc22

2006045797

ISBN-10 90-429-1809-8
ISBN-13 9789042918092
D. 2006/0602/97

This book is dedicated to
Jean and Jim Lindsay
and Johnna

With special thanks to
RB Reaves, Celest Martin, William Bartels, George Willis
Dorothy Donneley, Sandra Mejia, Marla Kozensky, Jack Heitner

CONTENTS

PREFACE

This study contributes to the many transatlantic connections scholars are now drawing between the English and American literary traditions. *Mystical Discourse* specifically contributes to the few but growing connections scholars are now discerning between Wordsworth and Whitman. I believe one reason scholars have discerned such connections is that both poets privileged a marginalized way of knowing which they expressed through a type of mystical language I call the 'cosmic' mode. This alternative way of knowing entails the merging of self and other, a living cosmos endowed with consciousness, a monistic ontology, love as a higher alternative to normal rational awareness, the privileging of sound and silence over traditional linguistic utterance, a poetics of prophesy, and an anti-religion.

To combat Enlightenment modes of ideation, Wordsworth and Whitman employed cosmic language as a weapon of ideological resistance, for it is highly subversive in several ways. First, such language collapses the foundation of Western thought – the subject/object dichotomy – without which there can be no dualism (Chapter 2). Second, it causes a radical orientation towards nature that overcomes what Heidegger called 'Gestell', the technological attitude, in which nature is subjugated for the use of humankind (Chapter 5). Third, it bridges the Cartesian schism, the separation of mind and matter (Chapters 3 & 5). Fourth, it democratizes the objects of the material world, including all of its human inhabitants (Chapters 3 & 8). Fifth, it forcefully challenges the rationalist paradigm in its privileging of childlike wonder and love as a more viable way of knowing than ratiocination (Chapters 6 & 9). Sixth, because it leads to subjectivity, it constitutes the first attack on the cherished, Western notion of objective truth (Chapter 6). Seventh, it calls into question the primacy of language, often requiring 'anti-language' for expression (Chapter 7). Eighth, it leads to a godlike persona and a quasi-religion, both of which challenge religious orthodox structures (Chapter 10). Last, cosmic rhetoric radicalizes the poetic medium itself in its call for the transformation of the reader's consciousness (Chapter 8).

To view mystical discourse in both poets as a form of ideological resistance compellingly refutes the oft-leveled condemnation of Romanticism as a visionary mode that estranges the poet from legitimate human concerns. Because mysticism is reason's repressed other, the utilization of cosmic rhetoric is a form of rebellion, an insurrection of a subjugated way of knowing that upsets what Foucault has called the 'totalitarian hierarchy of knowledges' in the West. This insurrection is an intimately human concern, but its praxis is consciousness change, not direct sociopolitical involvement. Wordsworth and Whitman embrace the cosmic mode as a challenge to the strictures of Enlightenment doctrines. Wordsworth uttered the war cry for this rebellion, and Whitman heeded the call to adventure, taking it to an even higher level.

CHAPTER I

A WORD ON METHOD

Marjorie Garber argues that political criticism has become passé. In her work *Academic Instincts* she demonstrates that many recent critics are calling for a return to a critique of the aesthetic. 'Almost everyone wants to talk about it: a concern with aesthetics and ethics; the reappearance of certain notions of "value" and "values" on the literary scene, has preempted the stage, moving critical attention away from the previous decade's concern with politics and cultural identity'. Garber also argues that such a turn of the wheel is quite natural, having been 'repeated in every literary-scholarly generation'.[1]

My study of Wordsworth and Whitman rides on the crest of this new wave. Although I find much of value in deconstruction (and even more in the work of Derrida himself), I have resisted the impulse to embrace it as a methodology because deconstruction is an inappropriate tool for reading the lyric. Steven Mack in his excellent dissertation, *Walt Whitman and the Struggle for a Pragmatic Vision of Spiritual Democracy*, says he finds more value in reconstructing Whitman's vision than he does in deconstructing it: 'To search for just the right thread to pull to unravel a poet who rejoices in his own contradictions strikes me as both pointless and a bit too easy'.[2] Joel Kenneth Jackson similarly attempts to restore Wordsworth's mystifications in his dissertation.[3] Both poets are full of contradictions and opposing ideological forces. Don Bialostosky argues that deconstruction is, in fact, one more construction, and does violence to Romantic poetry. 'Deconstruction rests on an error from which we can and should preserve ourselves'.[4]

---

[1] Marjorie Garber, *Academic instincts*, Princeton: Princeton University Press, 2001, 48.

[2] Stephen John Mack, *Walt Whitman and the struggle for a pragmatic vision of spiritual democracy* (Diss. University of Southern California, Los Angeles, California, 1997), 4.

[3] Joe Kenneth Jackson, *Wonder and defamiliarization in Wordsworth* (Diss. Syracuse University, New York, 1978), x.

[4] Don Bialostosky, *Wordsworth, dialogics, and the practice of criticism*, New York: Cambridge University Press, 1992, 154.

I should stress that in dismissing deconstruction I am by no means condemning it as a philosophy but rather the ways in which certain literary theorists have employed it as a methodology for *de*structive purposes, that is, to advance a political agenda in the name of exposing a given writer's complicity with hegemonic forces. Derrida was the alpha philosopher – the dominant thinker of our age, and it will take us many years to assess his impact on a variety of disciplines. Yet, it seems impossible that deconstruction's 'textual harassment',[5] as Peter Barry calls it, can do anything for the poetry of Wordsworth and Whitman but force a false confession made under the duress of an admittedly highly sophisticated methodology.

The other dominant modes of critical theory – neo-Marxism, cultural materialism, and Foucauldian-inspired new historicism are just as hostile to Romanticism. Jerome McGann, for instance, has argued that the lyric itself is 'an expression of the false consciousness of romantic ideology'.[6] Such a view, while interesting from a socioeconomic perspective, reduces the immense power of Romantic poetry to the deceived belief that class-based interests are not socially constructed but natural and universal. Lance Massey argues that such Marxist criticism, as well as poststructuralist theory, seeks if not to dethrone literature to demystify it. He also points out that such demystification on either logocentric or linguistic grounds or on the basis of cultural materialism 'sacrifices the capability to find out how literature does carry meaning – presence – or at least offers the illusion of doing so'.[7] Bialostosky similarly condemns the work of Clifford Siskin, whose iconoclastic historicizing of Wordsworth levels all concerns to 'social inequality' and produces 'an effect of alienation that demoralizes our professional identities without reconstituting them'.[8]

One of the latest trends in literary theory, Bahktinian dialogics, is also inimical to the Romantic lyric. According to Bahktin, all poetry is inadequate to writing towards truth 'because the process closes itself off to the palimpsest of the external; it denies history and its heteroglossic superfluity of meaning'.[9] The poetic process, Bahktin also wrote, 'is defined by a willful and permanent forgetting, an active refusal to allow the whole to be seen, and that part of the whole which is lost is the interaction of the world and the object over time, which has produced layers of supplementary or contradictory meaning'. For

---

[5] Peter Barry, *Beginning theory*, New York: Manchester University Press, 1995, 72.

[6] Qtd. in Onno Dag Oerlemans, *The dynamics of lyric and narrative in the poetry of Wordsworth and Whitman* (Diss. Yale University, New Haven, Connecticut, 1992), 23.

[7] Lance Massey, 'Tintern Abbey's "Tranquil Restoration": Toward a methodology of healing in an age of anxiety', in: *Publications of the Missouri Philological Association* 21 (1996), 45.

[8] Bialostosky, *Wordsworth, dialogics, and the practice of criticism*, 6.

[9] Qtd. in Oerlemans, *The dynamics of lyric and narrative in the poetry of Wordsworth and Whitman*, 18.

Bahktin, as for critics such as Alan Liu, prose is the ideal genre for the application of dialogics because the lyric is 'in the flight from history and the real'.[10] What this means of course is that such theorists are incapable of adequately reading poetry – a mode of knowing that resists the reductive and leveling influence of Marxist and Marx-inspired theories.

The influential feminist critic Elaine Showalter has decried the inability of much modern theory to yield satisfying interpretive results. She argues that the reigning critical schools are one more example of male demonstrations of dominance:

> The new sciences of the text based on linguistics, computers, genetic structuralism, deconstructionism, neo-formalism and deformalism, affective stylistics and psychoaesthetics have offered literary critics the opportunity to demonstrate that the work they do is as manly and aggressive as nuclear physics – not intuitive, expressive and feminine, but strenuous, rigorous, impersonal and virile [...] Literary science, in its manic generation of difficult terminology, its establishment of seminars and institutes of post-graduate study, creates an elite corps of specialists who spend more and more time mastering the theory, less and less time reading the books. We are moving towards a two-tiered system of 'higher' and 'lower' criticism, the higher concerned with the 'scientific' problems of form and structure, the lower concerned with the 'humanistic' problems of content and interpretation.[11]

While I agree almost in full with Showalter's condemnation of such aggressive literary theory, I disagree that it is necessarily 'manly', since there is a considerable number of feminist critics who embrace such theories. Her point is well taken, however, for it seems almost contradictory to read a genre as expressive and intuitive as the Romantic lyric through a rigorous, strenuous, 'scientific' lens.

Hélène Cixous argues that much modern critical theory proceeds from the wrong starting point, from a place of anger rather than reverence:

> Everything begins with love. If we work on a text we don't love, we are automatically at the wrong distance. This happens in many institutions where, in general, one works on a text as if it were an object, using theoretical instruments. It's perfectly possible to make a machine out of the text, to treat it like a machine and be treated by it like a machine. The contemporary tendency has been to find theoretical instruments, a reading technique which has bridled the text, mastered it like a wild horse with saddle and bridle, enslaving it. I am wary of formalist approaches, those which cut up structure, which impose their systematic grid.[12]

---

[10] Qtd. in idem, 110.

[11] Elaine Showalter, 'Towards a feminist poetics' (1979), in: K.M. Newton (Ed.), *Twentieth-century literary theory*, New York: St. Martin's, 1997, 218.

[12] Helene Cixous, 'Conversations (1988)', in: Newton, *Twentieth-century literary theory*, 227.

Cixous goes on to argue that the relationship between critic and text is similar to 'the work of love that can take place between two human beings'. 'To understand the other', she argues, 'it is necessary to go in their language, to make the journey through the other's imaginary'.[13] Much modern theory, however, is unable to enter into the language of a given writer, forcing a translation of the writer's language into that of the methodological apparatus. The critical theorist understands the writer, then, on his own terms, not on the writer's, which of course is a misreading.

I do not dispute that much of the theory I am dismissing is remarkably sophisticated, subtle, and potentially valuable in literary studies. What I am arguing against is the subordination of literature to theory and the hubris of theorists who look down upon literature. Most of the current theories came into vogue in the 1990s – a decade in which several critics proudly declared the 'primacy of theory'. This proclamation led to the breeding of scholars who seem to have lost the sensibility to appreciate fine writing. Their anger over sociopolitical issues has led to the creation of an atmosphere of disenchantment and disillusionment in the discipline. As John Heitner has argued, 'a renewal of the senses of wonder and mystery may be the most healthful of tonics for the contemporary critic'.[14]

I am also arguing against the frequent inability of contemporary theory to yield readings that do justice to the writers we esteem, particularly as it relates to the matter of spirituality – a concern near and dear to such writers but deemed irrelevant by the reigning critical schools. The project of demystification has led to an exclusive focus on race, gender, class, and sexual orientation, as if there are no other legitimate concerns for the literary scholar. I believe religious belief/spiritual orientation should be added to the list of primary concerns for contemporary theory. And the trend seems to be moving in this direction, for there is a 'relatively new and continuing effort in and beyond the academy to deal in a more rigorous fashion with the intersections of what is called – often quite vaguely – religion and the arts'.[15] In his essay 'The Need for a Religious Literary Criticism' Dennis Taylor argues for the need for ways of discussing religious or spiritual dimensions in works of literature:

> We live in an age of critical discourses that are expert in discussing the dimensions of class, gender, textuality, and historical context. Yet an important part of the literature we read goes untouched by her discourses, or it is deconstructed, historicized, sexualized, or made symptomatic of covert power relationships. The

---

[13] Cixous, 'Conversations', 226.

[14] John Heitner, *At the edge of consciousness*, Edina, MN: Alpha, 1986, 107.

[15] John Mahoney, 'Critical methodology and writing about religion and literature', in: *Religion and the Arts* 1 (1997) no.4, 90.

> negative hermeneutic of such reductive discourse has been thorough and successful [...] The need for a religious literary criticism not only is reflective of a current scholarly void, but also comes out of a spiritual hunger, felt by many teachers and students, for a way of discussing the intersections of their own spiritual lives with what they read.[16]

Taylor does not simplistically argue for a return to the hegemonic standard of previous religious critical discourse, and he acknowledges that the old terms such as 'transcendental', 'spiritual', 'divine', 'numinous', and 'mystical' are coded words with little content.[17] He argues that 'for an adequate reading of the religious dimensions of literary texts, we need languages that are critical and passionate, ecumenical and committed, detached and catholic. Such a language needs to enter into productive dialogue with our reigning discourses. It needs to appeal not only to the converted, but also to those with no pronounced commitments...'.[18]

This study of Wordsworth and Whitman is a specific response to Taylor's call for a new discourse of spirituality in literary studies. Throughout, I will engage many current critical concepts but without subordinating the 'spiritual' component in Romantic poetics. To dismiss this element in Wordsworth and Whitman and privilege a theoretical perspective is to ignore a central aspect of the work of quite possibly the two greatest Romantics. I will thus attempt to be as 'ecumenical' as possible, and I will engage the reigning theoretical perspectives to a considerable extent.

I am leery of any type of theory that subordinates and/or subjugates the text. To be sure, no work of literary criticism is free from methodology. Critics who say they do not embrace a methodology are merely saying they are not consciously aware of the methodology they are employing. All reading involves some type of interpretive strategy, whether conscious or unconscious. My 'method', therefore, will be something on the order of the 'Rasa' theory of Indian poetics, which seeks to identify the dominant tone – which in the case of Wordsworth and Whitman is mystical – in a given poet and to accept contradictory tones and not to impose on a text any arbitrary sense of unity. V.K. Chari's essay 'Whitman Criticism in the Light of Indian Poetics' is a good example of the application of Rasa, which, he says, 'conceives of the end of poetry not as the mere conveying of ideas or knowledge for its information value but as the presentation or evocation of emotions, such as erotic love, heroic enthusiasm, pathos, wonder, comic laughter, fear, disgust, serenity [...] and a host of other,

---

[16] Dennis Taylor, 'The need for a religious literary criticism', in: John L. Mahoney (Ed.), *Seeing into the life of things*, New York: Fordham University Press, 1998, 3.

[17] Taylor, 'The need for a religious literary criticism', 21.

[18] Idem, 27.

minor emotions…'.[19] The 'Rasa' tradition, according to Medhusudan Pati in her essay 'Wordsworth: An Indian View', 'offers a most congenial, hospitable environment for the romantic impulse'.[20]

Rasa directly contradicts Bahktinian dialogics, which says there is no dominant voice in a text, that all texts are polyvocal in being informed by multiple voices. In Rasa a poem is seen 'as an orchestration of several feeling tones, in which a major emotional theme develops into a dominant tone by subordinating various minor feelings, which become dissolved into a dominant impression. Aesthetic unity is achieved through the tension of diverse impulses'.[21] Rasa also deals with the unity/indeterminacy issue in a different way than deconstruction does; whereas deconstruction is concerned primarily with ideological (intellectual) fissures, Indian poetics attempts to account for *emotion* in a way that takes for granted that conflicting impulses are the bedrock of human feelings. Whereas deconstructors feel their purpose is vindicated when they expose 'aporias', Rasa critics are not overly concerned with such ideological matters. What counts for them is the heart, which is, incidentally, the vehicle of romantic poetry and of Wordsworth and Whitman's verse specifically, as the authors of *Start with the Sun* have observed.[22]

Let us turn, then, to a study of two of the most highly contradictory poets in the Romantic tradition with the idea of discerning several deep connections between them. My goal in the next chapter is to account for the reasons why some scholars have discerned a transatlantic bridge and to put forth my own particular thoughts on the issue.

---

[19] V.K. Chari, 'Whitman criticism in the light of Indian poetics', in: Ed Folsom (Ed.), *Walt Whitman: The Centennial essays*, Iowa City: University of Iowa Press, 1994, 241.

[20] Medhusudan Pati, 'Wordsworth: An Indian view', in: Visvanath Chatterjee (Ed.), *The Romantic tradition*, Calcutta: Jadavpur University Press, 1984, 64.

[21] Chari, 'Whitman criticism in the light of Indian poetics', 241.

[22] James E. Miller, Karl Shapiro, & Bernice Slote, *Start with the Sun: Studies in the Whitman tradition*, Lincoln, NE: University Press of Nebraska, 1960, 45.

CHAPTER II

THE TRANSATLANTIC BRIDGE[1]

'I will relate the story of Michael for the delight of a few natural hearts, for the sake of youthful poets, who among these hills will be my second self when I am gone'
(Wordsworth)

I

Despite that Wordsworth and Whitman are the two principal Romantics in the Anglo-American tradition, there have been surprisingly few comparative studies done on the two figures. To date there are only seven full-length comparative studies on them, all of which are unpublished doctoral dissertations. There are no full-length, published, comparative works on the two poets. Yet there are about a dozen article-length essays on them, as well as many passing comments made by either Wordsworthian or Whitmanian critics that connect these writers.

Part of the reason for this scholarly neglect is the Emersonian influence on Whitman, which is often attention-diverting and causes critics to interpret the American bard (quite reasonably so) strictly in terms of his major influence. It is also probable, however, that Whitman himself is partly responsible, as he was notorious for disavowing the impact other writers had on his verse. He denied, for instance, having read Emerson prior to the 1855 publication of *Leaves of Grass*, despite having written a review of one of Emerson's essays as early as 1842.[2] Whitman claimed he did not like Wordsworth because he 'lacks sympathy with men and women – that does not pervade him enough by a long shot'. He is also quoted as condemning the whole Lake School for beginning 'with the

[1] This chapter was previously published as '"That serene and blessed mood": Mystical discourse in Wordsworth and Whitman', in: *Studies in Spirituality* 14 (2004), 285-302.

[2] Jerome Loving, *Walt Whitman: The song of himself*, Los Angeles: University Press of California, 1999, 157.

rights of man' but then coming out 'for kingcraft, priestcraft, obedience…'.[3] Despite this supposed rejection of Wordsworth, Floyd Stoval argues that Whitman, in fact, did admire his English predecessor, citing the poet's 1846 review which placed Longfellow on the same platform with Bryant and Wordsworth. 'Considering that he rated Bryant as one of the best poets in the world', wrote Stoval, 'this is high praise for Wordsworth'.[4] Stoval concludes that 'in developing his literary method Whitman was undoubtedly influenced by his reading of the great romantic writers of his time' – Wordsworth and Coleridge among others.[5] Similarly, Walter Malone observes that Whitman made frequent use of the British magazines that were in circulation in his day – particularly the North British Review, the Edinburg Review, Blackwood's Edinburg Magazine, and the Westminster Review.[6] It is in all probability safe to assume that Whitman knew more of Wordsworth than he acknowledged. Despite Whitman's ruse, there are critics, albeit a small number, who have recognized a connection between the two poets. Let me take a few pages to survey this field of study.

Mark Delancey argues that Whitman demonstrates a 'Wordsworthian rhetoric of unity in coupling subject and object' – a rhetorical gesture in which 'different things become one thing, which speaks through them to identify each with all'.[7] Delancey also sees the conjoining of body and soul in Whitman as suggestive of the Wordsworthian relation between the 'celestial light' and 'the light of common day', as they are connected in the 'Intimations' ode.[8] Similarly, Robert Weisbuch states that the consensus from Matthiessen to the present is that 'Whitman's poetic of 1855 echoes Wordsworth's of 1800 in terms of […] their deep sense of the interpenetration of human thoughts and apparently inanimate objects'.[9]

Albert Cook believes what connects Wordsworth and Whitman is the subversion of the literary goal of 'point', which he describes as a predominant goal of 18th-century poetic style. 'Point' is a quality in speech or writing that arrests attention – a pungent, witty, or ingenious turn of thought well suited to epigram

---

[3] Qtd. in Richard Gravil, '"The Discharged Soldier" and the "Runaway Slave": Wordsworth and the definition of Walt Whitman', in: *Symbiosis* 1 (1997) no.1, 51.

[4] Floyd Stoval, *The foreground of Leaves of Grass*, Charlottesville: University Press of Virginia, 1974, 207.

[5] Stoval, *The foreground of Leaves of Grass*, 192.

[6] Walter Karl Malone, *Parallels to Hindu and Taoist thought in Walt Whitman* (Diss. Temple University, Philadelphia, Pennsylvania, 1964), 16.

[7] Mark Delancey, 'Texts, interpretations, and Whitman's "Song of Myself"', in: *American Literature* 61 (1989) no.3, 367.

[8] Delancey, 'Texts, interpretations, and Whitman's "Song of Myself"', 365.

[9] Robert Weisbuch, *Atlantic double-cross: American literature and British influence in the age of Emerson*, Chicago: University of Chicago Press, 1986, 179.

in that it invites a sense of completion or closure in being a parsimonious stylistic goal.[10] Wordsworth and Whitman frequently employ the opposite of point – amplitude – according to Cook, which accounts for the expansiveness, the open-ended, and the flowing qualities in their verse.

Richard Gravil believes Whitman read and was profoundly influenced by *The Prelude*, which was published in 1850 on Wordsworth's death – five years before the first publication of *Leaves*. He concedes that 'there is no textual evidence that "Song of Myself" answers *The Prelude*', but he believes 'very strongly' that it does. He goes as far as to say that 'Song of Myself' is the 'fulfillment' of Wordsworth's autobiographical epic in that it is filled with 'echoes and intensifications of *The Prelude*'.[11] Jennifer Kidney also argues that Whitman attempted to write his own version of *The Prelude* – 'an autobiographical poem with epic scope, which takes the form of a *nostos*, a return home, both physical and spiritual' (in abstract). She claims this nostalgia informs their attitudes towards language in that it is responsible for the attempts in both poets to 'attain a more primitive, pure, childlike language'.[12] And like Gravil, she concedes that the relationship between the two poets is one that may be assumed on the basis of historical facts, 'but it is not a biographically explicit relationship'.[13]

In his forceful challenge to Derrida, Daniel Kiefer links Wordsworth and Whitman in their appeal to 'immortal voice as protection against the mortality of physical sensation'. Kiefer says both poets are preoccupied with loss and the recapturing of childhood joy; both insist on an inward search; both displayed immense confidence in their own calling, a highly original style, and the desire to construct a long poem on the subject of the self.[15] 'Wordsworth's poetic project', he concludes, 'in retracing the mind's development, pointing to a prophetic grandeur, and yet returning to the common time, seems very like Whitman's'.[16] Like Kiefer, Erma Kelly sees a link between Wordsworth and Whitman in their view of childhood, 'especially the view of the child destined to become a poet'.[17] She argues, however, that both poets do not merely condemn 18th- and early

[10] Albert Cook, 'The transformation of "point": Amplitude in Wordsworth, Whitman, and Rimbaud', in: *Studies in Romanticism* 30 (1991) no.2, 171.

[11] Gravil, '"The Discharged Soldier" and the "Runaway Slave"', 51 & 66.

[12] Jennifer Kidney, *An American prelude: Nostalgia and the sense of death in American poetry* (Diss. Yale, New Haven, Connecticut, 1974), 9.

[13] Kidney, *An American prelude*, 79.

[14] Daniel Reynard Kiefer, *Figurations of poetic voice in Whitman and Wordsworth* (Diss. Yale University, New Haven, Connecticut, 1985), 13.

[15] Kiefer, *Figurations of poetic voice in Whitman and Wordsworth*, 13.

[16] Idem, 14.

[17] Erma Kelly, 'Whitman and Wordsworth: Childhood experiences and the future poet', in: *Walt Whitman Review* 23 (1977), 60.

19th-century views of the child as being not fully developed mentally and therefore of only limited interest; rather, they elevate the child 'to the status of a teacher because he is capable of insights that elude most grown men'.[18] The most important truth a child can possess 'is an intuitive grasp of the unity of the universe. This is the key insight that both poets strive to express, and an intuitive grasp of this insight makes the child a potential poet'.[19]

Onno Dag Oerlemans sees in Wordsworth and Whitman, despite a 'palpable ideological distinction between the two', a common bond 'in their lyricism in its anti-ideological force, its ability to convey knowing beyond ideology'.[20] Arguing against a historicist reading of either poet, Oerlemans believes the lyric is actually a transhistorical category of knowing better thought of as a form of 'unknowing' – a point that will take on special significance as my discussion progresses. Lawrence Kramer's comparative work on Wordsworth and Whitman yokes the two in terms of the 'recurrent representation of the mind as troubled or uneasy in the presence of an ocean or water'.[21] Kramer sees the pattern in both writers of the self forced to be emptied in the presence of something vast and sublime. The self submitting to such an enormous visionary presence, however, does so 'at the cost of pressing the mind to the brink of nonexistence'.[22] The typical romantic response, according to Kramer, is not submission but trope-making, which reasserts the self but in the process destroys the sublime moment. Harry Wilson in essence reinforces Kramer's thesis in that he reveals the ways in which 'nature determines that special analogy between speaker and object, which, in a sense, makes the speaker's response possible' (in abstract). Most of the major Romantics, he argues, project inner psychological and emotional states onto nature. Unlike Kramer, however, Wilson claims that such projection is not determined strictly by crisis or mental disorder, recurring as it does not only in moments of despair but also in those of peace.[23]

Robert Weisbuch in his excellent work *Atlantic Double-Cross* reads Whitman's 'Song of Myself' in terms of *The Prelude*, that is, as an epic-like poem merged with spiritual autobiography in which the poetic self plays the role of hero.[24] Barbara Herman also argues that both poets incorporate elements from both the epic

---

[18] Kelly, 'Whitman and Wordsworth', 62.

[19] Ibidem.

[20] Oerlemans, *The dynamics of lyric and narrative in the poetry of Wordsworth and Whitman*, vii.

[21] Lawrence Kramer, 'Ocean and vision: Imaginative dilemma in Wordsworth, Whitman, and Stevens', in: *Journal of English and Germanic Philology* 79 (1980), 210.

[22] Kramer, 'Ocean and vision', 211.

[23] Harry Wilson, *Psychological projection in six Romantic poems* (Diss. University of California, Davis, CA 1976), xi.

[24] Weisbuch, *Atlantic double-cross*, 178.

and prophetic traditions.[25] Herman claims both poets focus on spiritual and social concerns simultaneously, and that ultimately what each writes about most is the act of writing itself.[26] Justin Kaplan, one of Whitman's many biographers, similarly believed Whitman was the inheritor of the Wordsworthian/Romantic notion of the poet as the 'agency of a transcendent power' who 'created rapt verse in 'ecstasy of statement'.[27] According to Kaplan, Whitman's 1855 'Preface' was in the Wordsworthian tradition, but he also points out that it could never have been written on Wordsworth's side of the Atlantic.[28]

In this excellent body of scholarship on Wordsworth and Whitman what I perceive is the mystical rhetoric found so pervasively in the work of both poets. A glance at key phrases in the forgoing arguments bears out my assertion: 'coupling of subject and object', 'the interpenetration of thought and inanimate objects', 'physical and spiritual return home', 'immortal voice', 'prophetic grandeur', 'intuitive grasp of the unity of the universe', 'unknowing', 'spiritual autobiography', 'knowing beyond ideology', 'different things becoming one', 'expansion and amplitude', 'child consciousness', 'inward search', 'self-dissolution', and so on. All of these ideas are found pervasively in mystical discourse. A representative passage from each poet will also bolster my argument:

Wordsworth:

> [...] I at this time
> Saw blessings spread around me like a sea.
> Thus did my days pass on, and now at length
> From Nature and her overflowing soul
> I had received so much that all my thoughts
> Were steeped in feeling. I was only then
> Contented when with bliss ineffable
> I felt the sentiment of being spread
> O'er all that moves, and all that seemeth still... (1805 *Prelude* II. 413-421)

Whitman:

> A vast similitude interlocks all,
> All spheres, grown, ungrown, small, large, suns, moons, planets,
> All distances of place however wide,
> All distances of time, all inanimate forms,

---

[25] Barbara Herman, *The pleasure of heaven, pains of hell, intimations of immortality: Remembrance, repression, and reconciliation in Wordsworth and Whitman* (Diss. Texas Christian University, Fort Worth, Texas, 1991), 22.

[26] Herman, *The pleasure of heaven, pains of hell, intimations of immortality*, 15.

[27] Justin Kaplan, *Walt Whitman: A life*, New York: Simon & Schuster, 1980, 189.

[28] Kaplan, *Walt Whitman*, 189.

> All souls, all living bodies know they be ever so different, or in different worlds,
> All gaseous, watery, vegetable, mineral processes, the fishes, the brutes,
> All nations, colors, barbarisms, civilizations, languages,
> All identities that have existed or may exist on the school, or any globe,
> All lives and deaths, all of the past, present, future,
> This vast similitude spans them, and always has spann'd,
> And shall forever span them and compactly hold and enclose them. ('On the Beach at Night Alone' 4-14)

This 'sentiment of being over all that moves', this sense of all things encompassed by a 'vast similitude' pervades the verse of both poets; it informs not only their ontology and epistemology but also their ideas on self, nature, language, poetics, and religion. What I would like to suggest in particular is that the type of mysticism found in both Wordsworth and Whitman resists classification; there is a certain measure of indeterminacy in it that prevents one from calling it Taoist, Zen, Sufi, Native American, or shamanic without also being unable to account for certain elements in such a reading.

There is indeed mystical rhetoric in Wordsworth and Whitman, but I believe too many critics too enthusiastically read these poets as though they were mystics themselves, which is patently not the case. Evelyn Underhill, the premier scholar of mysticism in the 20th century, believed Wordsworth and Whitman were 'acquainted, beyond most poets and seers, with the phenomena of the illuminated life', but she also believed they were 'amongst those who cannot be called pure mystics'.[29] In her essay 'Wordsworth: An Indian View' Medhusudan Pati claims, citing the Indian mystic Aurobindo, that Wordsworth's 'mystical' experiences are incomplete, which is to say, they do not conform to traditional definitions of mysticism.[30] I believe the same is true of Whitman.

R.A. Gilbert argues that 'it does not follow that the ecstasy or exaltation expressed by a poet is necessarily a mystical experience'.[31] Gilbert claims it is necessary to take into account 'expressed or known beliefs and the lives of the poets concerned' when bestowing the title of 'mystic' on a writer.[32] No one to my knowledge has provided any kind of definitive proof that Whitman had experiences approaching those of the mystics, as Gay Wilson Allen has argued.[33] Malcolm Cowley, citing Richard Maurice Bucke, claims that Whitman's 'notebooks and manuscripts of the early 1850s are full of sidelong references to such an

---

[29] Evelyn Underhill, *Mysticism: The nature and development of spiritual consciousness*, Oxford: Oneworld, 1994 (orig. publ. 1911), 238.

[30] Pati, 'Wordsworth: An Indian view', 70.

[31] R.A. Gilbert, *The elements of mysticism*, Rockport, MA: Element, 1991, 53.

[32] Gilbert, *The elements of mysticism*, 53.

[33] Gay Wilson Allen, *The solitary singer: A critical biography of Walt Whitman*, Chicago: University of Chicago Press, 1955, 17-18.

experience, and they suggest that it was essentially the same as the illuminations or ecstasies of earlier bards and prophets'.[34] It seems fair to say, however, that if Whitman indeed had such an experience of mystical rapture there would have been more than *sidelong* references in his notebooks. What his (and Wordsworth's) prose writings reveal are experiences and states of consciousness *like* those we see in various types of mysticism but not quite measuring up to the standard. The difference is between simile and metaphor. The employment of mystical rhetoric by a writer, therefore, does not make one a mystic, but it does make one *like* a mystic.

To label Wordsworth and Whitman as actual mystics is to take the metaphor literally; in the process such a reading fails to recognize their 'literary' qualities. John Hobbs's essay 'Theodore Roethke: The Poet As Mystic' and John Holmes's dissertation 'William Blake's Place in the Mystical Tradition' are two examples of overzealously reading a poet as an actual mystic. More sophisticated is Shira Wolosky's essay, 'The Metaphysics of Language in Emily Dickinson', which places Dickinson's poems in the 'tradition of mystical discourse' but in a way that does not overlook the linguistic element.[35] In his 1815 'Preface' Wordsworth himself warned against 'people who read from religious or moral inclinations', because they are often 'beset with misconceptions and mistakes'. 'No lovers of the arts', he added, 'have gone further astray than the highest and the devout, the religious'.[36]

I do acknowledge the impossibility of distinguishing between mystical experience and the representation of it in words, as Kerry McSweeney argues.[37] All mysticism is literary mysticism, since all we have left of any mystical experience is the representation of it in words. My point is that to treat either Wordsworth or Whitman as a traditional mystic is to overlook their poetic achievement, which is a mistreatment of arguably the two greatest Romantic poets. As Donald Childs argues in his discussion of T.S. Eliot's mysticism, 'the question that must concern literary critics dealing with the mystical elements of a poet is, to what extent does the writer's interest in mysticism have an impact on his poetic style?'.[38]

---

[34] Malcolm Cowley, 'Introduction', in: idem (Ed.), *Leaves of Grass: The first (1855) edition*, New York: Viking, 1959, xii.

[35] Shira Wolosky, 'The metaphysics of language in Emily Dickinson', in: Philip Leonard (Ed.), *Trajectories of mysticism in theory and literature*, London: Macmillan, 2000, 25.

[36] William Wordsworth, *The Prelude: 1799, 1805, 1850* (Ed. Jonathan Wordsworth, M.H. Abrams, & Stephen Gill), New York 1979, 480 & 481. (All subsequent citations, unless noted, are from the 1805 text).

[37] Kerry McSweeney, *The language of the senses: Sensory-perceptual dynamics in Wordsworth, Coleridge, Thoreau, Whitman, and Dickinson*, Buffalo: McGill-Queen's University Press, 1998, 39.

[38] Donald Childs, 'T.S. Eliot: From varieties of mysticism to pragmatic poesis', in: *Mosaic* 22 (1989) no.4, 100.

In 'Wordsworth's Panentheism' Daniel Dombrowski argues that in discussing the spiritual component of the poet's verse it is important 'to avoid egregious errors in categorization and to affix labels without dogmatism so that the texts themselves can breathe', which is precisely why I am avoiding the term mystic.[39] Dombrowski claims the term 'panentheism' gets us closer to Wordsworth's thoughts on God, as he was neither a pantheist nor a classical theist. I agree with the general thrust of this argument, particularly considering that Evelyn Underhill's definition of mystical perception as 'the dual apprehension of the transcendent yet immanent God' is in accord with Dombrowski's definition of panentheism.[40] David Keubrich, however, argues that theism can affirm both God's immanent presence in history and his transcendence.[41] Keubrich also claims it is wrong to state that Christian mysticism denies the senses and the natural world.[42]

Because of such confusion, the type of mysticism found in Wordsworth and Whitman I would like to term 'cosmic' – a word designating a continuum of consciousness spanning both the experience of oneness and total unity with all nature and transcendent experiences and yearnings typically associated with Western mysticism. The cosmic will mean both natural and spiritual mysticism; it will include consciousness of this world and of the 'other'. Wordsworth and Whitman were neither pure transcendentalists nor pure pantheists and should be read as such. The word cosmic, I hope, will also capture the indeterminacy of the type of mysticism we see in both poets. The cosmic is neither Eastern nor Western, nor is it Christian or pagan, collapsing as it does the rigid boundaries separating various types of mystico-religious thinking. As such, I will situate my study between two critical poles – between those who debunk the 'religion' of Romanticism and those who too enthusiastically embrace Romanticism as a religion or who read Wordsworth and Whitman as actual mystics. In 'Poetics of Prophecy' Geoffrey Hartman ends his discussion with what he calls 'a hermeneutic that seeks to transcend the dichotomizing of religious and nonreligious modes'.[43] It is inappropriate to call either writer secular or religious, since the truth of mysticism in Wordsworth and Whitman lies somewhere in the middle.

The use of cosmic rhetoric by both poets leads to the merging of self and other, a living cosmos endowed with consciousness, a monistic ontology, love as a higher alternative to normal rational awareness, the privileging of sound and

---

[39] Daniel Dombrowski, 'Wordsworth's panentheism', in: *The Wordsworth Circle* 16 (1985) no.3, 140.

[40] Underhill, *Mysticism*, 246.

[41] David Keubrich, 'Whitman's new theism', in: *ESQ* 24 (1978), 230.

[42] Keubrich, 'Whitman's new theism', 232.

[43] Geoffrey Hartman, 'The poetics of prophesy', in: Lawrence Lipking (Ed.), *High romantic argument: Essays for M.H. Abrams*, Ithaca: Cornell University Press, 1981, 37.

silence over traditional linguistic utterance, a poetics of prophesy, and a subversion of orthodox religion – each of which will constitute a chapter in this study. Although cosmic rhetoric is in part rooted in the Romantic *Zeitgeist*, Wordsworth and Whitman transmuted it by employing it as a weapon of ideological resistance, for it is highly subversive in several ways. First, it collapses the foundation of Western thought – the subject/object dichotomy – without which there can be no dualism. Second, it causes a radical orientation towards nature that overcomes what Heidegger called 'Gestell', the technological attitude, in which nature is subjugated for the use of human kind. Third, it bridges the great Cartesian schism, the separation of mind and matter. Fourth, it democratizes the objects of the material world, including all of its human inhabitants. Fifth, it forcefully challenges the rationalist paradigm in its privileging of childlike wonder and love as a more viable way of knowing than ratiocination. Sixth, because it leads to subjectivity, it constitutes the first attack on the cherished Western notion of objective truth. Seventh, it calls into question the primacy of language, often requiring 'anti-language' for expression. Eighth, it leads to a godlike persona and a heterodox 'religion', both of which challenge religious orthodox structures. Last, it radicalizes the poetic medium itself in its call for the transformation of the reader's consciousness.

Cosmic rhetoric compellingly refutes the oft-leveled condemnation of Romanticism as a visionary mode that estranges the poet from legitimate human concerns. Because mysticism is reason's repressed other, as Derrida has argued, the use of cosmic rhetoric is a form of rebellion, an insurrection of a subjugated way of knowing that upsets what Foucault has called the 'totalitarian hierarchy of knowledges'[44] in the West, atop which reason reigns supreme. This insurrection is an intimately human concern, involving a reassertion of the primal, non-rational components of consciousness repressed by rationality. But its praxis is consciousness change, not direct sociopolitical involvement. Just as Bloom, Cixous, Kristeva, Barthes, Irigaray, Derrida, and other current thinkers have turned to mystical discourse to escape the confines of Eurocentric ideology, so did Wordsworth and Whitman embrace the cosmic rhetorical mode as a challenge to the oppressive dominance of Enlightenment modes of ideation. Wordsworth uttered the war-cry for this rebellion, and Whitman heeded the call to adventure, taking it to an even higher level.

The term 'cosmic consciousness' was coined by Richard Maurice Bucke, Whitman's literary executor and perhaps the most ardent of the 'Whitmaniacs' who believed the poet was something of a prophet or a seer. The authors of *Start with the Sun* also employ the term cosmic in defining the American poetic

[44] Michel Foucault, 'Lecture: 7 January 1976', in: K.M. Newton (Ed.), *Twentieth-century literary theory*, New York: St. Martin's, 1997, 129.

tradition inaugurated by Walt Whitman, which, as I already stated, they believe is rooted in Wordsworth and other Romantics. The cosmic for Miller, Shapiro, and Slote includes not only transcendent experiences but phenomena of the physical world, things frequently left out of Western/religious mystical perception.

Stanislav Grof, one of today's leading transpersonal psychologists, describes cosmic consciousness as a perceptual phenomenon:

> When we experience identification with the cosmic consciousness, we have the feeling of enfolding the totality of existence within us, and of comprehending the reality that underlies all realities. We have a profound sense that we are in connection with the supreme and ultimate principle of all Being. In this state, it is absolutely clear that this principle is the ultimate and the only mystery; once its existence is excepted, everything else can be understood from it and explained. The experience of cosmic consciousness is boundless, unfathomable, and beyond expression. Yet, even a short experiential exposure to it satisfies fully our craving for understanding. All questions about the mysteries of life seem to be answered and there is no need to go any further.[45]

This enfolding of all external things within the self is a critical feature of the mysticism in Wordsworth and Whitman. In *The Visionary Company* Harold Bloom contrasts Blake's attitude towards nature with Wordsworth's, arguing that Blake's doctrine is either that 'imagination destroys nature or nature destroys the imagination'.[46] In Wordsworth, however, Bloom sees a merging with nature, a coupling of subject and object that transcends the view of nature and mind as disparate things. Such an insight can also be applied to Whitman, who, as I will show, takes this merging to a new level.

II

There does seem to be a limited amount of critical recognition of the mystical connection between Wordsworth and Whitman. In his groundbreaking tome, *American Renaissance*, F.O. Matthiessen likens Whitman's notebook description of the 'divine power pouring through the poet' to Wordsworth's account in 'Tintern Abbey' of the mystical illumination in which we are laid asleep in body and become a living soul.[47] According to Matthiessen, 'there is no document more allied to Whitman's prefaces [...] than Wordsworth's preface to *Lyrical Ballads*'.[48] Matthiessen further argued that Whitman got from Wordsworth the conception

[45] Stanislav Grof, *The holotropic mind*, New York: HarperCollins, 1990, 164.
[46] Harold Bloom, *The visionary company*, Ithaca, NY: Cornell University Press, 1961, 128.
[47] F.O. Matthiessen, *American Renaissance*, New York: Oxford University Press, 1941, 540.
[48] Matthiessen, *American Renaissance*, 614.

that the universe was not a mechanism and the idea that 'man is integrally connected with what he sees, hears, and feels, that what he *is* cannot be separated from the impressions made by external nature upon his sensibility'.[49] Matthiessen devotes only a few pages to the Whitman/Wordsworth connection, however, as his massive work only deals with five American Romantics.

Seeing Whitman's spiritual democracy as being rooted in Wordsworth, John Bailey argued that both poets were pantheists:

> Now Whitman [...] owed a great deal more than he knew to Wordsworth. Or at least he was much more akin to Wordsworth than he knew. For it was Wordsworth more than anyone else who gave to poetry its freedom to call nothing common or unclean. When Whitman brought the average man into poetry he was only advancing in a path first cleared and leveled by Wordsworth.[50]

Bailey also claimed the power and beauty in both poets stemmed from another common element in their verse – an 'all-embracing human sympathy which sees wonder and feels love where others, till the poet helps them, see and feel nothing at all'.[51] Bailey is careful to point out what he feels is a difference in this pantheistic element found in both: Wordsworth's pantheism is always held in check by an unresolved transcendentalism, whereas for Whitman God is utterly in all things.[52] I disagree at least in part with Bailey's conclusion, since, as I will attempt to show, this 'unresolved transcendentalism' is not present in Wordsworth's earliest mystical passages. Like Mathiessen, Bailey only devotes a few pages to this mystical connection.

Perhaps taking his cue from Matthiessen and Bailey, Roger Asselineau argues that Whitman 'always has the sharp consciousness of the purely sensual source of his mystical intuitions. Instead of proceeding at once to a spiritualization, like the English Romantics or the American transcendentalists, he never forgets that his body is the theater and the point of origin for his mystical states'.[53] Although it is indisputable that body and soul are inseparably coupled in Whitman, there is a transcendentalist strain in his mysticism, particularly in the later years when he underwent bodily paralysis as a result of a series of strokes, at which point his mystical rhetoric takes an otherworldly turn. Asselineau does, however, insightfully identify a similarity in the aesthetics of both, arguing that Whitman's 'cosmic spirit' is 'nothing else than Wordsworth's and Coleridge's imagination'.[54]

---

[49] Idem, 615.

[50] John Bailey, *Walt Whitman*, New York: Macmillan, 1926, 65.

[51] Bailey, *Walt Whitman*, 66.

[52] Idem, 142.

[53] Roger Asselineau, *The evolution of Walt Whitman*, Iowa City: University of Iowa Press, 1999 (orig. publ. 1954), 4.

[54] Asselineau, *The evolution of Walt Whitman*, 99.

Asselineau's two-volume biography is highly informative, but it, too, devotes very little attention to the Wordsworthian connection, as his focus is on the American bard.

V.K. Chari, the first critic to undertake a full-length study of Whitman's mysticism, similarly pays very little attention to the common ground both poets share. In his chapter on the nature of consciousness, for example, Chari notes that 'Whitman, like Emerson, shared in the Romantic tradition of Coleridge and the German idealists, and his concern with the problems of consciousness was part of the contemporary Romantic concern with the human mind and its operations through the creative imagination'.[55] Significantly, Chari does not even mention Wordsworth in relation to the issue of consciousness when, in fact, it was one of his primary concerns. He does, however, later acknowledge that the depiction of a trancelike state found in one of Whitman's notebooks smacks of Wordsworth's 'serene and blessed mood' of 'Tintern Abbey'.[56] But that is the extent of his treatment of the connection in his superlative work.

In *Start with the Sun*, Miller, Shapiro, and Slote discuss the differences between the two primary poetic traditions in American literature – New Puritanism, a 'tradition of rigorously honed intellectualism in which the old worship of the soul has been replaced by the worship of the mind' – and New Paganism, which expresses a 'pagan joy and wonder in the natural world, the living cosmos'.[57] William Carlos Williams lamented the change in the American tradition from Whitman's new paganism to Eliot's 'rigorously honed intellectualism': 'I shall never forget the impression created by *The Waste Land*. It was as if the bottom had dropped out of everything. I had not known how much the spirit of Whitman animated us until it was withdrawn from us'.[58] The New Puritanism is rooted in 'the scholastics, the 17th-century verbal dramatists, and the 18th-century reasonable wits', whereas the New Paganism 'has its origin in the Romantics of the early 19th century – Blake and *Wordsworth*; a little of Shelley and Keats; Emerson and Thoreau'.[59] Since *Start with the Sun* is concerned primarily with the American tradition, though they do throw D.H. Lawrence into the mix, Miller, Shapiro, and Slote do not develop the Wordsworthian connection they identify. Although this work is groundbreaking and insightful, I object to the authors' labelling of Wordsworth and Whitman as 'nature mystics',

[55] V.K. Chari, *Whitman in the light of Vedantic mysticism*, Lincoln, NE: University of Nebraska Press, 1964, 20.

[56] Chari, *Whitman in the light of Vedantic mysticism*, 105.

[57] Miller, Shapiro, & Slote, *Start with the Sun*, 3 & 4.

[58] Qtd. in Sculley Bradley & Harold W. Blodgett (Eds.), *Leaves of Grass: A Norton critical edition*, New York: Norton, 1973, 905.

[59] Miller, Shapiro, & Slote, *Start with the Sun*, 4 (emphasis added).

which is really only part of the truth. On this matter, I agree with V.K. Chari, who similarly objects to the authors' reduction of mysticism in Whitman 'to a kind of biological or organic mysticism of the life force – a physical mysticism'.[60] As I hope to demonstrate, in both poets the matter is far more complicated.

In his dissertation on the critical writings of Wordsworth and Whitman, Abdelwahab Elmessiri makes some similar passing remarks regarding mysticism in both poets that I find problematic. He claims, for instance, the *later* Whitman was mystical and prophetic, whereas I will attempt to show the opposite – Whitman's most mystical passages are in his earliest verse. He also shockingly claims that because Whitman's monism is 'static and simple' (and therefore 'reductive'), his poetry 'remains of limited human interest'.[61] Regarding Wordsworth Elmessiri claims that 'time and again in his poetry Wordsworth tends to see man as part of nature who has no experience outside of it and who is entirely satisfied with its fixed forms'.[62] Just the opposite tendency is true in Wordsworth, however, for as I will argue, the poet (particularly the later orthodox poet) is by no means at ease with his own oneness with nature as he expressed it in his earliest verse. Elmessiri also concludes that 'the human mind as being passive and subservient to nature underlies many of Wordsworth's critical statements'.[63] This may or may not be true of Wordsworth's critical prose; it is certainly not true of *The Prelude,* in which it is clear that mind and nature are *co-creators.*

In a comparative essay on Wordsworth and Whitman, Gary Simon similarly makes some problematic statements regarding the mysticism in both poets. For example, Simon argues that 'Wordsworth's poetics do not always succeed in penetrating the inner spirit of things and consequently often fail to sustain mystical effects'.[64] When his 'transcendent lyricism does succeed, as in "Tintern Abbey", his poetics frequently lack the organicism necessary to lift the reader beyond the material realm'.[65] 'Whitman's melodies', Simon adds in contrast, 'carry his reader along the path of transcendency'.[66] As I hope to show, Wordsworth was much more of a transcendentalist than Whitman. Although his poetry is by no means otherworldly, there is nevertheless an all-pervasive urge towards transcendence in his verse. Although such an urge also permeates

---

60 Chari, *Whitman in the light of Vedantic mysticism,* 13.

61 Abdelwahab Elmessiri, *The critical writings of Wordsworth and Whitman: A study of the historical and anti-historical imaginations* (Diss. Rutgers, Camden, New Jersey, 1969), 129.

62 Elmessiri, *The critical writings of Wordsworth and Whitman,* 12.

63 Idem, 129.

64 Gary Simon, 'Craft, theory and the artist's milieu: The myth-maker and Wordsworth', in: *Walt Whitman Review* 22 (1976), 66.

65 Simon, 'Craft, theory and the artist's milieu', 66.

66 Ibidem.

Whitman's work, there is also a counter-urge which celebrates all things – weeds, prostitutes, fences, rocks, dockworkers, etc. – not in their spiritual/transcendental aspect but in their physicality.

In *The Language of the Senses* Kerry McSweeney discusses in a chapter on Wordsworth and Whitman the ways in which 'sensory-perceptual experience is shown to be a source or enabling condition of imaginative power in romantic writers'.[67] He claims sensory ratios are an essential constituent of both symbolic perception and expansion of consciousness experiences in both poets, 'descriptions or representations of which are a central feature of their work'.[68] McSweeney's challenge both to Derrida and De Man is a compelling refutation of the critical view of Romanticism as an attempt by the self to borrow the temporal stability it lacks from nature via the spiritualization of the symbol. In their flight 'from temporality and an authentically human destiny', according to such a deconstructive view, 'Romantic poets became trapped in the contradiction of a pseudo-dialectic between subject and object'.[69] As an antidote to this type of misreading, McSweeney offers Whitman's 'expansive celebration of symbolic perception' in verse-chant 6 of 'Song of Myself'. He claims the grass is a 'polysemous symbol, but it is not split up into a multiplicity of arbitrary signifiers [...] because there is a single perceiver with a radiating intensity of affirmative apprehension'.[70] McSweeney also demonstrates in Wordsworth how 'the dynamic interplay of eye and ear is a fundamental constituent of the 'spots of time' and related experiences', which thus has an important bearing on one of the most contentious areas in Wordsworth criticism – the mind/nature dialectic.[71] Where I disagree with McSweeney, however, is in his privileging of the eye over the ear, a point I will deal with more fully in chapter 7.

Lastly, Jeanne Bugliari's essay on Wordsworth and Whitman situates both poets within the idealist tradition. Bugliari acknowledges the disparate philosophies and marked discrepancies of style in both, but she also points out that such 'obvious stylistic and interpretive disparity tends to skewer their more basic agreements (without which, one might add, it were useless to contrast, since any such differentiation presumes a more general underlying comparison; otherwise, contrast is a mere exercise in irrelevancy)'.[72] I agree with her general assertion that 'each poet profoundly desired the mystical union of the soul with the

---

[67] McSweeney, *The language of the senses*, x.
[68] Ibidem.
[69] Idem, 25.
[70] Idem, 27.
[71] Idem, x.
[72] Jeanne Bugliari, 'Whitman and Wordsworth: The janus of nineteenth century idealism', in: *Walt Whitman Review* 19 (1973), 63.

infinite', but I find problematic her statement that both poets 'glorified objects of nature' merely as 'vehicles of transcendental experience through which they reached spiritual reality'.[73] This is only partly true of Wordsworth, as there is much in the 1805 *Prelude,* as well as his other pre-1807 verse, that runs against the grain of idealism. And it is even more incorrect to dismiss Whitman's conception of nature in such a Platonic way, for the natural, particularly the sexual, is celebrated in its own right in *Leaves of Grass.*

As the above discussion shows, there does seem to be some critical recognition of mystical rhetoric as a transatlantic bridge between Wordsworth and Whitman but only in either passing remarks or, at best, in article-length essays. To be sure, there are works devoted to examining each poet's mysticism individually. V.K. Chari's *Whitman in the Light of Vedantic Mysticism,* David Keubrich's *Minor Prophecy,* and George Hutchinson's *The Ecstatic Whitman* are excellent studies of the American poet's spirituality. In addition, there are a few dissertations likening Whitman's mysticism to Sufism, Taoism, and Tantrism, as well as several articles on the subject. Regarding Wordsworth there are works such as John Rudy's *Wordsworth and the Zen Mind* and M.H. Abrams's *Natural Supernaturalism,* not to mention a few dissertations and article-length essays on the mystical elements in his verse. To date, however, there are no full-length *transatlantic* studies of the mystical rhetoric in Wordsworth and Whitman. Since there is some scholarship on each poet's 'mysticism', a comparative study of the two would seem not only beneficial but necessary. My study contributes to this scholarly void.

III

In the next chapter I will put forth a nuanced definition of mysticism. Now, however, in anticipation of some possible objections to my thesis, I would like to state as clearly as possible what the 'cosmic' is not. First, in drawing this connection between Wordsworth and Whitman I am not covertly asserting the platitude that they were both Romantics. The cosmic is firmly rooted in the Romanticism of the 18th and 19th centuries. Both writers testified 'to a deeply significant experience in which an instant of consciousness, or else an ordinary object or event, suddenly blazes into revelation', as was typical of many romantic writers, according to M.H. Abrams.[74] Wordsworth and Whitman, however, amplified Romantic ideas and took the revelatory moment to a new level. No other poets in the anglophone tradition are more closely aligned in this sense than Wordsworth and Whitman.

---

[73] Bugliari, 'Whitman and Wordsworth', 64.

[74] M.H. Abrams, *Natural supernaturalism,* New York: Norton, 1971, 385.

Second, in the case of Wordsworth what we are dealing with is not simply Coleridgean metaphysics qua poetry, for it was precisely at the moment when Wordsworth shrugged off Coleridge's influence in *The Prelude* that he finds his 'cosmic' register. To be sure, the Coleridgean influence on Wordsworth is profound. When Wordsworth wrote his most cosmic verse, he was in almost daily contact with Coleridge. In *Biographia Literaria* Coleridge defines primary imagination 'to be the living power and prime agent of all human perception, and as a repetition in the finite mind of the eternal act of creation in the infinite I am'.[75] Clearly, such theories of the imagination are echoed repeatedly in Wordsworth's mystical verse. It is important to remember, however, that Coleridge ruined his poetic gifts by becoming enthralled by German metaphysics, an immersion in philosophy Wordsworth never undertook. After all, he never completed his planned philosophical magnum opus, *The Recluse*. Wordsworth claimed, in fact, never to have read any of the German philosophers Coleridge was studying, according to Rosemary Ashton.[76] Despite Derrida's blurring of the boundaries between philosophy and literature, it is important to remember that the one privileges mind stuff, the other (particularly the genre of Romantic poetry) privileges feelings.

In the case of Whitman the cosmic element is not merely Emersonian transcendentalism. Whitman told John Burroughs that prior to 1855 he had never read Emerson. Yet, as I have already pointed out, Whitman wrote an article in March 1842 for the *New York Aurora* in which he praised Emerson's style and the content of his lectures. Similarly, in the December 15, 1847 issue of the *Brooklyn Daily Eagle* Whitman quoted a whole paragraph from one of Emerson's 'inimitable lectures'.[77] Despite his later denial of Emerson's influence, Whitman told John Townsend Trowbridge, 'I was simmering, simmering, simmering [...] Emerson brought me to a boil'.[78] Clearly, Emerson made possible much of Whitman's poetic achievement. It is important to remember, however, that 'Emerson boasts (albeit perhaps ambivalently) of having declined to exert a personal influence on others that might have warped them from their own orbits'.[79] 'Throughout his writings, Emerson represents himself as an experimenter, a questioner or, a seeker, rather than a guide or a sage'.[80] Emerson exerted indisputably the

---

[75] Samuel Taylor Coleridge, *Biographia literaria*, London: Dent, 1993, 167.

[76] Rosemary Ashton, *The life of Samuel Taylor Coleridge*, Oxford: Blackwell, 1997, 4.

[77] Kuniko Yoshizaki, 'The Oriental sources of Walt Whitman', in: *Kyushu American Literature* 20 (1979), 14.

[78] Qtd. in Yoshizaki, 'The Oriental sources of Walt Whitman', 14.

[79] Catherine Tufariello, 'The remembering wine: Emerson's influence on Whitman and Dickinson', in: Joel Laporte & Saundra Morris (Eds.), *The Cambridge companion to Ralph Waldo Emerson*, New York: Cambridge University Press, 1999, 162.

[80] Tufariello, 'The remembering wine', 162.

profoundest influence on Whitman's poetry, but this impact is frequently overstated, as there are profound differences between the two. 'With Emerson', argued Lewis Mumford, 'one surveys the world from a glacial summit: the air is rarefied, and at this distance even the treacherous places in the landscape seem orderly and innocent. With Whitman one sees the heights from the bosom of the valley'.[81] Matthiessen claimed that 'Whitman bridged the gap between the material and the ideal in a way that Emerson could not'.[82] More important, much of the spirituality that Whitman's verse exhibits was far more broadly diffused in 19th-century America than is generally recognized, as David Reynolds points out in his cultural biography, *Walt Whitman's America*. Whitman's spirituality is informed not only by Emersonian transcendentalism but also by Swedenborg, Harmonialism, Mesmerism, Elias Hicks and the Quakers, the Persian poets, and many other influences.

Third, the cosmic is not Platonism per se but a reworking and a subverting of the Platonic. In *Wordsworth and the Zen Mind* John Rudy demonstrates the ways in which the mystical elements in Wordsworth's verse transcend Platonic idealism. In *Whitman in the Light of Vedantic Mysticism* V.K. Chari offers a similar perspective on Whitman's subversion of Plato. Willis Barnstone in his excellent work *The Poetics of Ecstasy* distinguishes between two categories of mysticism – monism and theism, that is, 'total union' or mere 'conjunction'.[83] In Plato, he argues, 'we have a spiritual dualism, a theistic form of mysticism. In theistic mysticism there are always two identities'.[84] Particularly in Whitman, but in Wordsworth as well, the cosmic seems to blur the distinction between self and other, although there are also mystical moments in which there are two identities. The cosmic in both poets, therefore, seems to warrant both labels at once. Matthiessen's labeling of Whitman's dominant mode of thought as Fichtean 'material ideality' could be applied to Wordsworth as well.[85] Given that Plato considered all poets to be deficient artists (he called them imitators) in their perception of ideal forms, it would seem an injustice to interpret Wordsworth and Whitman through a framework that sees them as being 'out of touch with the real'.[86] In *Natural Supernaturalism* M.H. Abrams distinguishes between the *exoteric* and the *esoteric* traditions in Western religion, which were spawned by Plato and Plotinus respectively. He argues that the Romantics are more in line with

[81] Qtd. in Bradley & Blodgett, *Leaves of Grass*, 851.

[82] Matthiessen, *American Renaissance*, 522.

[83] Willis Barnstone, *The poetics of ecstasy: Varieties of* ekstasis *from Sappho to Borges*, New York: Holmes, 1983, 8.

[84] Barnstone, *The poetics of ecstasy*, 9.

[85] Matthiessen, *American Renaissance*, 525.

[86] Plato, 'The Republic', in: Allan Gilbert (Ed.), *Literary criticism: Plato to Dryden*, Detroit: Wayne State, 1962, 42 & 46.

the esoteric tradition (Neoplatonism). It is doubtful, however, that either Wordsworth or Whitman read any of Plotinus' texts, which means if there is a Neoplatonic influence on their mysticism it is an indirect one at best.

Fourth, the cosmic is not necessarily the sublime, although there is significant overlap between the two. The Romantic sublime is more closely aligned with that of Longinus, for whom the sublime was related to 'ecstasy' and 'transport', according to Willis Barnstone.[87] The Romantic sublime does not necessarily involve the Burkean element of terror; or rather, terror can be present, but it is not an essential ingredient. Often in Wordsworth, Whitman, and other Romantics, ordinary objects, places, or events can take on an almost supernatural character. Consequently, Christopher Salvesen argues that to speak of the 'Wordsworthian' sublime 'is to talk about something substantially different from "the Sublime" itself'.[88] As a form of perception the sublime refers to 'the process of physically transcending external limits while simultaneously crossing a psychological boundary of consciousness', according to James Twitchell.[89] The sublime is 'that experience both above the slush of matter and beyond self-consciousness of the poet'.[90] As Twitchell points out, however, 'if we become merged with the infinite, the process of sublimation ceases. The awareness of altered consciousness is replaced by an entirely new consciousness' of the transcendent realm.[91] As an aesthetic category, the sublime can lead to the edge of the liminal, but it can go no further. It is, therefore, more this-worldly than otherworldly.

Fifth, the cosmic is not a throwback to the Cartesian separation of mind and matter or the essentialism of liberal humanism. In later chapters I will demonstrate the ways in which Wordsworth and Whitman attempted to heal the wounds of such a schism. John Rudy argues that in Wordsworth there is the revelation of the 'fundamental emptiness', the 'essencelessness' of all things, including consciousness itself.[92] I would extend this argument to Whitman as well, for he, too, sees 'a world of things uncolored or unadorned by the imaginative application of a cultural overlay of images extracted from a human spiritual or religious tradition [...] Cognition so conceived is not an act of discovery so much as a surrender to being, a yielding of the separate self to a condition of identity with, rather than apprehension of, "the life of things"'.[93]

---

[87] Barnstone, *The poetics of ecstasy*, 3.

[88] Christopher Salvesen, 'Aspects of the Romantic sublime', in: *Charles Lamb Bulletin* 50 (1985), 38.

[89] James B. Twitchell, *Romantic horizons: Aspects of the sublime in English poetry and painting, 1770-1850*, Columbia: University of Missouri Press, 1983, 3.

[90] Twitchell, *Romantic horizons*, 9.

[91] Idem, 42.

[92] John G. Rudy, *Wordsworth and the Zen mind: The poetry of self-emptying*, Albany: SUNY, 1996, 4.

[93] Rudy, *Wordsworth and the Zen mind*, 5.

Sixth, the cosmic is not merely 'displaced Protestantism', as Harold Bloom has argued, nor is it strictly an appropriation of the prophetic/biblical tradition, as Abrams, Hartman, and others have claimed. Surely, the spiritual elements in Wordsworth and Whitman are informed by Christianity, but there are also subversive elements in their rhetoric that render both poets incompatible with Western orthodox religion.

Last, I am not imposing my belief system on Wordsworth and Whitman but merely describing a phenomenon of consciousness as it appears in their verse. One can be a thoroughgoing atheist and still undertake an academic study of mysticism. As William James put it, belief in the existence of God is irrelevant in religious studies.[94] Mystical perception itself, as modern researchers are finding out, is associated with alterations in brain wave patterns, not with mere beliefs. EEGs have revealed slower brain waves such as alpha and theta patterns in meditators who enter 'trancelike' states.[95] Often, mystical perception can either destroy cherished beliefs or at the least run against the grain of religious and/or moral orthodoxy.

IV

In reading Wordsworth and Whitman against each other I am not suggesting that there is a direct connection, but I am hoping to reveal a stronger link than has been previously accepted. As Richard Gravil has argued, the relationship is not biographically explicit, but it exists nevertheless. In his study of Whitman and Rumi, Ghulam Muhammed Fayez says the great number of striking parallel ideas, images, and techniques in both attests more to the 'universal nature of mystical experience' than the possible influence of Rumi on Whitman.[96] Mysticism is a phenomenon of consciousness, and, although it is historically conditioned, it also transcends time and place. For this reason Aldous Huxley called it the 'perennial philosophy' in his excellent study by the same name. Whitman may have cultivated his cosmic rhetoric independently, perhaps as a result of some kind expansion of consciousness experience, but it is highly plausible that Wordsworth's 'mysticism' also influenced his rhetoric. Either way, the connection between the two is profound.

As editor of a collection of comparative essays on Heidegger and Asian thought, Graham Parkes claims 'the criteria for the success of a comparative

---

[94] William James, *The varieties of religious experience*, New York: Penguin, 1985 (orig. publ. 1902), xx.

[95] William Bevis, 'Emerson: Ecstasy and aphorism', in: *Studia Mystica* 5 (1982) no.3, 47.

[96] Ghulam Muhammed Fayez, *Mystic ideas and images in Jalal al-Din Rumi and Walt Whitman* (Diss. University of Arizona, Phoenix, 1978), vii.

study of two thinkers from different traditions are no different from those pertaining to a discussion of a single philosopher. The question in both cases is, simply: does the study enhance our understanding of the philosopher's thought, of the problems engaged by it – and of ourselves and the world'.[97] In reading Wordsworth and Whitman against each other I am hoping to enhance critical awareness of both; I am hoping to shed light on problems in their verse that cannot be approached in any other way; and I am hoping to enhance our own understanding of the problems both poets engaged in their work. Since the cosmic elements in their verse cannot be accurately pegged as any type of traditional mysticism, the way to understand Whitman best is to read him against another poet such as Wordsworth – someone similar enough in general spirit to allow for an illustration of common elements but also far enough removed so as to facilitate an understanding of the ways in which each poet stands on his own distinctive ground.

I will attempt to subject the cosmic rhetoric in both poets to a kind of descriptive phenomenology of mystical perception, which is to say, I will try to discern the state of consciousness and dominant feelings, as well as the accompanying existential realizations, that both poets tried to bring to the reader, as David Keubrich does in *Minor Prophecy* – his study of the prophetic aspects of Whitman's rhetoric. It goes without saying that I will be engaging in *very* close textual analysis. Although the New Critics have been buried, the close reading of formal analysis persists in (and actually makes possible) the work of most current theoretical schools. I acknowledge that this study in some ways goes against the grain, but as J.L. Mehta observes in his comparative discussion of Heidegger and Vedanta, 'there are no rules for a game of this kind, only the playing of the game can generate the rules, if at all'.[98]

---

[97] Graham Parkes, 'Introduction', in: idem (Ed.), *Heidegger and Asian thought*, Honolulu: Hawaii University Press, 1990, 5.

[98] Qtd. in Parkes, *Heidegger and Asian thought*, 15.

Chapter III

COSMIC PERCEPTION AND THE RHETORIC OF UNITY

'The mind of man is framed even like the breath
And harmony of music,
There is a dark
Invisible workmanship that reconciles
Discordant elements, and makes them move
In one society'
(Wordsworth)

I

As I have indicated in the previous chapter, scholars generally do not like the term mysticism because it often evokes images of amorphousness. In her study of Tennyson, Ashton Nichols claims 'the literary application of the word mystic degenerates into a vagueness that only confuses our understanding'.[1] Michael Spencer in his essay on T.S. Eliot similarly claims that 'the word has taken on such a wide field of meaning that trying to discuss the mysticism of various authors is like wandering off into a morass'.[2] A look at the various readings of mysticism in Wordsworth and Whitman proves the point: Critics have likened Whitman's mysticism to Sufism, Taoism, shamanism, Vedanta, Tantrism, Swedenborgianism, and many other types of spirituality. In Wordsworth there is a continuum spanning such interpretations as the Zen readings of John Rudy and Paulino Lim to N.D. O'Donoghue's concept of the 'mystical imagination'.[3] Critics have

[1] Ashton Nichols, 'The epiphanic trance: Why Tennyson is not a mystic', in: *Victorian Poetry* 24 (1986) no.2, 132.

[2] Michael D. Spencer, 'Mysticism in T.S. Eliot's four quartets', in: *Studies in Spirituality* 9 (1999), 232.

[3] John G. Rudy, *Wordsworth and the Zen mind: The poetry of self-emptying*, Albany: SUNY, 1996; Paulino Lim, 'Zen and Wordsworth', in: *The Wordsworth Circle* 7 (1976), 129-132; N.D. O'Donoghue, 'Mystical imagination', in: James Mackey (Ed.), *Religious imagination*, Edinburgh: Edinburgh University Press, 1986, 186-205.

also read him in Taoist terms, as a 'sacred' poet (in Mircea Eliade's[4] sense of the word), and as a 'panpsychist'. To speak of mysticism in either poet, therefore, is not to say much at all, since too many scholars understand the term to mean different things.

For scholars such as Nichols, mysticism really means Western mysticism, particularly the Christian variety, which is why she excludes Tennyson from the mystical tradition. For other critics, mysticism is a subversion of Christianity. Gary Simon, for instance, argues that Whitman's universe is pantheistic.[5] For V.K. Chari, mysticism is Vedanta, which is why he is so uneasy with Miller, Slote, and Shapiro's likening of Whitman's mysticism to a mysticism of the life force, a physical mysticism.[6] Whereas Jerome Loving claimed that by the time Whitman wrote *Leaves of Grass* he had become an 'idealist' and also that his mystical claims ceased by the time of the 1860 'Calamus' poems,[7] Gay Wilson Allen and Roger Asselineau both argued that mystical perception is indeed the root center of all of Whitman's verse.[8]

In Wordsworth the matter of mysticism is equally problematic. Whereas Lawrence Kramer reveals the ways in which Wordsworth (and Whitman) exert imaginative power that resists 'the oceanic feeling',[9] Mary Wedd argues that for Wordsworth the imagination links the individual with the spiritual world. James Twitchell claims that the Romantic artist keeps to the margin of the transcendent because to cross over is to sacrifice the self and the imagination,[10] but James Glimm argues that 'the sensations accompanying illumination, as described by the religious mystics, corresponds to a striking degree with the highest imaginative experiences described in the poetry of Wordsworth'.[11] Harold Bloom actually denied the poet's mysticism. He believed 'it is a laziness of our imaginations that causes us to call this vision mystical, for the mystical is finally ineffable and Wordsworth desires to be a man talking to men about matters of common experience'.[12]

---

4 Mircea Eliade, *Shamanism: Archaic techniques of ecstasy* (trans. Willard R. Trask), Princeton: Princeton University Press, 1974 (orig. publ. 1951).

5 Simon, 'Craft, theory and the artist's milieu', 65.

6 Chari, *Whitman in the light of Vedantic mysticism*, 12.

7 Loving, *Walt Whitman*, 181.

8 Gay Wilson Allen, *A reader's guide to Walt Whitman*, Syracuse: Syracuse University Press, 1970, 129; Asselineau, *The evolution of Walt Whitman*, 90.

9 Kramer, 'Ocean and vision', 210.

10 Twitchell, *Romantic horizons*, 73.

11 James Glimm, *Five essays on mystical experience in the works of Wordsworth, Coleridge, and Shelley* (Diss. University of Texas, Austin, 1968), 6.

12 Bloom, *The visionary company*, 136.

Because there is so much confusion over the term mysticism, I would like to turn the discussion towards a definition, which, I hope, will provide a situating context for the type of cosmic rhetoric found in the verse of Wordsworth and Whitman. In doing so I hope to demonstrate the connection between both poets in such mystical language. I believe the critical record is better served, however, if I avoid frequently used labels such as Zen, Taoist, Sufi, Christian, and the like, and simply read each poet in terms of the phenomenology of the mystical experience itself. There is mysticism in both poets but it is best understood as a phenomenon of consciousness rather than any type traditional spirituality.

II

To define mysticism I must engage in a *via negativa* of my own and describe what it is not. First, mysticism is not synonymous with irrationality. Particularly in academia, mysticism is often considered to be a sort of disconnected, irrational form of thought. In such a mindset, anything unexplainable within the confines of logic is incorrectly labeled mystical. Although mystics claim to transcend the mind, and although there is indisputably a non-rational component in mysticism, it is incorrect to say mysticism is irrational. Second, mysticism is not that which is inexplicable or vague. Although there is an ineffable quality to mystical states, it is incorrect to call a poorly articulated thought mystical. Third, mysticism is not magic. Whereas the latter works within the realm of illusion, the former is an attempt to apprehend higher truths. There is also an element of artificiality in magic that is not found in mysticism. Despite the sense of wonder that magic tricks induce in the observer, there is always a sense of the factitious in them, whereas many mystics claim that altered states of consciousness are more real and more authentic than physical reality. Fourth, mysticism in its classic sense is not to be confused with such psychic arts as telepathy, telekinesis, clairvoyance, and astral projection. Although Jess Byron Hollenback argues that all such experiences exist on a continuum, with mystical union on one end and psychism on the other, mystical scholars are generally concerned with the former. Fifth, mysticism is not to be equated with the mysterious or that which is not fully explainable, such as the pyramids, u.f.o. sightings, and strange lake creatures. Such things are mysterious, not mystical. Sixth, mysticism is not religion. Whereas the one involves direct experience with the sacred – however it is defined – the other typically requires some sort of intermediary such as the clergy, ritual, religious texts, or someone else's mystical experience. Last, mysticism is not the complete cessation of being. Those who misunderstand the Buddhist concept of *nirvana* – which is not a concept at all – view it as a total nothingness, when in fact it is actually the affirmation of a positive through negative language, as Thomas Merton and D.T. Suzuki have argued. Mystics frequently claim that the experience is often a realization of true identity.

So then, what is mysticism? The word 'mystic' has its origins in the ancient Greek mystery schools. 'A mystic', writes F.C. Happold, 'was one who had been initiated into one of these mysteries, through which he had gained an esoteric knowledge of divine things and been reborn into eternity. His object was to break through the world of history and time into that of eternity and timelessness'.[13] But surely the mystical experience in its generic sense stretches back to the dawn of humankind. All cultures, both east and west, 'primitive' and modern, seem to have their mysticisms. Since scholars are not in total agreement as to the essential elements (if any exist at all), it is necessary to look at some of the ways in which mysticism has been defined.

Although William James preceded her, Evelyn Underhill is almost universally acknowledged as the premier scholar of mysticism in the 20th century. I will begin, therefore, with one of her definitions:

> Mysticism [...] is not an opinion: it is not a philosophy. It has nothing in common with the pursuit of occult knowledge. On the one hand it is not merely the power of contemplating eternity: on the other, it is not to be identified with any kind of religious queerness. It is the name of that organic process which involves the perfect consummation of the Love of God [...] [I]t is the art of establishing [man's] conscious relation with the Absolute.[14]

Mysticism is not about what one believes; it is not about opinion, as Underhill asserts. In fact, the mystical experience often occurs in direct opposition to one's belief system. Such conversion experiences usually serve to profoundly alter a set of beliefs. Jesus, Siddhartha Gautama, and Saul of Tarsus are three obvious examples, but there are countless others, who, after experiencing some aspect of the sacred, have viewed the world in a radically altered manner. Underhill's definition, despite that it actually comprises only one type of mysticism – theistic mysticism, which is to say, union with God – captures the essence of what constitutes the experience, which is experience itself versus belief in a moral or religious code. At the heart of mystical consciousness is love and one's experiential relationship to it. 'Mysticism means direct, immediate experience of ultimate reality', as Wayne Teasdale put it.[15] Underhill also adds that '[m]ysticism, in its purer form, is the science of ultimates, the science of Union with the Absolute,

---

[13] F.C. Happold, *Mysticism: A study and an anthology*, New York: Penguin, 1990 (orig. publ. 1963), 18.

[14] Underhill, *Mysticism*, 24.

[15] Wayne Teasdale, *The mystic heart*, Novato, CA: New World, 1999, 20.

and nothing else, and the mystic is the person who attains to this union, not the person who talks about it'.[16]

Also at the heart of Underhill's definition is the notion that mystical consciousness is an organic process, which is to say that all people possess the capacity for it, not just an elect, chosen few. 'Mysticism', according to Freke and Gandy, 'is a natural state of consciousness which has been experienced by people of all cultures, at all times in history – by followers of every religion and no religion[...]. It is the spontaneous experience of a wider reality, beyond the limited horizon of ordinary existence'.[17] Although such experiences can be induced, there is in them an involuntary element. According to Zen practitioners, for instance, *satori* is a completely spontaneous explosion of consciousness in which the meditator is consumed in a momentary yet life-altering flash of higher awareness that can occur at any given moment. (The Zen Master Bobo Roshi was said to have experienced *satori* while visiting a prostitute).

There is an element of sameness in mysticism, both in terms of its many different manifestations and in terms of its perceptions. It 'is a phenomenon that seems to occur in all religions and cultures', according to Bruno Borchert.[18] '[Mysticism] is different in external form, but in essence everywhere it is the same: *it is the experiential knowledge that, in one way or another, everything is interconnected, that all things have a single source*'.[19] Richard Maurice Bucke coined the term 'cosmic consciousness' to explain this 'interconnected' way of seeing things, which is more of an intuitive knowing than it is a factual understanding.[20] Bucke also asserts that cosmic consciousness is an evolutionary leap from what he calls 'self consciousness', which is itself a leap from 'simple consciousness', or animal consciousness.[21] The prime characteristic of cosmic consciousness is 'a consciousness of the cosmos, that is, of the life and order of the universe' – a penetration beyond the veil of discreteness to an 'illumination which alone would place the individual on a new plane of existence – would make him almost a member of a new species'.[22]

For the scholars of the purist camp, however, the experience is incomplete without the element of love, which is the foundation of mystical consciousness.

---

[16] Underhill, *Mysticism*, 25.

[17] Timothy Freke & Peter Gandy, *The complete guide to world mysticism*, London: Piatkus, 1997, 9.

[18] Bruno Borchert, *Mysticism: Its history and challenge*, York Beach, ME: Weiser, 1994 (orig. publ. 1989), 11.

[19] Borchert, *Mysticism*, 11.

[20] Richard Maurice Bucke, *Cosmic consciousness*, New York: Penguin, 1991 (orig. publ. 1901), 3.

[21] Bucke, *Cosmic consciousness*, 16.

[22] Ibidem.

According to Borchert, the mystical experience can best be described in terms of being in love with another person. 'Replace [the one with the other], and you have a rough and ready description of mysticism in general. As a matter of fact, mystical experience is often felt and described by mystics, themselves, in terms of being in love, and their lives are a love affair with the all-embracing reality that permeates and surpasses mundane existence'.[23]

Mysticism, then, is the perception of the universe and all of its seemingly disparate entities existing in a unified whole bound together by love. Black Elk, a native American medicine man, used the term 'sacred hoop' to express such an insight. As a result of mystical consciousness, 'opposites tend to meet and coincide', wrote Thomas Merton, 'for the realm of spiritual experience is no longer the realm of strict logic in which A and not-A are irreconcilably set apart and opposed. In point of fact, it is by forgetting the immediate data of sense and letting go all preoccupation with material concerns that one enters into the kind of cosmic fellowship and unity with all being that [mystics speak of]'.[24] One of Black Elk's 'visions' captures this transcendence of 'strict logic': 'I looked about me and could see that what we then were doing was like a shadow cast upon the earth from yonder vision in the heavens, so bright it was and clear. I knew the real was yonder and the darkened dream of it was here'.[25]

In mystical consciousness there is a sense of the peeling back of a layer (or layers) to discover what has been concealed. 'When you have *satori*', said an unknown Zen master, 'you are able to reveal a palatial mansion made of precious stones on a single blade of grass; but when you have no *satori*, a palatial mansion itself is concealed behind a single blade of grass'. This discovery yields

> an extension of normal consciousness, a release of latent powers and a widening of vision, so that aspects of truth unplumbed by the intellect are revealed to [the mystic]. Both in feeling and in thought he apprehends an immanence of the temporal in the eternal and the eternal in the temporal. In the religious mystic there is a direct experience of the presence of God. Though he may not be able to describe it in words, though he may not be able logically to demonstrate its validity, to the mystic the experience is fully and absolutely valid and is surrounded with complete certainty. He has been 'there', he has 'seen', he 'knows'.[26]

The end of mysticism, however, is not this discovery of latent power or hidden knowledge. In fact, mysticism has nothing to do with acquisition for the self but rather the opposite. Mystical consciousness 'is not individualistic', according to

---

[23] Borchert, *Mysticism*, 40.

[24] Thomas Merton, *Mystics and Zen masters*, New York: Farrar, 1967, 139.

[25] Qtd. in John G. Neihardt, *Black Elk speaks*, Lincoln, NE: University Press of Nebraska, 1979 (orig. publ. 1932), 169.

[26] Happold, *Mysticism*, 18.

Underhill. 'It implies, indeed, the abolition of individuality; of that hard separateness, that 'I, Me, Mine' which makes of a man a finite isolated thing. It is essentially a movement of the heart, seeking to transcend the limitations of the individual standpoint and to surrender itself to the ultimate reality; for no personal gain, to satisfy no transcendental curiosity, to obtain no other-worldly joys, but purely from an instinct of love'.[27]

Although some scholars hold rigidly to definitions of what they believe constitutes the mystical experience, it is important to remember that mystical consciousness can be experienced by degrees. Since it does not always occur in a blinding flash of illumination, it would be more appropriate to say that mystical consciousness is a continuum spanning the gulf between feelings of oneness with things traditionally seen outside of the individual self and the ultimate awareness that comes with mystical union, conjunction, and/or self-annihilation. Mystical consciousness, as such, can be defined as a direct apprehension of the sacred or spiritual that leads to perceptions unavailable in the normal waking state. Mysticism, then, is a movement of consciousness – a dynamic scientifically observed by researchers at the Monroe Institute who claim that specific alterations in brain wave functioning occur when subjects enter 'mystical' or trance states.[28]

According to the respondents to a questionnaire that Marghanita Laski employed in her research, mystical consciousness brings with it feelings of unity, eternity, release, new life, satisfaction, joy, salvation, beauty, and insight.[29] What is lost in mystical consciousness, according to the same questionnaire, are feelings of individuality and difference, time, place, limitation, worldliness, desire, sorrow, and sin.[30] Those who experience ecstasies and mystical visions typically report an expansion into a greater sense of identity, as well as a sense of wholeness and the restoration of missing aspects of themselves. What they lose is an underlying sense of isolation, the guilt associated with sin, the sense of sorrow and unhappiness, as well as the reference points of time and space.

What D.T. Suzuki said of *satori* – the equivalent of *nirvana* in Zen Buddhism – seems to capture the seemingly random element in the causes of mystical consciousness: 'Satori is experienced in connection with any ordinary occurrence in one's daily life [...] Someone takes hold of you, or slaps you, or brings you a cup of tea, or makes some most commonplace remark, or recites some passage from a sutra or from a book of poetry, and when your mind is right for its outburst, you come at once to satori'. Of course, mystical consciousness can be

27 Underhill, *Mysticism*, 25.
28 Robert A. Monroe, *Far journeys*, New York: Doubleday, 1985, 16.
29 Marghanita Laski, *Ecstasy in secular and religious experiences*, Los Angeles: Tarcher, 1961, 30.
30 Laski, *Ecstasy in secular and religious experiences*, 31.

induced by less mundane triggers such as meditation, prayer, as well as many of Laski's more spectacular ones – mountains, music, sex, art, etc. The point, however, is simply that there is no single cause of mystical consciousness, and it can occur seemingly anywhere and to anyone.

The rhetoric of Wordsworth and Whitman partakes of this mystical discourse in a variety of ways, the discussion of which constitutes the body of my study. In this chapter, however, I would like to focus on the rhetoric of 'cosmic unity', by which I mean the interconnection of all things. Wordsworth and Whitman both participate in mystical discourse by employing such rhetoric to a striking degree of frequency and similarity. It is one of the many, and perhaps the most striking, of the connections between the two poets. The rhetoric of unity accounts in large part for the unconscious and conscious transatlantic bridges scholars have discerned in their verse. It also serves as the basis for the many different ways in which the mysticism of both poets has been interpreted.

III

Perhaps Whitman's best example of the perception of cosmic unity comes in verse-chant 5 of 'Song of Myself', in which the speaker invites his soul to loaf with him on the grass:

> I mind how once we lay such a transparent summer morning,
> How you settled your head athwart my hips and gently turn'd over upon me,
> And parted the shirt from my bosom-bone, and plunged your tongue to my bare-stript heart,
> And reach'd till you felt my beard, and reach'd till you held my feet.
> Swiftly arose and spread around me that peace and knowledge that passed all argument of the earth,
> And I know that the hand of God is the promise of my own,
> And I know that the spirit of God is the brother of my own,
> And that all the man ever born are also my brothers, and the women my sisters and lovers,
> And that a kelson of the creation is love,
> And limitless are leaves stiff or drooping in the fields,
> And brown ants in the little wells beneath them,
> And mossy scabs of the worm fence, heap'd stones, elder, mullein and poke-weed.[31]

[31] Walt Whitman, 'Song of Myself', in: Bradley & Blodgett, *Leaves of Grass*, 86-98. (All subsequent Whitman citations, unless noted, are from this edition).

In strikingly sexual imagery, the speaker is ravished by his own soul, which leaves him with an understanding beyond all the argument of the earth – the wisdom that he is cosmically connected not only to all men and women but also to the minor details of life, such as brown ants, a pile of stones, and even weeds. Roger Asselineau has shown that this passage meets William James's criteria for mystical experience, arguing that it reveals a noetic, ineffable, transient and passive state of being.[32] To this I would add that it also contains an element in Underhill's definition of mystical states – love – since the 'understanding' the speaker is left with is not an intellectual acquisition of any sort but the perception that love binds together all seemingly discrete things. I agree with James Miller's comment, however, that the passage should be read as the dramatic representation of a mystical experience rather than a mere description of such a state.[33] The poetic qualities, such as alliteration, repetition, parallelism, and the appeal to the senses are too striking to be subsumed by a reading of the passage as mere description of experience.

Wordsworth employs the same rhetoric in 'Tintern Abbey', in which he speaks of

> [...] that blessed mood,
> In which the burden of the mystery,
> In which the heavy and the weary weight
> Of all this unintelligible world,
> Is lightened – that serene and blessed mood,
> In which the affections gently lead us on,
> Until, the breath of this corporeal frame
> And even the motion of our human blood
> Almost suspended, we are laid asleep
> In body, and become a living soul:
> While with an eye made quiet by the power
> Of harmony, and the deep power of joy,
> We see into the life of things. (37-49)

Just as Whitman passes all of the argument of the earth, Wordsworth experiences the lifting of the weary weight of the unintelligible world, that is, of the questioning intellect that tries (but fails) to apprehend the mystery of being. His blessed mood triggers a shifting of awareness akin to sleep in that it causes a temporary forgetting of the body. The resulting perception is one of harmony and joy, and he thus 'sees into the life of things', which is to say, he sees that all things participate in the harmony of this serene and 'blessed mood'. The form

[32] Asselineau, *The evolution of Walt Whitman*, 17-18.

[33] James E. Miller, *A critical guide to Leaves of Grass*, Chicago: University of Chicago Press, 1957, 47.

of consciousness he depicts transcends normal awareness; it is light, tranquil, liquid, and sanctimonious. This soul awareness is beyond rationality, as it enables the speaker to discern a sense of unity behind the seeming discord of the world, beyond the fragmentation yielded by logic. Such consciousness brings with it an accompanying insight into the impenetrable, the ability to *see into* things. But this is not to be confused with a heightened visual sense, for Wordsworth's insight is predicated upon the blinding of the corporeal sense.

There appears to be a difference between the two poets in how they arrive at the perception of unity: Whereas Whitman celebrates the body, as it cosmically copulates with the soul in a spiritual marriage, Wordsworth transcends the body altogether. As Roger Asselineau observes, 'Whitman never forgets that his body is the point of origin for his mystical states'.[34] Wordsworth, on the other hand, often (but not always) locates his point of origin in the imagination – the doorway to the otherworld. But such a view is often taken to untenable extremes. Asselineau himself believed that the experience depicted in Whitman's verse-chant 5 is a 'mystical state possibly induced during masturbation'.[35] Similarly, Wordsworthian critics are frequently off the mark in calling the poet a strict transcendentalist who Platonically denies the physical world. To be sure, there is a body-denying/world-denying element in Wordsworth's rhetoric, but such a denial can be found in Whitman's rhetoric as well, particularly that of the later years.

The issue is not with either poet per se but with the dualistic mindset critics often bring to bear in their interpretations of Wordsworth and Whitman's mysticism. The cosmic rhetoric in both actually subverts the dualism of Western thinking. V.K. Chari, despite his seeming uneasiness over the physical elements of Whitman's mysticism, does acknowledge that the latter's poems 'are exceptionally free from the spirit of dualism – of matter and spirit, subject and object, the sensible and suprasensible – which is so prominent in Christian and Platonic mysticism'.[36] John Rudy similarly observes in Wordsworth's poetry the existence of 'a prejudgmental, pre-reflective consciousness so deeply aligned with a perceived matrix of creative forces that it is impossible to say where the world's energies leave off and those of the poet begin'.[37] It is just as incorrect, therefore, to interpret Wordsworth's passage as world-denying Platonism as it is to interpret Whitman's as a physical, possibly autoerotic, moment. In both cases, rather, there is a collapsing of the boundary between this world and the other. Although 'laid asleep in body', and although he has become a 'living soul', Wordsworth

[34] Asselineau, *The evolution of Walt Whitman*, 18.
[35] Idem, 113.
[36] Chari, *Whitman in the light of Vedantic mysticism*, 114.
[37] Rudy, *Wordsworth and the Zen mind*, 13.

sees into the life of things in this world. And Whitman, although he similarly sees into the life of things, also possesses a knowledge beyond this world. While it is important not to homogenize the cosmic rhetoric in both poets, for there are palpable distinctions, it is necessary to recognize the ways in which both poets subverted Western dualism. As Whitman wrote in 'A Song for Occupations', 'Strange and hard that Paradox true I Give / Objects gross and the unseen soul are one' (216).

In her comparative study of Whitman and the American Indian tradition, Norma Wilson claims the difference between a mystic and a visionary is that 'the mystic submits to a divine order so that earthly life becomes unimportant', whereas the visionary 'lives actively on this earth, as a revolutionary attempting to bring about the ideal earthly existence'.[38] As I have argued in the previous chapter, I do not believe either Whitman or Wordsworth deserves the label of mystic, but I also reject the title of visionary, as it denies the transcendental element. Whitman wrote in 'To Think of Time':

> I swear I think now that every thing without exception has an eternal soul!
> The trees have, rooted in the ground! The weeds of the sea have! The animals!
> I swear I think there is nothing but immortality!
> That the exquisite scheme is for it, and the nebulous float is for it, and the cohering is for it!
> And all preparation is for it – and identity is for it – and life and materials are altogether for it! (440)

In Whitman's rhetoric all things have both a physical *and* a transcendental aspect; all things cohere in a 'nebulous float' – a cosmic liquid from which all materials derive existence, as Helen Davis has observed. This liquid is not merely the physical ocean, however, for even oceans die, and Whitman's nebulous float is immortal. Whitman's 'cosmic solution' is not only a symbol of death, for it also 'chants life and the immortal birth of eternal rhythmic tides which pulsate in every living thing'.[39]

Similarly, to call Whitman a visionary is to deny all of the many moments in his mystical passages when the ego-self seems to be overcome by a force much larger and greater than itself, when it submits to the divine order. In verse-chant 5 of 'Song of Myself' he is cosmically ravished by his soul. In 'The Mystic Trumpeter', after hearing non-physical music, he proclaims, 'O trumpeter, methinks I am myself the instrument thou playest / Thou melt'st my heart, my brain –

---

[38] Norma Wilson, 'Heartbeat: Within the visionary tradition', in: Geoffrey M. Sill (Ed.), *Walt Whitman of Mickle Street*, Knoxville: University of Tennessee Press, 1994, 226.

[39] Helen Benigni Davis, 'The cosmic solution in Walt Whitman's Leaves of Grass', in: *The Cloverdale Review* (1992-93), 99-100.

thou movest, drawest, changest them at will' (50-51). In countless other such passages forces act upon the poetic persona, who almost helplessly receives the action. Admittedly, there are also moments in Whitman's verse in which the poetic persona reverses roles and becomes the force acting on other people, places, and things. What I am suggesting is simply that Whitman can be called neither a mystic nor a visionary; the title of 'cosmic poet' is more appropriate.

Wordsworth, too, might be called a visionary in terms of the ideal existence he puts forth in his verse. Arguably there is very little real-world strife in his poetry; all is harmonious, unified, and beautiful in the Wordsworthian world. For this reason, in fact, he has been charged by a number of Marxists with 'denying' history and the sociopolitical actualities of his day. To call him a visionary, however, is to forget his spiritualizing of the physical world:

> To every natural form, rock, form or flower,
> Even the loose stones that cover the highway,
> I gave a moral life – I saw them feel,
> Or linked them to some feeling. The great mass
> Lay bedded in a quickening soul, and all
> That I beheld respired with inward meaning.
> Thus much for the one presence, and the life of the great whole.
> (*The Prelude* III. 130-137)

For Wordsworth, all material things are held together by a quickening soul – 'one presence' – which, like Whitman's nebulous float, provides both meaning and existence to all physical forms. Such rhetoric may seem to deny the physical existence of things by attributing their origin to some nonphysical, transcendental source, but to interpret Wordsworth's cosmic unity in this way is, once again, to impose dualistic thinking on an expression of nonpolar thought.

'[B]y describing the effect and impressions of illumination in terms of ordinary consciousness', writes James Glimm, 'Wordsworth democratized transcendent encounter and set a paradigm for mystical description in secular literature'.[40] One of the ways in which Wordsworth and Whitman are connected is in the democratic principles they bring to transcendent language. Such rhetoric permeates Wordsworth's verse, as Glimm argues, and quite plausibly could have influenced Whitman, who took the democratization of transcendent encounter to a new level. All aspects of nature in his verse are alive with consciousness. His 'Song of the Redwood Tree' is one such example: As the poem opens the speaker hears an impalpable, though discernible, 'prophecy' – the voices of the dying Redwood trees lovingly giving themselves up to the axe and the march of

[40] Glimm, *Five essays on mystical experience in the works of Wordsworth, Coleridge, and Shelley*, ii.

progress. 'Farewell my brethren / Farewell O earth and sky, farewell ye neighboring waters / My time has ended, my term has come', says one tree (6-8). The speaker has the special capacity to hear the 'wood-spirits', which sing a mighty death-chant but also assert their life:

> You untold life of me,
> And all you venerable and innocent joys,
> Perennial hardy life of me with joys 'mid rain and many a summer sun,
> And the white snows and night and the wild winds;
> O the great patient rugged joys, my soul's strong joys unreck'd by man,
> (For know I bear the soul befitting me, I too have consciousness, identity,
> And all the rocks and mountains have, and all the earth,)
> Joys of the life befitting me and brothers mine,
> Our time, our term has come. (24-32)

The chant rises to what the speaker calls an 'ecstatic' level, as the trees sing the praises of 'a superber race', for whom they, as 'forest kings', will 'abdicate' their majestic thrones in order to serve the new race of Americans. Whitman's rhetoric of unity attributes life not only to trees but also to rocks, mountains, and even the earth itself. All things, animate and 'inanimate' participate in the same miracle of life, which is consciousness itself. 'To me', Whitman wrote, 'Every hour of the light and dark is a miracle / Every cubic inch of space is a miracle / Every square yard of the surface of the earth is spread with the same / Every one of the interior swarms with the same' ('Miracles' 17-20).

Whitman embraced the Wordsworthian democratization of transcendent encounter so thoroughly that he claimed in 'Starting from Paumanok' he would sing its praises in every one of his poems:

> I will not make poems with reference to parts,
> But I will make poems, songs, thoughts, with reference to ensemble,
> And I will not saying with reference to a day, but with reference to all days,
> And I will not make a poem nor the least part of a poem but has reference to the soul
> Because having look'd that the objects of the universe, I find there is no one nor any particle of one but has reference to the soul. (172-176)

Whitman subverted the distinctions one normally imposes on objects of perception, homogenizing all things and thus obliterating all boundaries between them. Helen Davis points out that human identity was, for Whitman, a 'temporary thrusting' from the cosmic solution in which the soul partakes of 'love and earthly identity' but then 'returns to the solution'.[41] To this I would add that

[41] Davis, 'The cosmic solution in Walt Whitman's Leaves of Grass', 95.

in Whitman's poetic not only human identity but all individual identity emerges from and ultimately merges back into the great whole, the cohesion that makes all things coincide.

Another way in which Wordsworth and Whitman are connected is in the consciousness dilation occurring before (and thus making possible) moments of cosmic unity. To a striking degree, both poets repeatedly depict moments in which the poetic persona experiences the obliteration of finite consciousness and the ensuing liquidity of cosmic consciousness. Such moments can occur as a result of a natural scene, but there are many exceptions to this rule, particularly in Whitman but also in Wordsworth. 'Composed upon Westminster Bridge' is a clear example of a cosmic perception occurring in a city:

> Earth has not anything to show more fair:
> Dull would he be of soul who could pass by
> A site so touching in its majesty:
> This city now doth, like a garment, wear
> The beauty of the morning; silent, bare,
> Ships, powers, domes, theaters, and temples lie
> Open unto the fields, and to the sky;
> All right and glittering in the smokeless air.
> Never did sun more beautifully steep
> In his first splendour, valley, rock, or hill;
> Ne'er saw I, never felt, a calm so deep!
> The river glideth that his own sweet will:
> Dear God! the very houses seem asleep;
> And all that mighty heart is lying still! (1-14)

In *Limits of Mortality* David Ferry sees the final line as suggesting 'that this city is not merely sleeping but dead, its heart stilled', arguing that Wordsworth 'looks at London and sees it as a corpse and admires it as such, welcomes a death which is the death of what the city has come to stand for in his symbolic world'.[42] Such a reduction is almost as absurd as Asselineau's attributing of Whitman's mystical moment to masturbation. Ferry's psychoanalytic reading is also not unlike Barbara Johnson's interpretation of muteness in Keats as a celebration of female silence, a symptom of female oppression. Dennis Taylor refutes such a view, arguing that 'there is an idea of muteness which is still a value to be sought, and to be distinguished from the gagging of women'.[43] Silence in Wordsworth is nourishing and should not be interpreted as some type of regressive, Freudian death wish. The poet sees not death, but life – more specifically, One Life –

[42] David Ferry, *The limits of mortality: An essay on Wordsworth's major poems*, Middletown, CT: Wesleyan University Press, 1959, 114.

[43] Taylor, 'The need for a religious literary criticism', 8.

which he describes in terms of a single heart lying still. To be sure, the heart is not beating, but it is also not dead. The city is not a corpse but an emblem of this nourishing silence. In the *stillness* the poet discerns not death but calm, quietude, and a nourishing sense of consciousness dilation. It is a soothing stillness, a beautiful silence that reveals a splendor pervading valley, rock, and hill. It is a calm so deep it makes the poet call out to his dear God – and a sight so touching that only the dull of soul could pass by without experiencing an expansion of consciousness that opens 'unto the fields, and to the sky'.

Wordsworth has a similar moment of dilation in the second book of *The Prelude*, in which he discusses feeling connected in an almost religious way to nature. This sense of unity comes to him 'strengthened with a superadded soul', which is to say, he does not feel as though he is superimposing this sense onto nature; rather, it seems to have a life of its own (II. 328):

> [...] before the vernal thrush
> Was audible, among the hills I sate
> Alone upon some jutting eminence
> At the first power of morning, when the vale
> Lay quiet in an utter solitude.
> How shall I trace the history, where seek
> The origin of what I then have felt?
> Oft in those moments such a holy calm
> Did overspread my soul that I forgot
> That I had bodily eyes, and what I saw
> Appeared like something in myself, a dream,
> A prospect in my mind. (339-352)

In a moment of stillness, even before the singing of birds is audible, the poet internalizes the silence of the scene, which becomes for him a moment of 'holy calm' that permeates his entire sense of being. This cosmic sense overtakes him much like it does in 'Tintern Abbey' in that it causes him to transcend his bodily senses. Interestingly, what he sees appears 'like something in myself', having a dreamlike or imaginative quality. Subject and object merge in this moment; he becomes what he sees, and what he sees has become him.

In his moments of dilation Whitman likewise merges entirely with what he perceives. He, too, not only sees the unity but embraces it and *becomes* it. In 'We Two, How Long We Were Fool'd' he even brings the reader into the similitude:

> We two, how long we were fool'd,
> Now transmuted, we swiftly escape as nature escapes,
> We are Nature, longer have we been absent, but now we return,
> We the calm plants, trunks, foliage, roots, bark,
> We are bedded in the ground, we are rocks,
> We are oaks, we grow in the openings side-by-side, [...]

> We are two fishes swimming in the seat together, [...]
> We are also the course smut of beasts, vegetables, minerals, [...]
> We are two resplendent suns, we it is who balance ourselves orbic and stellar, we
> are as two comets, [...]
> We are seas mingling, we are two of those cheerful waves rolling overeach other
> and interwetting each other, [...]
> We are snow, rain, cold, darkness, we are each product and influence of the globe,
> We have circled and circled till we have arrived home again, we two,
> We have voided all but freedom and all but our own joy. (1-19)

Asselineau claims there is no monism in Walt Whitman, arguing that Whitman 'passed from a materialism colored with spirituality to a spiritualism tinged with materialism'.[44] But if monism is defined as the 'doctrine that mind and matter are formed from one substance or principal of being', as it is by the authors of *The American Heritage College Dictionary*, then Whitman's poem proves Asselineau wrong. His refusal to see monism where it clearly exists is actually his refusal to relinquish his grip on the Western, dualistic mode of thinking. 'We Two' is a clear blurring of the boundaries separating individual and whole. Poet and reader overcome the 'illusion' of separate identities, becoming Nature itself and merging with, or rather returning to, the original source of Being. Whitman would later write in 'I Sing the Body Electric', 'I see my soul reflected in nature [...] I see through a mist, One with inexpressible completeness' (72, 73).

Significantly, Whitman circles the globe in his poem, using a symbol of unity – the round earth itself – to signify cosmic cohesion. As Dwight Kalita has pointed out, the poet was fond of using the image of the circling globe in his verse to symbolize his 'central idea of the regenerative and mystic union of body and soul'.[45] He used the image of the globe to explode the notion of disparate consciousnesses, for both poet and reader become liquefied and thus obliterated, overcoming the illusory sense of separate existence and melting back into unity. Such a transmutation back into that which is without division runs against the grain of Whitman's gospel of the Democratic individual. Politically-minded critics often overlook this cosmic element in Whitman's rhetoric, reading as they do his understanding of democracy too literally and ignoring the sense of cosmic unity that underscores it.

'Out Of the Rolling Ocean the Crowd' is a similar statement of the unity theme:

---

[44] Asselineau, *The evolution of Walt Whitman*, 31.

[45] Dwight Kalita, 'Walt Whitman: Ecstatic sea-voyager', in: *Walt Whitman Review* 21 (1975), 15.

Out of the rolling ocean the crowd came a drop gently to me,
Whispering *I love you, before long I die,*
I have travel'd a long way merely to look on you to touch you,
For I could not die till I once look'd on you,
For I fear'd I might afterward lose you.
Now we have met, we have looked, we are safe,
Return in peace to the ocean my love,
I too am part of the ocean my love, we are not so much separated,
Behold the great rondure, the cohesion of all, how perfect! (1-9)

Using another favorite image – the ocean – as Kalita also points out, Whitman is again pointing to the ephemeral quality of individual existence. The soul is merely a drop in a vast cosmic sea, which Whitman again describes in terms of 'rondure' and 'perfect' cohesion. This oceanic unity subverts death, containing in it a Wordsworthian quality of utter 'peace'. It empowers the poet with the vision that looks through death and sees only an all-pervading, unifying calm. The individual droplet loses its sense of self in returning to the ocean, but it gains the magnitude of the entire cosmic solution. Droplet becomes ocean – individual becomes all – in this cosmic swelling of consciousness.

One of Wordsworth's 'Lucy' poems, with which Whitman was almost surely familiar, similarly contains a death-subverting sense of unity, as well as the image of the round earth:

A slumber did my spirit seal;
I had no human fears:
She seemed a thing that could not feel
The touch of earthly years.
No motion has she now, no force;
She neither hears nor sees;
Rolled round in earth's diurnal course,
With rocks, and stones, and trees. (1-8)

Some critics have interpreted the Lucy poems as an expression of Wordsworth's fear of losing someone he loved – perhaps Dorothy. Regardless of whether the death depicted in the poems was real or imagined, what is of interest, at least in 'A Slumber', is the speaker's perceptual movement from naivete to the awareness of death and the unity beyond mortality. She (whoever *she* is) has no motion and no force, that is, her physical identity has ceased, for she 'neither hears nor sees'. Paradoxically, however, she rolls around in earth's daily course, having merged with the 'rocks, and stones, and trees'. Just like Whitman's later globe image, Wordsworth's suggests not only unity but an enlargement of identity via the cessation of individuality. The poem's subject has crossed the death threshold but has, nevertheless, *emerged* as something much larger in melting into the circling globe. To mix the metaphor, the drop has reentered the ocean and has swelled to become the ocean itself. The poet experiences a similar enlargement of consciousness as a result of Lucy's death. 'Lucy touches his inner levels of consciousness', according to James Glimm, 'so he moves beyond ordinary perception. She is a mystery that makes him think of the outer boundaries of the universe'.[46] The second stanza indicates he has awoken from his slumber of innocence to a new understanding of the outer boundaries of individual consciousness.

Unlike Wordsworth, Whitman frequently in his poems becomes other *people*, experiencing the same Wordsworthian sense of cosmic enlargement but by melting into other human beings. His famous poem 'The Sleepers' is the clearest representative example. The poem opens with the speaker wandering in some type of vision, 'lost to myself' and 'confused' because of the radical alteration in consciousness the expanded awareness brings (4). In his nighttime dreamscape the speaker sees a phantasmagoria of other dreamers and passes his hands soothingly in front of them as they sink into fitful sleep. Then, in a critical moment, he pierces the darkness and the earth recedes into the night. He calls what is 'not the earth' just as beautiful as the globe itself. Having crossed this threshold of consciousness, he states, 'I dream in my dream all the dreams of the other dreamers / And I become the other dreamers' (126). The experience leaves him with the knowledge that 'The universe is duly in order, everything is in its place' (155). With this sense of harmony and cohesion, he sees all sleepers at once as the poem closes:

> The sleepers are very beautiful as they lie unclothed,
> They flow hand in hand over the whole Earth from East to West as they lie on clothed,
> The Asiatic and African are hand in hand, the European and American are hand in hand,
> Learn'd and unlearn'd are hand in hand, and male and female are hand in hand,
> The bare arm of the girl crosses the bare breast of her lover, they press close without lost, his lips pressed against her neck,
> The father holds his grown or ungrown son in his arms with measureless love, and the son holds the father in his arms with measureless love [...] (161-167)

The nighttime journey leaves him with the vision of the unity of all opposites, such as East and West and the scholar and the illiterate, as well as of the interlocking of all things great and small, sacred and profane, healthy and diseased, in a oneness that spans and also transcends the entire earth. His discovery of this

[46] Glimm, *Five essays on mystical experience in the works of Wordsworth, Coleridge, and Shelley*, 29.

sense of cosmic unity leads to a rectification of wrongs, as 'The call of the slave is one with the master's call, and the master salutes the slave', and 'The felon steps forth from the prison' (170, 171). It leads to the healing of sickness as 'the insane becomes sane, the suffering of sick persons is reliev'd' (171). It leads to an all-pervading sense of human consonance.

Despite that many who met Wordsworth thought he was cold and somewhat arrogant, the persona in his poetry is not without human warmth. While home on summer break from Cambridge, for instance, the poet recalled in *The Prelude* the moment when a *human* quality began to intermingle with his love of nature:

> Nor less do I remember to have felt
> Distinctly manifested at this time
> A dawning, even as of another sense,
> A human-heartedness about my love
> For objects hitherto the gladsome air
> Of my own private being, and no more –
> Which I had loved, even as a blessed spirit
> Or angel, if he were to dwell on earth,
> Might love in individual happiness. (222-230)

He has grown to love the things of nature the way human beings love one another, which is to say, he has realized that the unity of all life is made possible by the dawning of this new cosmic sense of love:

> A newborn feeling. Its spread far and wide:
> The trees, the mountains shared it, and the brooks,
> The stars of Heaven, now seen in their old haunts –
> [...] Whatever shadings of mortality
> Had fallen upon these objects heretofore
> Were different in kind: not tender – strong,
> Deep, gloomy were today, and severe, the scatterings
> Of childhood, and moreover, had given way
> In later used to beauty and to love
> Enthusiastic, to delight and joy. (241-255)

From this point onward, the poet approaches all things of the natural world with a sense of warm love and reverence. He not only feels at one with nature but loves it as if it were an extension of himself. It is also worth noting that Wordsworth bridges the gulf between self and nature via this newly dawned sense of human heartedness in his love for the natural world. Perhaps it is a stretch to say so, but he has become intimate with the world. Although Wordsworth probably would have cringed at how far Whitman would later take such union, copulating with the world as he does, he (Wordsworth) nevertheless achieves an unprecedented sense of union with nature.

Whitman's 'Mystic Trumpeter' similarly causes in him the dawning of a new sense. The 'bodiless' musician's music, which vibrates capriciously through the air, 'descends like dew upon' him (16). In strikingly biblical language he describes the effect of the strange music as a 'holy calm' that transmutes his nighttime walk into 'the walks of Paradise' (17). In his consciousness dilation he perceives the underlying unity of the cosmos in terms of love:

> Love, that is all the earth to lovers – love, that mocks time and space,
> Love, that is day and night – love, that is son and moon and stars,
> Love, that is crimson, sumptuous, sick with perfume,
> No other words but words of love, no other thoughts but love. (39-42)

Whitman's love, while it is clearly cosmic in proportion, also contains erotic overtones. It is 'crimson, sumptuous, sick with perfume'. His love is more primal than Wordsworth's, more primitive and uninhibited. His love is a sort of spiritualized sexual love, another blurring of the boundary between matter and spirit:

> Blow again the trumpeter! and for thy theme,
> Take now be in closing theme of all, the solvent and the setting,
> Love, that is pulse of all, the sustenance and the pang,
> The heart of man and woman all for love,
> No other theme but love – knitting, enclosing, all-diffusing love. (30-34)

In her dissertation on Wordsworth and Whitman, Barbara Herman sees a critical distinction between the two poets in the 'suppressed sexuality of Wordsworth and the open celebration of the sensual in Whitman'.[47] The above passages seem to prove the point, but I would caution against reading Wordsworth as sexually repressed in the Freudian sense. Wordsworth wrote, as did Whitman, in an era when the mention of sexuality in literature was unacceptable. Clearly, Whitman defied such constraints by openly singing the praises of sex and by elevating the erotic to divine status. In Wordsworth there is no such celebration or elevation, but his verse is overwhelmingly sensu*ous*. There is an erotic connection to nature in Wordsworth, but it is of the muted, English, 18th-century kind. Wordsworth's is an innocent eroticism. His celebration of valleys, mountains, streams, trees and birds and his sense of joy whenever he returns to his natural home (as though he is being reunited with a lover) are clear examples.

To reduce the sense of cosmic love in both poets to the erotic, however, is to overlook the expansiveness of the sentiment. Erotic love, while it can cross the boundaries of individuality, is confined to the physical body. Cosmic love, on

---

[47] Herman, *The pleasure of heaven, pains of hell, intimations of immortality*, 41.

the other hand, contains the erotic and much else besides; it is copulation on a cosmic scale. As both poets show, it knits together all disparate entities. The difference between a Freudian reading and a cosmic one is essentially the difference between metaphor and metonymy: The Freudian says cosmic love is transmuted eroticism energy; the cosmic poet says erotic coupling is a microcosm of the macrocosm, a diminutive version of the love binding together all life.

Wordsworth frequently bestowed upon characters in his verse the understanding of cosmic love. 'The Pedlar' is one such example, for he learns at the tender age of six 'the deep lesson of love' (211):

> Oh! then what soul was his when on the tops
> Of the high mountains he beheld the sun
> Rise up, and they the world in life. He looked;
> The ocean and the earth beneath him lay
> In gladness and deep joy. The clouds were touched
> And in their silent faces did he read
> Unutterable love. Sound needed none,
> Nor any voice of joy: his spirit drank
> The spectacle; sensation, soul, and form
> All melted into him; they swallowed up
> His animal being: in them did he live,
> And buy them did he live: they were his life.
> In such access of mind. In such high hour
> Of visitation from the living God,
> Thought was not. In enjoyment it expired.
> No thanks he breathed, he proffered no request;
> Rapt into still communion that transcends
> The imperfect offices of prayer and praise,
> His mind was a Thanksgiving to the Power
> That made him: it was blessedness and love.[48]

The experience contains nearly all of the elements of mystical perception: self-dissolution, ineffability, the wisdom beyond thought, communion and bliss, visitation from God, and, most important, 'unutterable love'. The pedlar sees love in the earth and the ocean, and he reads love in the silent faces of the clouds. Significantly, he becomes aware of unifying properties of love from his high perspective on the mountaintop, often an emblem for expanded awareness in cosmic literature. His consciousness has dilated in his 'intercourse' (239) and 'communion' (234) with nature, and he spends much of his earlier years 'possessed'

[48] Taken from William Wordsworth, *Selected poems* (Ed. John O. Hayden), New York: Penguin, 1994, 218-240.

(240) by this loving union. Not unlike the amorous wetness that underlies Whitman's cosmic love, Wordsworth's passage also contains liquid imagery: the world is bathed in light, and the pedlar's spirit 'drank / The spectacle', as 'All melted into him'. The images are devoid of fixed boundaries, as the clouds are flowing and the rolling earth and *ocean* lie beneath. Even the sentiments the poet conveys are fluid and expansive such as gladness, deep joy, and, of course, love.

Interestingly, what catalyzes the pedlar's perception of cosmic unity is the image of the rising sun as its diffusive light bathes the world in golden splendor. Bernice Slote, discussing what she calls the tradition of 'life writers' (which consists of Lawrence, Crane, Thomas, and Whitman), claimed that those who 'have a sense of the cosmos and who in their art perform the ritual of union' express with symbolic complexity 'that man may find himself both human and divine as he returns to touch the earth with awareness and love, and joins the sun's creative stream'.[49] As I pointed out in the previous chapter, the authors of *Start with the Sun* mention in passing that this tradition is rooted in Wordsworth (among others). The pedlar's experience captures why Miller, Shapiro, and Slote saw a transatlantic continuity between both poets.

Considered in the light of such scholarship, Wordsworth's connection to the sun takes on an added significance. Early in *The Prelude* he makes clear his orientation towards the sun:

> [...] already I began
> To love the sun, a boy I loved the sun
> Not as I since have loved him – as a pledge
> And surety of our earthly life, a light
> Which while we view we feel we are alive –
> But for this cause, that I had seen him lay
> His beauty on the morning hills, had seen
> The western mountain touch his setting orb
> In many a thoughtless hour, when from excess
> Of happiness my blood appeared to flow
> With its own pleasure, and I breathed with joy. (177-188)

As a boy, Wordsworth loves the sun not because it gives him a sense of security but for its own power and beauty and the pleasure, happiness and joy it instills in him. However unconsciously, the boy is apprehending the interrelation of all life through the perception of the supreme symbol of unity from the earthly perspective – the sun. He loves the sun not because it does anything at all but simply because it *is*, because it reflects the mystery of *being*. Later in the same book Wordsworth's sun wisdom leads to a perception of unity:

[49] Miller, Shapiro, & Slote, *Start with the Sun*, 229.

[...] I at this this time
Saw blessings spread around me like a sea.
Thus did my days pass on, and now at length
From nature and her overflowing soul
I had received so much that all my thoughts
Were steeped in feeling. I was only then
Contended when with bliss ineffable
I felt the sentiments of being spread
O'er all that moves, and all that seemeth still,
O'er all that, lost beyond the reach of thought
And human knowledge, to the human eye
Invisible, yet live with to the heart,
O'er all that leaps, and runs, and shouts, and sings,
Or beats the gladsome air, o'er all that glides
Beneath the wave, yea, in the wave itself
And mighty depth of waters. Wonder not
If such my transports were, for and all things
I saw one life, and felt that it was joy;
One song they sang, and it was audible –
Most audible then when the fleshly ear,
O'ercome by a grosser prelude of that strain,
Forgot its functions and slept undisturbed. (88)

He feels the sentiment of being spread over all physical things, likening it to the flowing and fluid images of air and water, which clearly suggest the lack of boundaries in typical oceanic feelings. He feels transported beyond the range of human knowledge and physical perception. Wordsworth not only sees but hears the unity of one life, perceptions at once physical and spiritual. He hears the 'one song' with his 'fleshly ear', but the music is more audible when the physical ear forgets its function and sleeps.

Whitman's 'Song at Sunset' is a similar tribute to the sun in which the poet, at the 'Hour prophetic' (2) sees as the sun goes down the grandeur and the good in all physical life, including 'even the tiniest insect' (11). Like Wordsworth, he perceives beyond the physical realm, seeing the illustriousness of 'unnumber'd spirits' (10) and the 'spirituality of things' (39). The sun for both poets is a portal to the other world, at once a physical emblem of the divine unity and a physical manifestation of such unity. Considering that nearly all of the matter constituting the earth, including the atoms in all sentient beings, was once part of the huge, yellow fireball we call the sun, and considering that at the moment of the Big Bang *all* matter and space in the universe emerged from a microscopic nugget that would make a grain of sand look colossal, both poets' claim of cosmic unity is not nearly as far-fetched and deceived as it may sound. In one sense all life does indeed derive from a single source.

Dilation of consciousness in Wordsworth and Whitman does not always have to occur as a result of being in the presence of the sun or the ocean or some other magnificent physical spectacle. The catalyst for such experiences, in fact, can often be quite mundane. In *The Prelude* Wordsworth claims to have been able to cultivate a strange state of mind in which the 'ballast of familiar life' (VII. 631) would leave him while he would walk the streets of London, and the faces of everyone he met would be 'a mystery' (VII. 629). On one such occasion he happened upon a blind beggar who had a piece of paper containing his life's story affixed to his chest. The image induces in the poet something like a Zen moment of Satori in that he realizes that 'this label was a type / Or emblem of the utmost that we know / Both of ourselves and of the universe' (VII. 260).

Brooke Hopkins likens such Wordworthian moments to what Rudolph Otto called the 'numinous', which is something like 'holy' in terms of otherness and mystery but without the moral component typically associated with the term.[50] In the moment he learns of the mystery beyond knowing, that is, that the knowledge we have both of ourselves and of the universe is superficial and obstructive in that it prevents us from the unknowing of expanded awareness. Wordsworth likens the effect of the label to 'the might of waters', which is to say, although it is a seemingly insignificant image, it carries much weight indeed (VII. 644). The look on the blind beggar's 'fixed face and sightless eyes' seems to the poet as if he has been 'admonished from another world' (VII. 622-623). Through the seemingly trivial encounter with a beggar and the sympathy he inspires, Wordsworth has a life-altering experience in which he catches a glimpse of the otherworld. His perception razes to the ground the edifice of limited ego-awareness and leads him to a greater sense of the mystery of being.

Whitman reports a similar encounter in 'Sparks from the Wheel' in which he joins a group of children watching a knife grinder sharpen a knife:

> This scene and all its belongings, how they seize and affect me,
> The sad sharp-chinn'd old man worn clothes and broad shoulder-band
> of leather,
> Myself effusing and fluid, a phantom curiously floating, now here absorbed and
> arrested.
> The group, (and unminded point set in a vast surrounding,)
> The low hoarse purr of the whirling stone, the light-press'd blade,
> Diffusing, dropping, sideways-darting, in tiny showers of gold,
> Sparkles from the wheel. (9-16)

[50] Brooke Hopkins, 'The mystical dimensions of Wordsworth's poetry', in: *Studia Mystica* 4 (1981) no.2, 50.

Like Wordsworth, he experiences a very mundane catalyst of consciousness expansion in watching the knife grinder. Significantly, he joins a group of children, which suggests the childlike sense of imaginative wonder and the hypnotic reverie the sparks from the grinding wheel induce in him. He is staring at the wheel and cultivating the type of thoughtless knowing that accompanies many types of prolonged gazing. This might best be described as Wordsworth's 'wise passiveness', a state of mind similar to that of the daydream. Unlike Wordsworth, who is admonished from the otherworld, Whitman remains very much within the realm of the senses, depicting in detailed fashion the particulars of the scene and leaving it up to the reader to discern the hypnotic state of wonder and mystery that such details evoke.

Both writers clearly saw an underlying unity not only in the natural world but also among all people. 'Passing stranger', Whitman wrote in 'To a Stranger', 'you do not know how longingly I look upon you [...] I have somewhere surely lived a life of joy with you' (1, 3). The cosmic sense of connection to and attraction towards other people is at the heart of Whitman's 'Calamus' sentiment, which he calls 'adhesiveness', and which many modern critics have interpreted strictly in terms of homoeroticism. While I do not dispute that such eroticism informs much of Whitman's poetry, I would also argue that it is important to situate the theme of comradeship within a larger spiritual context, as David Keubrich points out in *Minor Prophecy*: 'When Calamus is placed within the context of Whitman's larger religious vision, it becomes clear that its fundamental level of meaning is not a gospel of homosexuality but of a mystical love which the religious personality traditionally affirms to be the soul's proper sustenance and best means of union with divinity'.[51] My only objection to Keubrich's argument is that it too fixedly holds to a Christian interpretation of Whitman's spirituality, which is clearly at odds with the homoerotic element. Nevertheless, the point is Whitman's sense of unity with other people was not merely homosexual attraction (which is no doubt part of it) but the more inclusive connection involving same-sex and heterosexual eroticism and an all-encompassing cohesion transcending physical love. Perhaps, as Kuebrich also argues, Whitman was consciously working with Platonic conceptions of love in his Calamus poems, which, if true, severely weakens the argument of those who read adhesiveness in *Leaves of Grass* as disguised homosexuality.

Wordsworth did not embrace other people with so much warmth and invitation, preferring to cultivate his sense of cosmic unity often in the solitude of nature. In isolation, however paradoxically, he discovered a sense of connection

[51] David Keubrich, *Minor prophesy: Walt Whitman's new American religion*, Bloomington: Indiana University Press, 1989, 149.

and community. As he explains in his planned but abortive masterpiece, 'The Recluse', the title of which indicates his love of solitude, he prefers to be away from the 'multitude whose eyes are doomed / To hold a vacant commerce day by day / With objects wanting life – repelling love' (594-596):

> From crowded streets remote
> Far from the living and dead wilderness
> Of the thronged World, Society is here
> A true Community – a genuine frame
> Of many into one incorporate.
> *That* must be looked for here; paternal sway
> One household, under God, for high and low,
> One family and one mansion [...]. (612-619)

What he really seems to be objecting to is not so much the presence of other people per se but of other people who lack the understanding of cosmic unity. Such people are the types found in cities who engage in empty commerce and activities that quell the spirit of love and unity. He is objecting to his own loss of this consciousness when in the midst of such throngs, for in nature he can achieve a sense of communion and a sense of all people merged 'into one incorporate'.

IV

George Hutchinson has argued that Whitman performed a shamanic role in *Leaves of Grass* as a spiritual medicine man whose ecstatic mode was meant to assure his nineteenth-century contemporaries 'that the powers that control the world are near and can be invoked'.[52] A Shaman's function in a society, says Hutchinson (who draws heavily on Mircea Eliade's work), is to respond to pressures that pose a threat to the unity of a group. Whitman, he argued, was working out in his poetry the anxieties of political disunion, for the stability of the Federal government was seriously in question leading up to and during Whitman's period of poetic production. Wordsworth, it could also be argued, was similarly performing a shamanic role of his own. When he published *Lyrical Ballads* with Coleridge in 1798, the promise of the French Revolution had degenerated into Robespierre's 'reign of terror', and the hope of a unified France under the Revolution's guidance was destroyed. There was also the threat of disunion in Britain as a result of the French situation, as sympathies were divided. Both poets,

[52] George B. Hutchinson, *The ecstatic Whitman*, Columbus, OH: Ohio State University Press, 1986, 12.

according to such a view, serve to allay fears of tribal separation by singing a gospel of metaphysical unity in their verse. While I do not disagree with this argument, I would caution against totalizing (and thus reducing) the rhetoric of cosmic unity in such a way. To be sure, a poet can serve as a form of tribal cement, but to read the rhetoric of unity in Wordsworth and Whitman in strictly sociological terms is to do injury to the states of consciousness they were attempting to convey. The shamanic interpretation is valid, therefore, but it yields only one perspective, and it cannot entirely account for the subjective aspects of mystical rhetoric.

At the other extreme are critics such as Jonathan Wordsworth, who actually denied the transcendental character of Wordsworth's 'great whole', arguing that in his verse the poet 'evokes moods that are very closely analogous to perceptions of the supernatural, but which never in fact cross the borderline'.[53] He goes so far as to say that Wordsworth is actually practicing a 'slight of hand' in attributing spiritual status to rocks, trees, and flowers.[54] Such dismissals are a misreading, however, for they overlook Wordsworth's poetic intention of giving 'the charm of novelty to things of everyday, and to excite a feeling analogous to the supernatural', as Coleridge stated in *Biographia Literaria*.[55] Karl Walter Malone has claimed that 'those who deny Whitman's mysticism are in a particular difficulty, for they will find him a greater enigma than those who acknowledge his mysticism' – a point that applies to Wordsworth as well.[56] What such criticism implicitly betrays is the critic's own Western understanding of spirituality, which says the material can never be spiritual. In its indeterminacy, the rhetoric of unity subverts such dualistic thinking.

Qian-zhi Wu notes in his study of Wordsworth and Taoism the injury critics often do to the poet's verse in interpreting his sense of unity as a kind of psychological malady. 'Even though in his poetry Wordsworth himself hails the essential oneness of the universe and celebrates the joy of complete unity of the mind with the spirit of the external world', laments Wu, 'critics [...] still insist that the poet was laboring under some kind of delusion'.[57] Critics have faulted Whitman for such rhetoric, as well. Richard Volney Chase argued that such a 'vast cosmic democracy, placid, without episode, separation or conflict [...] finally ruined Whitman as a poet, submerging as it did, his chief forte and glory

---

[53] Jonathan Wordsworth, M.H. Abrams, & Stephen Gill (Eds.), *The Prelude 1799, 1805, 1850: authoritative texts, context and reception, recent critical essays*, New York: Norton, 576.

[54] *The Prelude 1799, 1805, 1850*, 576.

[55] Coleridge, *Biographia literaria*, 168-169.

[56] Malone, *Parallels to Hindu and Taoist thought in Walt Whitman*, 9.

[57] Qian-zhi Wu, *The Wordsworthian imagination: Seeing nature as it is. A Taoist reading of Wordsworth* (Dissertation Cornell University 1988), 5.

– his entirely original, vividly realistic presentation of the comedy and pathos of "the simple separate person"'.[58] To dismiss the rhetoric of unity in such a way, however, is to destroy the entire foundation of Wordsworth and Whitman's vision. It is also to ignore one of the most striking aspects of their poetry, and it overlooks the most traversable of the transatlantic bridges between them. More important, it denies these poets their weapon of choice, for they used cosmic rhetoric as a form of ideological resistance – as a way to embrace an alternative to the dualism of Western rationality. Cosmic rhetoric, as we have seen, collapses the subject/object dichotomy, which is in many ways the foundation of Western thought. The Romanticism of Wordsworth and Whitman at its core is highly subversive. It may not have led to direct political revolution, but it did effect a quantum leap in consciousness, the likes of which we have not experienced since.

[58] Richard Volney Chase, 'Oneself I Sing' (1955), in: *Leaves of Grass*, 893.

Chapter IV

EGOLESS EGOTISM AND THE COSMIC SELF

The Question of Being[1]

'We sense in this philosophy both a tendency towards an extreme individuality and a tendency towards a deeply-felt totality'
(Jean-Paul Sartre on Existentialism)

'Self is an ongoing construction re-created in each moment through our choices'
(Jean-Paul Sartre)

I

Self in Whitman is frequently problematic for critics, who often read such lines as, 'I am large, I contain multitudes' – as solipsism. In his essay on Emily Dickinson's mysticism, Steve Carter remarks that because Dickinson does not 'sacrifice her self-will to a set of doctrines or rules outside of herself', she is 'as *egotistical* as Whitman'.[2] Both poets, he argues, 'retain their identities as they allow natural psychic processes to operate'.[3] Carter's comments are representative of many critics who view Whitman as the bard of individualism, as the poet who sang a gospel of the separate self. Some of these critics have expressed disappointment over Whitman's rhetoric of cosmic unity, claiming that such talk of merging destroys the individualist strain in *Leaves of Grass*. In his comical essay on the poet, D.H. Lawrence similarly expressed dissatisfaction over Whitman's rhetoric of unity:

> Now Whitman's way to Allness, he tells us, is through endless sympathy, merging. But in merging you must emerge away from something, as well as towards

[1] This chapter was published as 'Egoless "egotism" in Wordsworth and Whitman: The paradox of self', in: *Studia Mystica* 24 (2003), 72-103.

[2] Steve Carter, 'Emily Dickinson and mysticism', in: *ESQ: A Journal of the American Renaissance* 241 (1978) no.1, 91. (emphasis added)

[3] Carter, 'Emily Dickinson and mysticism', 91.

> something, and in sympathy you must depart from one point to arrive at another. Whitman lays down this law of sympathy as the one law, the direction of merging as the one direction. Which is obviously wrong [...] We know, as a matter of fact, that all life lies between two poles. The direction is twofold. Whitman's *one direction* becomes a hideous tyranny once he has attained his goal of Allness. His One Identity is a prison of horror, once realized.[4]

According to such views, Whitman's virtue lies in his celebration of the isolated *cogito* of Cartesian philosophy, and when he lapses into his rhetoric of unity, he does injury to his verse. The question remains, however, whether the self he celebrates is the individual ego or something quite different altogether.

Ever since Keats's labeling of the Wordsworthian mode as the 'egotistical sublime', Wordsworth also has been charged with solipsism. The egotistical sublime, according to Frederick Garber's understanding of Keats's charge, 'is an overwhelming public assertion of the poet's self and identity, the burden of character that denies the integrity of the object outside of it'.[5] In other words, the poet does not merely describe objects of nature but projects his own subjective state onto natural objects and then describes not the object itself but his own inner state. As William Hazlitt argued after Keats, Wordsworth 'does not present the reader with a lively succession of images or incidents, but paints the outgoings of his own heart, the shadings of his own fancy'.[6] 'In his most characteristic mode', writes Garber, '[Wordsworth's] own perception is the central activity in the poem'.[7] According to this view, the poet's ego-self is what is celebrated, not the natural world or some transcendent realm.

Ann Mellor has argued that Wordsworth embodies a 'Masculine Romanticism', which she claims 'has traditionally been identified with the assertion of a self that is unified, unique, enduring, capable of initiating activity, and above all aware of itself as a self'.[8] Mellor contrasts Wordsworth's 'solipsistic' Romanticism with his sister Dorothy's, whose sense of self 'is fluid, relational, exhibiting the permeable ego boundaries Chodorow attributed to the social construction of the feminine gender in those Western cultures in which females are assigned the role of primary infant caregiver, of mother'.[9] Conclusions such as these have compelled Geoffrey Hartman to observe that 'the charge of solipsism or egotism

---

[4] D.H. Lawrence, 'Whitman' (1921), in: Bradley & Blodgett, *Leaves of Grass*, 846.

[5] Frederick Garber, 'Point of view and the egotistical sublime', in: *English Studies* 49 (1968), 417.

[6] Qtd. in Garber, 'Point of view and the egotistical sublime', 411.

[7] Idem, 409.

[8] Qtd. in John L. Mahoney, *William Wordsworth: A poetic life*, New York: Fordham University Press, 1997, 145.

[9] Qtd. in Mahoney, *William Wordsworth*, 156-157.

has never been totally laid to rest' in Wordsworth.[10] Even in such fundamental works as *Introducing Romanticism,* Duncan Heath and Judy Boreham argue that solipsism was characteristic of many Romantic artists, the 'inevitable outcome of romantic aspirations'.[11]

To combat the charge of egotism against both poets, some critics have interpreted comments seemingly expressed from the isolated *cogito* as instances of expanded mystical awareness in which self is transcended and the speaker is empowered by forces greater than himself and thus given sway over the objects of his perceptions. V.K. Chari, for instance, argues that self in Whitman is not a 'windowless monad' but the 'immortal self', which is the same as the 'great cosmic power'.[12] Chari interprets Whitman's self in Vedantic terms, that is, self is Atman (soul), which is ultimately identical with Brahman (oversoul). John Rudy similarly deals with the charge of solipsism in Wordsworth by interpreting self in Zen terms. In Wordsworth 'the human imagination is the power to drop the self and to see with or through that which one at first perceives as other'.[13] For Rudy, Wordsworth annihilates the ego-self, much like Zennists do, so that 'at any moment in his poetry he is without conscious center'.[14]

Just as critics of the egotist camp seem to misread self in Wordsworth and Whitman, so do the mystical apologists, although I do acknowledge my own indebtedness to such readings. Chari's interpretation of self as *atman* denies the actual separate personality Whitman put forth in his verse – the 'Turbulent, fleshy, sensual, eating, drinking and breading' persona of 'Song of Myself' and other poems (498). Ward Paul Welty argues that when Whitman referred to himself as a 'kosmos', he was designating the microcosmic aspects of the macrocosm, the larger whole.[15] While I agree with such a reading, it is important to remember that the persona as *kosmos* is only one of many in *Leaves.* Rudy's reading of a Zen persona in Wordsworth's poetry is likewise not thoroughly compelling. There certainly may be many moments when Wordsworth's speaker is without conscious center, but to apply this statement to all of his verse overenthusiastically sees Zen 'emptiness' where it often does not exist. The 'cosmic' self stands somewhere between these two poles, defying both solipsism

---

[10] Geoffrey Hartman, '"Was it for this...?": Wordsworth and the birth of the gods', in: Karen Hanson & Herbert Marks (Eds.), *Romantic revolutions*, Bloomington: Indiana University Press, 1990, 9.

[11] Duncan Heath & Judy Boreham, *Introducing Romanticism*, New York: Totem, 1999, 81.

[12] Chari, *Whitman in the light of Vedantic mysticism*, 130.

[13] Rudy, *Wordsworth and the Zen mind*, 203.

[14] Idem, 40.

[15] Ward Paul Welty, *Walt Whitman, Kosmos: A study of the persona of 'Song of Myself'* (Diss. Drake University, Des Moines, Iowa, 1980), 90.

and mystical self-transcendence. The cosmic self collapses distinctions between these categories, as it is difficult to label either poet as egotist or mystic. While there is something of a Promethean strain in Wordsworth and Whitman in their stealing of the consciousness of the gods and bringing it to the earthly self, there are also moments when human consciousness is elevated to divine heights.

II

It is not without some justification that critics as far back as his contemporaries saw Wordsworth as an egotist. Prior to him, it was unacceptable to be so subjective, to privilege one's own perceptions and states of feeling over the 'objective' world. In an 1804 letter to Richard Sharp, Wordsworth expressed his uneasiness over the composition of a long, autobiographical poem then under construction: '[I]t seems a frightful deal to say about one's self, and of course will never be published (during my lifetime, I mean), till another work [The Recluse] has been written and published, of sufficient importance to justify me in giving my own history to the world'.[16] Wordsworth felt he had to apologize for talking about himself so much, and only in publishing another long poem in which he put forth his philosophy would he feel justified in publishing his autobiographical epic. Of course, he only finished a fragment of *The Recluse*, and, consequently, *The Prelude* was not published until he died in 1850.

Isaiah Berlin argued in *Roots of Romanticism* against the notion of separate Romantic movements, yoking all of them together by means of two fundamental, unifying concepts – will and subjectivity – which he believed constituted the Romantic sentiment. Wordsworth was breaking new ground in his cultivation of the 'egotistical' sublime, which accounts for his uneasiness over talking about himself so much. He was not only subverting the poetic taste of his day but also contributing to the shattering of the Enlightenment illusion of objectivity. Subjectivity was the new 'truth', but it was not universally embraced, as Romanticism was not a wholesale rejection of Enlightenment doctrines but a transmutation of *some* of these doctrines. More important, Wordsworth began talking about himself not in the radical milieu of American individualism but in polite English society, much of which was still steeped in orthodox notions of subservience to one's superiors.

Whitman, on the other hand, was almost unabashed about embracing Romantic subjectivity. '*Leaves of Grass* indeed (I cannot too often reiterate) has

---

[16] Qtd. in Wordsworth, Abrams, & Gill, *The Prelude 1799, 1805, 1850*, 532.

mainly been the outcropping of my own emotional and other personal nature', he wrote in 'A Backward Glance O'er Travel'd Roads', 'an attempt, from first to last, to put *a Person*, a human being (myself, in the latter half of the Nineteenth Century, in America,) freely, fully and truly on record' (453-456). He claimed he 'could not find a similar personal record in current literature that satisfied me', which sounds as though he is admitting having read *The Prelude* but also expressing his dissatisfaction over the way in which Wordsworth went about pouring forth his subjective world; it also sounds as though he sensed Wordsworth's reservations about celebrating his personality.

But Whitman was not without his own reservations. In *Good-Bye My Fancy* he wrote, 'I will not reject any theme or subject because the treatment is too personal. As my stuff settles into shape, I am told (and sometimes myself discover, uneasily, but feel all right about it in calmer moments) it is mainly autobiographic, and even egotistic after all – which I finally accept and am contented so'.[17] He was more at ease in talking about himself than was Wordsworth, but only in calmer moments, which indicates he, too, struggled with the anxiety over the question of solipsism. Ultimately, however, his autobiographic impulse prevailed, for he later claimed that his poetic ambition was 'to articulate and faithfully express in literary or poetic form, and uncompromisingly, my own physical, emotional, moral, intellectual, and aesthetic Personality [...] and to exploit that Personality, identified with place and date, in a far more candid and comprehensive sense than any hitherto poem or book' ('Backward Glance' 60-65). He also wrote in 'By Blue Ontario's Shore':

> It is not the earth, it is not America who is so great,
> It is I who am great or to be great, it is You up there, or anyone,
> It is to walk rapidly through civilizations, governments, theories
> Through poems, pageants, shows, to form individuals.
> Underneath all, individuals,
> I swear nothing is good to me now that ignores individuals,
> The American compact is altogether with individuals,
> The only government is that which makes minute of individuals,
> The whole theory of the universe is directed unerringly to one single individual – namely to You. (251-259)

On an unprecedented scale, Whitman put forth in his verse a gospel of the sanctity of individual consciousness. For him, each person contains a uniqueness greater even than whole governments and civilizations. Each person is sacred; the individual in a paradoxical way is larger than the whole. 'I absorb you all in myself, and become the master myself', he wrote in 'By Blue Ontario's Shore'.

[17] Qtd. in Bradley & Blodgett, *Leaves of Grass*, 770.

'America isolated yet embodying all, what is it finally except myself? These States, what are they except myself?' (307-310).

Richard Gravil has concluded that 'Song of Myself' is distinguished from its Wordsworthian predecessor by (among other things) its 'unashamed adoption of an intensified egotistical sublime as the appropriate mode of an American Bard'.[18] Whitman took Wordsworthian subjectivity to a new level, intensifying it and resolving for himself the uneasiness accompanying such a celebration of the self. 'One main contrast of the ideas behind every page of my verses, compared with established poems, is [...] the quite changed attitude of the ego, the one chanting or talking, towards himself and towards his fellow-humanity', he boldly asserted in 'A Backward Glance'. 'It is certainly time for America, above all, to begin this readjustment in the scope and basic point of view of verse; for everything else has changed' (87-93). Perhaps in a roundabout manner Whitman was acknowledging the space cleared by Wordsworth in noting that everything had changed in terms of the ego's relation to its 'fellow-humanity'. Regardless, he knew he was not on a very well worn path.

Gravil also argues that Wordsworth 'invites the question' of solipsism because he *appears* to be a poet 'whose work rarely seems concerned with relation to other human beings'.[19] To be sure, Wordsworth's way to unity with his fellow human beings generally was found through solitude. Whereas Whitman liked to ride on trolley cars and ferries to be near as many people as possible, Wordsworth lived removed from such human contact. Although he declared in *The Prelude*: '[M]y heart / Was social and loved idleness and joy', (III. 235-236) he also acknowledged that he 'was taught to feel – perhaps too much – / The self-sufficing power of solitude' (II. 76-77). 'The Green Linnet' is emblematic of Wordsworth's inclination towards solitude. In the poem he depicts a typical Romantic bird 'perched in ecstasies' – a spirit who presides over the natural scenes singing his song of sweetness and joy (27). Interestingly, however, the linnet is 'Too blest with anyone to pair / Thyself thy own enjoyment' (23-24). Like the poet himself, the ecstatic bird is content to be 'sole in thy employment', existing apart from the 'one band' of birds, butterflies, and flowers. He is, however, inseparably connected to the entire natural scene in his 'dominion' over it. Similarly, in one of his many direct addresses to Coleridge in *The Prelude*, Wordsworth overtly states his theme 'Not of outward things / Done visibly for other minds [...] but of my own heart' (III. 176, 179). In a very real sense Wordsworth's world is a solitary one, a unified universe because there exists in it only one consciousness. Although he was clearly not as bold as Whitman in

[18] Gravil, '"The Discharged Soldier" and the "Runaway Slave"', 48.

[19] Richard Gravil, 'Wordsworth's ontology of love in "The Prelude"', in: *Critical Quarterly* 16 (1974), 236.

his defense of his celebration of self, Wordsworth nevertheless sings the song of the 'simple separate person'. He, too, is a chanter of personality.

What is interesting about both poets, however, is the countercurrent of self-transcendence (or self-dilation depending upon how it is interpreted) in their verse. In *Critical Theory and Practice* Keith Green and Jill LeBihan claim that 'psychoanalysis transformed any belief in a unified self' – attributing the shattering of the illusion of a unified identity to Freud.[20] Crediting Freud with such a discovery, however, reveals the authors' Eurocentric bias, as Buddhists had destroyed such notions thousands of years earlier. 'Self is a fever; self is a transient illusion, a dream', said the Buddha.[21] Long after the Buddha (but well before Freud and psychoanalysis) Wordsworth and Whitman similarly subverted the notion of a fixed, unified self. But they both did so in a milieu largely incapable of recognizing the genius of their endeavor, a historical context still fettered by the conceptual straitjacket of the Enlightenment, a context that engendered the undeserved charge of solipsism. In both poets there are countless oceanic moments when the borders of individual consciousness fall away, the result of which is not a being perceiving but Being becoming aware of itself through individual perception, as Heidegger might have said. The celebration of individual being in both poets should be clear. Let me now turn to a discussion of Being, of the 'pleasurable sense of all-oneness' that accompanies oceanic moments.[22]

III

In one of the distinctions he sees between Wordsworth and Whitman, Gravil states that while 'Wordsworth's self encounters numerous concrete others [...] Whitman merges others into himself or into what has been called an intersubjectivity'.[23] While it is generally true that the other people Wordsworth encounters remain 'other', Gravil's comment needs some qualification. In Book 12 of *The Prelude*, for instance, Wordsworth speaks of his love for public roads (just as Whitman later did in 'Song of the Open Road'), which exert a considerable influence over his consciousness because of the merging he experiences while traversing them:

---

[20] Keith Green & Jill LeBihan, *Critical theory and practice*, New York: Routledge, 1999, 142.

[21] Qtd. in S. Abhayananda, *History of mysticism: The unchanging testament*, Naples, FL: Atma, 1987, 71.

[22] Borchert, *Mysticism*, 13.

[23] Gravil, '"The Discharged Soldier" and the "Runaway Slave"', 53-54.

I love a public road: few sites there are
that please me more – such object hath had power
O'er my imagination since the dawn
Of childhood, when its disappearing line
Seen daily afar off, on one bare steep
Beyond the limits which my feet had trod,
Was like a guide into eternity,
At least to things unknown and without bound. (142-151)

The language he employs is oceanic: the site of the road in the distance overwhelms him, momentarily obliterating consciousness of self. The road's disappearing line seems to him an emblem of that which is beyond the temporal realm, that which is eternal and therefore boundless. On such solitary journeys the line separating self and other melts and allows him to see 'into the depth of human souls' where he reads the 'passions of mankind' (XII. 165, 164). Although he does not enter the dream of other dreamers, as Whitman does, Wordsworth merges in metaphysical sympathy with the 'uncouth vagrants' and 'bedlamites' he encounters on the boundless road (157, 156). In what is more than mere human empathy, he sees deeply into souls that 'To vulgar eyes' 'appear to have no depth at all' (167, 166). He alone can discern in these boundless moments the interconnections among all people because he has in some way moved beyond the confines of the isolated *cogito*, apprehending beyond the limits of finite perception.

Such moments also render problematic Gravil's reading of *The Prelude* as merely the presentation of 'the history of a self in process of creation' versus 'Song of Myself', which portrays 'the ecstasies of a present self of transcendental reach'.[24] Robert Weisbuch, upon whose work Gravil draws heavily, similarly concludes that 'in British Romanticism the self is expressed. In American Romanticism self is created, then externalized, then granted sway over externality'.[25] In both cases the Wordsworthian self lacks potency, or so the argument implicitly goes, because it cannot self-transcend, because it remains fixed within imposed boundaries.

Wordsworth's vision atop Mount Snowdon, however, which he recounts in Book 13 of *The Prelude*, refutes such views of the limited, impotent self: As he is ascending the mountain, the ground in front of him appears to brighten, bathed in light that falls 'like a flash' (XIII. 39). Finding himself amidst a 'huge seat of mist', he sees about a third of a mile away 'a blue chasm, a fracture in the vapor, / A deep and gloomy breathing-place, through which / Mounted the

[24] Idem, 53.
[25] Weisbuch, *Atlantic double-cross*, 218.

roar of waters, torrents, streams / Innumerable, roaring with one voice' (XIII. 57-68). The experience results in what John Rudy has called 'an implosive unity' – a 'oneness in which all distinctions fall inward on each other'.[26] It seems to Wordsworth that in the blue chasm nature had lodged 'The soul, the imagination of the whole' (XIII. 66). He hears through the chasm the roaring waters of Oneness, which he interprets metaphorically. Nature is demonstrating to him the equivalent of the human imagination, the blue chasm of the mind through which pour the energies of divine inspiration.

He is so empowered by the experience that later in the evening the scene appears in memory as 'The perfect image of a mighty mind, / Of one that feeds upon infinity / That is exalted by an under-presence, / The sense of God, or whatsoe'er is dim / Or vast in its own being' (XIII. 70-74). His reaction to the experience enables him to expand the self beyond normal limits. The same power he observed on the mountain is a 'genuine counterpart / And brother of the glorious faculty / Which higher minds bear with them as their own' (XIII. 90-92). The energies of a majestic natural seen have dilated the self, giving it a measure of potency it had not previously possessed by a transference of nature's poetic strength. Higher minds (poets, that is) 'from their native selves can send abroad / Like transformation, for themselves create / A like existence' (XIII. 93-95). Imagination for Wordsworth is the link between being and Being, the perception of which empowers the self by elevating being to Being, dissolving the distinctions between the two.

In his excellent dissertation, 'Wonder and Defamiliarization in Wordsworth', Joe Kenneth Jackson puts forth a description of the sublime experience that seems to shed light on the paradoxical nature of the transcended-yet-empowered Wordsworthian self. In the first part of a two-phase process 'the self is stopped, baffled, or overwhelmed by [a] vast object, too large for imaginative comprehension', such as the blue chasm on Mount Snowdon. 'The second phase is paradoxical', writes Jackson, 'involving two contrary movements or a kind of splitting of the self'.[27] The great object, whether it be a mountain, an ocean, a majestic natural seen, or even a city at rest, 'expands the imagination, taking the self beyond its limits in an identification with the object'. At the same time, however, the self becomes aware of its own relative insignificance 'and experiences a kind of self-abasement'.[28] There are thus two, almost conflicting, forces imposed on the self in such moments. On Mount Snowdon Wordsworth experiences an oceanic moment in which he perceives a oneness, a unification of

[26] Rudy, *Wordsworth and the Zen mind*, 23.
[27] Jackson, *Wonder and defamiliarization in Wordsworth*, 48.
[28] Ibidem.

opposites, in hearing the mighty 'roar of waters' (XIII. 59) amidst a 'still ocean' (XIII. 44). Self is temporarily dissolved, as the magnitude of the spectacle makes him aware of his own relative insignificance. Later that night in a moment of meditation, however, he transmutes the power of nature into imagination, which elevates the self to the blue chasm's status and thus restores the self's sense of empowerment. Lance Massey has pondered what would happen if the 'internal dialogue between subject and Other merged' in Wordsworth's poetic. He concludes that 'there would be a unity – a self-contained wholeness. But it is precisely this singularity that needs objectification in order to exist'.[29] In order to perceive Being, in order to apprehend it from the limited human perspective, therefore, a being must objectify Being and thereby create a schism in the singularity. Subject and object must forever remain separate from the self's perspective. Only when self is transcended, transmuted, dissolved, and thus elevated to the status of Being itself can it collapse division and enter into monistic oneness.

The boat-stealing incident in Book I of *The Prelude* reveals a similar sense of vacuity of the ego that leads to self dilation. After rowing out into the middle of the lake, 'a huge cliff / As if with voluntary power instinct, / Upreared its head' (I. 378-380). The crag seems 'like a living thing' to him, appearing to follow his boat's course on the lake (I. 383). He is overpowered by the magnitude and the majesty of the cliff, experiencing an annihilation of self that sends him home 'with grave / And serious thoughts' that haunt him for many days afterwards (I. 389-390). In this moment of ego evacuation Being has experienced itself, for the poet claims that because of his encounter with something greater than himself, his 'brain / Worked with a dim and undetermined sense / Of unknown modes of being' (I. 391-393). Which is to say, he experiences nothing discernible to the isolated *cogito*: 'There was a darkness – call it solitude / Or blank desertion – no familiar shapes / Of hourly objects, images of trees, / Of sea or sky, no colors of green fields' (I. 394-397). He sees nothing at all, in fact, but only 'huge and mighty forms that do not live / Like living men', which 'moved slowly through my mind / By day, and were the trouble of my dreams' (I. 398-400). He cannot articulate these unknown modes of being, for to do so would be to objectify what transcends the subject/object dichotomy. He can only describe what he experiences in terms of a nothingness – what he calls darkness and blank desertion. He has ventured beyond the utterable.

Farther removed from the 18th century and its notions of the sublime, Whitman does not need the catalyst of some overwhelming natural force to experience the emptiness of ego. Although the ocean can play a role, typically self-tran-

[29] Massey, 'Tintern Abbey's "Tranquil Restoration"', 52.

scendence can occur spontaneously in his poems. Whitman already possesses a sense of the 'illusion' of individual identity, as he can see through the constructedness of individual selfhood. He does not, therefore, need to experience the ego annihilation and consequent empowerment that occurs as a result of an encounter with a sublime catalyst. Whitman's self seems already split. In verse-chant 4 of 'Song of Myself', for instance, he describes this dual consciousness:

Trippers and askers surrounded me,
People I meet, the effect upon me of my early life or of the ward and city I live in, or the nation,
The latest dates, discoveries, inventions, societies, authors old and new,
My dinner, dress, associates, looks, complements, dues,
The real or fancied indifference of some man or woman I love,
The sickness of one of my folks or of myself, or ill-doing or loss or lack of money, or depressions or exaltations,
Battles, the horrors of fratricidal war, the feature of doubtful news, the fitful events;
These come to me days and nights and go from the again,
But they are not the Me myself. (66-74)

The speaker knows his individual identity is constituted by his engagement in life, by the authors he reads, the latest news, the way he dresses, his own right or wrong actions, his experiences with people, etc. He knows these provide him with a sense of individual identity, but he also has a sense of the artificiality of this ego-self:

Apart from the pulling and hauling stands what I am,
Stands amused, complacent, compassionating, idle, unitary
Looks down, is erect, or bends an arm on an impalpable certain rest,
Looking with side-curved head curious what will come next,
Both in and out of the game and watching and wondering at it. (75-81)

He is both in and out of life, at times detached and wondering what it is all about and at others actively engaged. V.K. Chari calls this 'the activity of the dynamic self', which 'consists of a centrifugal and centripetal movement, a constant outgoing and return to the nucleus'.[30] Chari claims this constant 'self-merging and self-extricating' in Whitman 'is the way in which the dynamic self measures itself out and feels its own resilience'.[31] What is of interest here is the centrifugal movement away from individuality, the aspect of self that Whitman claims is not the 'Me myself' – the not-self, or *anatman* as Buddhists would call it.

---

[30] Chari, *Whitman in the light of Vedantic mysticism*, 110.
[31] Ibidem.

Whitman's verse is awash in such moments of self transcendence. In 'That Shadow My Likeness' he questions whether the part of himself that 'goes to and fro seeking a livelihood, chattering, chaffering' is really the final source of identity. 'How often I find myself standing and looking at it where it flits', he declares. 'How often I question and doubt whether that is really me' (1-3). In 'As I Ebb'd with the Ocean of Life', which is often interpreted as a moment of poetic self-doubt, he feels as though he is 'at the utmost a little washed up drift' (22). His sense of insignificance is so overpowering that he *merges* himself with the scene, becoming 'as part of the sands and drift' (24). Once again, he claims 'the real Me stands yet untouched, untold, altogether unreached / Withdrawn far, mocking me with mock-congratulatory signs and bows' (28-29). In 'Are You the New Person Drawn toward Me' he asks, 'Do you see no further than this façade, this smooth and tolerant manner of me? / Do you suppose your self advancing on real ground toward a real heroic man? / Have you no thought O dreamer that it may be all maya, illusion?' (6-8).

In 'To You' Whitman includes the reader in this sense of self-dissolution: 'Whoever you are, I fear you are walking the walks of dreams, / I fear these supposed realities are to melt from under your feet and hands' (1-2). Individual identity in such rhetoric is liquid, fluidly dissolving in the face of the speaker's perception. 'Even now your features, joys, speech, house, trade, manners, troubles, follies, costume, crimes, dissipate away from you, / Your true soul and body appear before me, / They stand forth out of affairs, out of commerce, shops, work, farm, clothes, the house, buying, selling, eating, drinking, suffering, dying' (4-5). In *The Doors of Perception* Aldous Huxley distinguished the individual mind from 'Mind at Large', which has to be 'funneled through the reducing valve of the brain and nervous system. What comes out of the other end is a measly trickle [...]'.[32] Whitman, no doubt, celebrated the individual, but he also frequently shows individual consciousness as a reduction of Being, as a diminutive version of Huxley's Mind at Large.

Like Wordsworth's verse, there are in Whitman's moments in which the reducing valve of the human ego is bypassed and Being floods individual consciousness. In 'Passage to India', a later poem steeped in the rhetoric of Indian spirituality, he depicts the soul at the end of its journey as it approaches God: 'The seas all cross'd, weather'd the capes, the voyage done, / Surroundest, copest, frontest God, yieldest, the aim attain'd, / As fill'd with friendship, love complete, the Elder Brother found, / The Younger melts in fondness in his arms' (220-223). Significantly, the individual personality *melts* in the arms of God; mind has become Mind at Large. In an oceanic moment the individual droplet of selfhood

[32] Aldous Huxley, *The Doors of Perception & Heaven and Hell*, New York: Harper, 1963, 23.

returns to the cosmic sea. Since several critics have noted Whitman's belief in reincarnation, there is no need to discuss the matter here at any length other than to say such a belief provided the poet with a structure for his oceanic views concerning selfhood. 'To be in any form, what is that?' he asked in 'Song of Myself'. '(Round and round we go, all of us, and ever come back thither)' (611-612). An individual's separate sense of being was temporary for Whitman, as the soul returns to Being upon the cessation of its individual form in an endless cycle of separation and return.

Whitman sings of the 'simple separate person', but it is also important to remember that he utters 'the word Democratic, the word En-masse' ('One's-Self I Sing' 1-2). 'Song of Myself' similarly opens: 'I celebrate myself, and sing myself, / And what I assume you shall assume, / For every atom belonging to me as good belongs to you' (1-3). As is the case with Wordsworth's verse, then, Whitman's contains both individualist and self-transcending strains, and, like Wordsworth, Whitman deliberately confuses the boundaries separating the two. For this reason, Roger Asselineau has called Whitman a 'mystical individualist', which, of course, is an oxymoron.[33] In traditional mysticism one's individuality must be relinquished in order to apprehend mystical unity. But in Whitman (and in Wordsworth) the separate self is sometimes not transcended but enlarged, which, in fact, can be viewed as a form of transcendence. The fact remains, however, the self does not empty in such moments but gorges itself on what it encounters.

In verse-chant 15 of 'Song of Myself' Whitman lists in one of his famous 'catalogues' a variety of discrete images, at the end of which he proclaims, 'And these tend inward to me, and I tend outward to them, / And such as it is to be of these more or less I am, / And of these one and all I weave the song of myself' (327-329). He moves beyond the confines of individuality, *becoming* the objects of his perception. 'Of every hue and caste am I, of every rank and religion, / A farmer, mechanic, artist, gentleman, sailor, Quaker, / Prisoner, fancy-man, rowdy, lawyer, physician, priest' (346-348). Yet, however paradoxically, he retains his selfhood. In a moment of self-assertion he proudly declares, 'I resist anything better than my own diversity' (349). The cosmic self can be called a type of egoless egotism, not quite an annihilated self but also definitely not a purely solipsistic one. In 'Song of Myself' Whitman thus wrote, 'I hear and behold God in every object, yet understand God not in the least, / Nor do I understand who there can be more wonderful than myself' (1281-1282).

In verse-chant 5 of 'Song of the Open Road' Whitman similarly asserts individual selfhood:

[33] Asselineau, *The evolution of Walt Whitman*, 145.

From this hour I ordain myself loos'd of limits and imaginary lines,
Going where I list, my own master total and absolute,
Listening to others, considering well what they say,
Pausing, searching, receiving, contemplating,
Gently, but with undeniable *will*, divesting myself of the holds that would hold
me. (emphasis added, 53-57)

On the face of it this passage is an almost Satanic or Byronic assertion of the will. Whitman refuses to recognize any superior above himself. Although he will listen to others and consider what they say, he will not be bound by any limitations imposed from without, which he sees as illusory – the imaginary lines of humanmade rules, morals, creeds, religions, and the like. To read the passage strictly as a Byronic/Satanic assertion of the will, however, is to tell only half of the story. Whitman radically proclaims the sanctity of his will but he does so from a cosmically enlarged perspective, not from the petty ego-self, which becomes clear in the next stanza:

I inhale great draughts of space,
The East and the West are mine and the North and the South are mine,
I am larger, better than I thought,
I did not know I held so much goodness.
All seems beautiful to me,
I can repeat over to men and women.
You have done such good to me I would do the same to you,
I will recruit for myself and you as I go,
I will scatter myself, and men and women as I go,
I will toss a new gladness and roughness among them,
Whoever denies me it shall not trouble me,
Whoever accepts me he or she shall be blessed and shall bless me. (58-68)

Whitman takes the engorgement of self to a level approaching what would be considered heresy in the Christian tradition. Self has expanded to a godlike stature; he is so large and so good he has some of his *self* to spare, scattering it among the men and women he encounters along the way. He even blesses and is blessed by them. Just as Wordsworth is able to transcend time and catch a glimpse of eternity on his public road, so is Whitman able to transcend space, inhaling 'great draughts' of it and encompassing vast regions in all directions at once. He is large; he contains multitudes. Whitman is 'a man preoccupied of his own soul', as he says in 'Assurances'. But when he says such things he is often doing so (though not always) from an unusual, cosmic point of view.

A comment William James made in *The Varieties of Religious Experience* helps to shed light on the issue of self in Whitman:

Walt Whitman owes his importance in literature to the systematic expulsion from his writings of all contractile elements. The only sentiments he allowed himself

> to express were of the expansive order; and he expressed these in the first person, not as your mere monstrously conceited individual might so express them, but vicariously for all men, so that a passionate and mystic ontological emotion suffuses his words, and ends by persuading the reader that men and women, life and death, and all things are divinely good.[34]

Although Whitman was expressing his expansive sentiments vicariously for all people, he was also speaking in the first person as a monstrously conceited individual, contrary to James's comment. Perhaps 'monstrously conceited' is not the proper label, but the point is to deny the separate self is to make Walt turn over in his grave. Whitman's conception of selfhood could be expressed only as paradox – in seemingly contradictory terms of unbridled will and subjectivity and of the relinquishment of the will to the great cosmic unity.

IV

The notion of will, so prominent in both Wordsworth and Whitman, is thus a barrier preventing their entrance into the mystics' domain. The ideal in mysticism, particularly in the Eastern schools, is the relinquishment of ego's attachments, that is, the cessation of the will. The second Noble Truth in Buddhism, for instance, is *tanha*, which is usually translated as desire for private fulfillment, or 'those inclinations which tend to continue or increase separateness'.[35] According to Indian thought, one must act, one must engage in and be engaged by life but only in the spirit of non-attachment (*vairag*). Such a theme recurs throughout the *Bhagavad Gita*:

> Be intent on action
> not on the fruits of action;
> avoid attraction to the fruits
> and attachment to inaction!
>
> Perform actions, firm in discipline,
> relinquishing attachment;
> be impartial to failure and success –
> this equanimity is called discipline.[36]

In the Upanishads, most of which predate the *Gita*, there is the notion that when 'all desires that cling to the heart are surrendered, then a mortal becomes immortal, and even in this world he is one with Brahman. When all the ties that

[34] James, *The varieties of religious experience*, 85.
[35] Huston Smith, *The world's religions*, San Francisco: Harper, 1991, 102.
[36] *The Bhagavad-Gita* (trans. Barbara Stoler Miller), New York: Bantam, 1986, II. 44-48.

bind the heart are unloosened, then a mortal becomes immortal. This is the sacred teaching'.[37] Immortality, then, is found in the death (transcendence) of the little self. In Taoism there is the concept of *wu wei*, which means effortless action. One should not *try* to do anything, according to this idea, but relinquish the desire for a particular outcome and simply act. In doing so the ego is relinquished, and the Tao acts through the person. Ego and its primary instrument – the will – are thus obstacles that must be overcome in most forms of mystical thought. '[G]ood', wrote Huxley, 'is the separate self's conformity to, and finally annihilation in, the divine Ground which gives it being; evil, the intensification of separateness, the refusal to know that the Ground exists'.[38]

According to Heidegger, ego perpetuates itself through the instrument of the will. 'Will constantly posits value', writes Heidegger scholar Akihiro Takeichi, 'and by positing the condition for itself, will secures itself. This means that for will to be will it needs to posit itself (and thereby it maintains and enhances itself) by constantly positing an object'.[39] The subject, therefore, remains forever a subject by constantly objectifying its world. Because ego is an illusion, and because will lacks a ground, it 'always needs to ground itself by positing anything other than itself'.[40] The annihilation of self, therefore, is accomplished by the relinquishment of the will, by overcoming that which 'separates us from the life of the planet, which keeps us apart from one another, which makes us feel self-conscious, inadequate, lonely, suspicious, possessive, jealous, awkward, fearful, and hostile; which thwarts our deepest desire, which is to be one with all creation', as Friebert and Young put it.[41]

There are moments in Wordsworth's verse when self is annihilated. In Book 8 of *The Prelude* he speaks of 'a time of greater dignity, / Which had been gradually prepared, and now / Rushed in as if on wings – the time in which / the pulse of being everywhere was felt' (VIII. 477-480). The boundary between being and Being seems to have been transgressed, as the experience overtakes his consciousness. Interestingly, the passage is stated in the passive voice: The pulse of being rushes in and, as he says, everywhere *was felt* by him. As a result of this self-annihilation, all boundaries dissolve in a moment, and 'all of several frames of things, like stars / Through every magnitude distinguishable, / Were

---

[37] 'Katha Upanishad', in: *The Upanishads* (trans. Juan Mascaro), New York: Penguin, 1965, 66.

[38] Aldous Huxley, *The perennial philosophy*, New York: Harper, 1944, 184.

[39] Akihiro Takeichi, 'On the origin of Nihilism: In view of the problem of technology and karma', in: Parkes, *Heidegger and Asian thought*, 177.

[40] Takeichi, 'On the origin of Nihilism', 177.

[41] Arthur Clements, 'Mysticism, science, and the task of poetry', in: *Studia Mystica* 9 (1986) no.4, 46.

half confounded in each other's blaze, / *One Galaxy* of joy and life' (emphasis added, VIII. 481-484). He also speaks of a feeling of 'being rapt away / By the divine effect of power and love' – a consciousness so overwhelming that he acknowledges 'dependency sublime' (VIII. 490-491, 494).

In Whitman's much-commented-upon mystical experience in verse-chant 5 of 'Song of Myself', the speaker is similarly the recipient of the action. In fact, he is cosmically raped by his own soul: 'I mind how once we lay such a transparent summer morning, / How you settled your head athwart my hips and gently turn'd over upon me, / And parted the shirt from my bosom-bone, and plunged your time to mind bare-script heart, / And reach'd till you felt my beard, and reached till you held my feet' (87-90). Here, too, ego is dissolved, which leaves the speaker with 'the peace and knowledge that passed all the argument of the earth' (91). It leaves him with a cosmic understanding: 'And I know that the hand of God is the promise of my own, / And I know that the spirit of God is the brother of my own, / And that all the man ever born are also my brothers, and the women my sisters and lovers, / And that a kelson of the creation is love' (92-95). Like Wordsworth, Whitman experiences self-dissolution, which then leads to a rhetoric of cosmic unity. In the annihilated state all things animate and inanimate – people, 'heap'd stones', weeds, and even fences – seem connected. Subject and object have merged, and the subsequent perception is of monistic oneness.

In both poets, however, the self is often empowered, as I have previously demonstrated. James Miller has noted that in 'Song of Myself' the 'self is not, as in the traditional mystical experience, submerged or annihilated, but rather celebrated; the senses are not humbled but glorified'.[42] Miller argued that Whitman subverts Evelyn Underhill's 'Mystic Way' – a pattern she discerned in most mystical experiences. After the self awakens, it needs to purify itself, according to Underhill; it needs to be transcended before the goal of union can be achieved. Whitman, however, does not follow this pattern, inverting it in his defiant celebration of the senses, which, as Miller observed, the poet insists on taking with him to the higher perception of mystical unity. Yet, Miller goes on to read 'Song of Myself' through Underhill's pattern, which, as V.K. Chari objected, 'forces the poem into a predetermined mold'.[43] In other words Whitman's 'mysticism' is more problematic than even Miller seems to realize. 'Whitman's philosophy', according to John Roche, 'demands that he expands his ego; wisdom comes not from denial but from dilation'.[44]

---

[42] Miller, *A critical guide to Leaves of Grass*, 10.

[43] Chari, *Whitman in the light of Vedantic mysticism*, 122.

[44] John Roche, 'Democratic space: The ecstatic geography of Walt Whitman and Frank Lloyd Wright', in: *Walt Whitman Quarterly Review* 6 (1988) no.1, 23.

Wordsworth, too, privileges the senses. Although there is a transcendent element in his rhetoric, Wordsworth's focus, not unlike that of any other poet, is primarily on an appeal to the senses, particularly to vision and hearing. Harold Bloom has said the logic of the 'Intimations' ode 'only plays at being a logic of concepts', when in fact it 'is concerned not with the tradition of conceptualization but with the flowing given of our sensuous experience' – an observation that can be extended to much of Wordsworth's verse.[45] Jean Hagstrum has also observed that 'in Wordsworth sensation and imagination interlock', which leads her to the conclusion that sexuality 'remains an ever-present force' in his poetry.[46] Interestingly, Hagstrum argues that the erotic is present even in transcendental moments. In what most critics have seen as an asexual, body-denying selection of poems, then, Bloom and Hagstrum recognize an unignorable sensuous/sensual strain. Other critics such as Klaus Peter Mortenson, however, have pointed out just the opposite, seeing in the Wordsworthian sublime 'a transformation in which the normal five senses are replaced by another inner sense opening up an insight into cosmic correspondences, thereby raising the sensory above the concrete and individually limited, to the universal, the divine totality'.[47] Wordsworth's cosmic rhetoric, however, demanded both the reality of sensory experience and of the transcendence of the senses. To deny either aspect is to do a great injustice to his verse.

Wordsworth and Whitman have been faulted for not moving out of the confines of selfhood. In his comparative study Luke Powers argues for Blake and Whitman's position in the mystical tradition, but he also says the difference between the two is that whereas Blake relinquishes self and privileges the spirit world, 'Whitman always holds mastery over himself, and, even in his most intoxicated lunges or pirouettes, never once loses control'.[48] Although there are clear exceptions (more than Powers acknowledges) to such an argument, the point is well taken. Whitman too often does not let go, does not relinquish self in the traditional mystical manner. Wordsworth, according to Michael G. Cooke, similarly tries to regain control after 'visionary' or what I have called oceanic moments, the result of which is a loss of the perception of cosmic unity and the gaining of a controlled sense of selfhood. 'The "all" eludes the romantic writer, even where an innovative cohesion and continuity can be shown to be intrinsic',

---

45 Bloom, *The visionary company*, 173.

46 Qtd. in Philip Rule, 'The gendered imagination in religion and literature', in: Mahoney, *Seeing into the life of things*, 64.

47 Klaus Peter Mortensen, *The time of unrememberable being: Wordsworth and the sublime, 1787-1805*, Copenhagen: Museum Tusculanum, 1998, 37.

48 Luke A. Powers, 'The poem "That Print Cannot Touch": Interweavings in the poetry of Walt Whitman and William Blake', in: *The Cloverdale Review* (1992-93), 58.

writes Cooke.[49] When Wordsworth tries to articulate Being, he fails, of course, for as Heidegger argued, Being is not individual, and it is thus impossible to observe or examine it.[50] When Wordsworth, as a being, attempts to describe Being, he reduces it to the individualist perspective and thus fails to capture what is so elusive. As a poet, however, it is his job to try, despite that he is ultimately doomed. He was a mystical writer, after all, not a mystic who happened to write poetry.

Cooke also points out a major phenomenon of the Romantic period in England and Germany, namely, 'the poising of the individual yearningly between annihilation and omnipotence'[51] – an insightful encapsulation of the two seemingly contradictory strains in the poetry of Wordsworth and Whitman. Oceanic moments dissolve, however fleetingly, the ego and the will, as Lawrence Kramer has pointed out in his excellent comparative essay on Wordsworth and Whitman. When the self is confronted with annihilation, according to Kramer, it can refuse being 'pressed to the brink of non-existence' and reassert its imaginative power by engaging in trope-making.[52] In other words, the poet can establish dominance over the threatening sublime object by signifying it in a reductive way, that is, by describing it in poetic terms, thereby stripping it of its power over the self.[53] Kramer's argument begs the question, however: What is a *poet* to do? In merely articulating such moments in figurative language, will reasserts and re-secures itself by attempting to objectify what is beyond the subject/object dichotomy. When it does so Being is necessarily reduced; the droplet emerges in an illusory separation from the ocean. Surely all mystics who attempt to convey their experiences through language are complicit in such a 'belittling' of the object that triggers oceanic consciousness.[54] As James Twitchell argues, 'clearly something will have to be sacrificed if the poet decides to cross into that liminal world [...] he will have to give up language and thus give up art. So he keeps to the margin'.[55] Wordsworth longs for the liquidity of his consciousness. 'O glide, fair stream! for ever so, / Thy quiet soul on all bestowing', he says of the Thames River, 'Till all our minds for ever flow / As thy deep waters now are flowing' ('Remembrance of Collins' 5-8). Whitman, too, as the chanter of death, repeatedly desires the dissolution of self, the 'free flight into the wordless', as he

[49] Michael Cooke, 'Romanticism and the paradox of wholeness', in: *Studies in Romanticism* 23 (1984) no.4, 437.

[50] Eric Lemay & Jennifer Pitts, *Heidegger*, New York: Writers & Readers, 1994, 40.

[51] Cooke, 'Romanticism and the paradox of wholeness', 436.

[52] Kramer, 'Ocean and vision', 212.

[53] Ibidem.

[54] Idem, 229.

[55] Twitchell, *Romantic horizons*, 73.

calls it in 'A Clear Midnight' (1). Both poets, however, also undermine their own desire for self-annihilation not only in their overwhelming assertion of self but in their mere attempt to employ language to convey such consciousness.

V

For Wordsworth and Whitman, being was a mystery. If asked, neither poet could have articulated a coherent philosophy of selfhood. Such an endeavor would take someone more systematic like Heidegger (who, incidentally, shares much in common with Eastern thought and with the Romantics, and who has been charged pejoratively with engaging in paradoxical, mystical thinking). Both poets, nevertheless, suggest the inability of the human perspective to grasp the ultimate mystery of Being. In 'Star-Gazers' Wordsworth's speaker happens upon a crowd of spectators taking turns looking through a telescope. But strangely, 'One after one they take their turn, nor have I one espied / That doth not slackly go away, as if dissatisfied' (31-32). Hoping to pierce the mystery of Being, of consciousness itself, the star-gazers go away 'less happy than before', which suggests the inability of individualized human consciousness to apprehend Being. In 'When I Heard the Learn'd Astronomer' Whitman does a bit of stargazing of his own. After he listens to a lecture and sees 'the proofs, the figures' (2) and the 'charts and diagrams' (3) ostensibly explaining the mystery of existence, he becomes 'tired and sick' (5) and wanders off by himself into the 'mystical moist night air' (7). Like Wordsworth's star gazers, he himself is completely dissatisfied with the astronomer's explanation of Being, finding his own answer to the mystery by looking 'up in perfect silence at the stars' (8). In the stillness of the night, as the poems suggests, he knows without knowing; he apprehends the mystery which can only be expressed as perfect silence.

Several critics have noted the many different selves in Whitman – a shape shifting poet whose solution to the great mystery of identity was to be protean, to 'never stop for long in any one guise [...] never to be trapped in one limited skin'.[56] Richard Volney Chase similarly recognized Whitman's 'fluid, unformed personality [exulting] alternately in its provisional attempts to define itself and in its sense that it has no definition'.[57] Dennis Donahue claims that if Whitman found two things traditionally considered enemies, he would declare their unity and 'make them friends in a larger community', which explains 'why Whitman was never troubled by the problem of every other major romantic poet – the

---

[56] Daniel Hoffman, 'Hankering, gross, mystical, nude: Whitman's "self" and the American tradition', in: Sill, *Walt Whitman of Mickle Street*, 5.

[57] Chase, 'Oneself I sing (1955)', 890.

nature of the self'.[58] Clearly, however, Whitman *was* troubled by the nature of the self, and his answer to the problem was (at least in part) made possible by Wordsworth and his handling of the issue, whether directly or indirectly.

Wordsworth did not have the benefit of Whitman's America – a milieu resonating with the music of hope, promise, possibility, and renewal, but he surely did well considering his own social context. As I pointed out earlier, Weisbuch argues that whereas in American Romanticism self is created, on the other side of the Atlantic it is merely expressed. Considering the foregoing discussion, however, such a comment seems unfair at least to Wordsworth, whose fluid sense of self permeates his verse. In 'Rhetoric' Stanley Fish has distinguished between two interpretations of the self, or two species of humankind, which he calls (using Richard Lanham's terms) 'homo seriosus' and 'homo rhetoricus'. The former 'species' possesses a 'central self, an irreducible identity', whereas 'rhetorical man is an actor', as he 'is trained not to discover reality but to manipulate it. Reality is what is accepted as reality, what is useful'.[59] To be sure, Wordsworth is not the great shape-shifter that Whitman was, but he was protean in his own right, if to a lesser degree. In his ultimate subjectivity and anti-essentialism, Wordsworth, like Whitman, anticipated Merleau-Ponty's existentialist doctrine: 'I am the absolute source – my existence does not stem from my antecedents, from my physical and social environment; instead it moves out towards them and sustains them, for I alone bring into being for myself [...] the tradition which I elect to carry on [...]'.[60]

He, too, is the center of the world. Just as Whitman wondered, 'what is a man anyhow? what am I? what are you?' so did Wordsworth question the fixity of individual consciousness, frequently both obliterating and expanding it in his verse ('Song of Myself' 391). Just as Whitman said, 'In all people I see myself', so did Wordsworth see himself in all of nature, projecting consciousness outward and absorbing into himself the world's natural energies (401). Just as Whitman declared, 'To me the converging objects of the universe perpetually flow', (403) so did Wordsworth internalize the 'beauteous pictures' of nature to the point of 'A consciousness of animal delight, / A *self-possession* felt in every pause / And every gentle movement of my frame' (emphasis added, *The Prelude*, IV. 392, 397-399). Just as Whitman said of himself, 'There was a child went forth every day, / And the first object he look'd upon, that object he became' (There Was a

[58] Qtd. in Bradley & Blodgett, *Leaves of Grass*, 964.

[59] Stanley Fish, 'Rhetoric', in: Frank Lentricchia & Thomas McLaughlin (Eds.), *Critical terms for literary study*, Chicago: University of Chicago Press, 1995, 208.

[60] Maurice Merleau-Ponty, 'Preface to "Phenomenology of Perception"' (1962), in: Richard Kearney & Mara Rainwater (Eds.), *The continental philosophy reader*, New York: Routledge, 1996, 80.

Child' 1-2), so did Wordsworth write, 'There was a boy' in whom nature 'carried far into his heart the voice / of mountain torrents' (*Prelude* V. 364, 383-84). Geoffrey Hartman has argued that *The Prelude* is a '*Bildungsroman* that takes the child from solipsism to society and from his unconsciously apocalyptic mind, dreaming of an utterly different world, to a sense of realities'.[61] To read the work as an 'epic of the emergence of an *individual* consciousness out of a field of forces that includes imagination, nature, and society', however, is to ossify the self in a way Wordsworth would not have intended or appreciated.

In a passage worth quoting in full, Whitman pondered the question of being in 'Democratic Vistas':

> There is, in sanest hours, a consciousness, a thought that rises, independent, lifted out from all else, calm, like the stars, shining eternal. This is the thought of identity – yours for you, whoever you are, as mine for me. Miracle of miracles, beyond statement, most spiritual and vaguest of earth's dreams, yet hardest basic fact, and only entrance to all facts. In such devout hours, in the midst of these significant wanders of Heaven and earth, (significant only because of the Me in the centre,) creeds, conventions, fall away and the calm of no account before this simple idea. Under the luminousness of real vision, it alone takes possession, takes value. Like the shadowy dwarf in the fable, once liberated and looked upon, it expands over the whole Earth, and spreads to the root of Heaven.
> The quality of BEING, in the object's self, according to its own central idea and purpose, and of growing therefrom and thereto – no criticism by other standards, and adjustments thereto – is the lesson of Nature. (in *Specimen Days & Collect* 239-240)

Perhaps because they could not answer the question of being in a rational manner, both poets turned to the lesson of nature. And in the natural world they found the answer: 'One impulse from a vernal wood / May teach you more of man', wrote Wordsworth, 'Of moral evil and of good, / Than all the sages can' ('The Tables Turned' 21-23). Whitman claimed in 'Song of Myself' to 'speak at every hazard, / Nature without check with original energy' ('Song of Myself' 12-13). Let us turn to a discussion of nature in both poets to attempt to understanding their relation to it, to discern in their cosmic rhetoric why the natural world played such a central role.

[61] Qtd. in Abrams, *Natural supernaturalism*, 132.

CHAPTER V

THE LIVING COSMOS

Healing Descartes' Wound

'When you have Satori you are able to reveal a palatial mansion made of precious stones on a single blade of grass; but when you have no Satori, a palatial mansion itself is concealed behind a simple blade of grass'
(unknown Zen master)

'Methinks that there abides in thee
Some concord with humanity'
(Wordsworth in 'To the Daisy')

'Bring all the art and science of the world, and baffle and humble it with one spear of grass'
(Whitman)

I

Despite the misguided view of Romantic poets railing against the evils of progress and calling for a simpler, more primitive way of life, Wordsworth and Whitman had positive views towards science. They were, after all, products of the Enlightenment culture, which said that the extension of learning could solve all human problems. But it was the Cartesian worldview out of which modern science was born that both poets also vehemently reacted to and ultimately rejected. 'The curse of irresistible progress is irresistible regression', wrote Horkheimer and Adorno, because 'the intellect is separated from sensuous experience in order to subjugate the sensuous'.[1] The Cartesian separation of mind and matter led to the privileging of the intellectual over the natural, which culminated in humankind's objectification of the natural world. 'What science wants to learn from nature

[1] Max Horkheimer & Theodor Adorno, 'The concept of Enlightenment', in: Richard Kearney & Mara Rainwater (Eds.), *The Continental philosophy reader*, New York: Routledge, 1996, 199-211 (orig. published 1947), 207.

is how to better exploit it for man's end', argued Horkheimer and Adorno. 'Enlightenment behaves towards things as a dictator toward man. The man of science knows things insofar as he can use them for his own ends'.[2]

Actually, Descartes merely articulated and codified the general attitude towards nature that informs the entire Western tradition. Unlike many other traditions, particularly those in the East, the Judeo-Christian Bible does not place nature on an equal footing with human beings. 'The Bible is unlike the mythology of other races', notes Bruno Borchert. 'Scant respect is paid to nature and the cosmos. The heavenly bodies are lower creations, and mankind stands apart from them'.[3] Such disrespect is established in the first chapter:

> God said, 'Let the earth bring forth living creatures, according to their various kinds: cattle, creeping things, and wild animals, all according to their various kinds'. So it was; God made wild animals, cattle, and every creeping thing, all according to their various kinds; and he saw that it was good. Then God said, 'Let us make human beings in our image, after our likeness, to have *dominion* over the fish in the sea, the birds of the air, the cattle, all wild animals on land, and everything that creeps on the earth.[4]

So there is at the outset of the Western tradition a schism between human beings and the natural world, as though each excluded the other – as though the one subjugated the other. In *The Perennial Philosophy* Aldous Huxley decried such attitudes towards nature:

> [M]an no longer regards Nature as being in any sense divine and feels perfectly free to behave towards her as an overweening conqueror and tyrant. The spoils of recent technological imperialism have been enormous [...] What is obvious, however, is that the advantages accruing from recent technological advances – or, in Greek phraseology, from recent acts of *hubris* directed against Nature – are generally accompanied by corresponding disadvantages, that gains in one direction entail losses in other directions, and that we never get something except for something.[5]

In such a worldview the cosmos no longer reveals 'a higher order, a supreme intelligence. [I]t is just nature – to be conquered and manipulated for technological, material gain'.[6]

What underlies such arrogant attitudes is actually a sense of helplessness. Newton's mechanical model of the universe, though it empowered humankind with a significant advancement in scientific knowledge, also significantly reduced

[2] Horkheimer & Adorno, 'The concept of Enlightenment', 200.

[3] Borchert, *Mysticism*, 117.

[4] Emphasis added, Genesis 1:24-26.

[5] Huxley, *The perennial philosophy*, 79-80.

[6] Michael Gellert, *Modern mysticism: Jung, Zen, and the still good hand of God*, York, ME: Nicholas-Hays, 1994, 204.

humankind's position, alienating the race and leaving it 'with no particular role to play in the scheme of things and no meaningful relationship to the inexorable forces that drive on the larger world of brute insensate matter'.[7] Western attitudes towards the natural world in general and the scientific revolution in particular, therefore, produced a thorough disenchantment with nature, which came to be seen as so much objective stuff, as so many observable and thus explainable laws. As a result, there has developed a rift between knowledge and wisdom – a felt gap 'that has the consequence of divesting our lives of meaning', as Simon Critchley has recently observed.[8] Even Edmund Husserl, himself a mathematician, condemned the 'mathematicization of nature', which he believed led to the erroneous notion that science is a totalizing system purporting to explain all aspects of human experience, when, in fact, scientific thought 'belongs to a determinate social and historical context'.[9] Which is to say, the byproduct of the context should not be subordinated to the context itself; human culture should not be totalized by one of its tools.

Heidegger similarly observed the problems arising from Cartesian dualism, which presupposes a fixed self that centers the world entirely on the self and leads to what he called *Gestell* – the technological attitude that divides the world by stripping it of any intrinsic value. The technological attitude causes human beings to lose respect for nature. More significantly, however, it causes a loss of the recognition of Being itself.[10] *Gestell* is the process by which the original harmony of Being becomes 'framed' or split up – an individuation that destroys the oneness in which all individual beings (Dasein) participate.[11] Borrowing a term from the German mystic Meister Eckhart, Heidegger argued that the remedy for *Gestell* was *Gelassenheit* – the cessation of the will to will, a form of detachment not without many parallels in Eastern thought, as Joan Stambaugh points out.[12] Human beings, according to Heidegger, could overcome the evils of the Cartesian separation of mind and nature by the relinquishment of the will, the releasement of one's attachments to objects. Gelassenheit, however, is not a form of passivity but a kind of openness to Being, a receptivity to that which transcends individual selfhood. Gelassenheit is the kind of consciousness found in Wordsworth and Whitman in moments when the fluid self is transcended, dissolved, or expanded.

---

[7] Danah Zohar, *The quantum self*, New York: Quill, 1990, 17.

[8] Simon Critchley, *Continental philosophy*, New York: Oxford University Press, 2001, 8.

[9] Edmund Husserl, 'The Vienna lecture and phenomenology' (1935), in: Richard Kearney & Mara Rainwater (Eds.), *The Continental philosophy reader*, New York: Routledge, 1996, 11.

[10] Lemay & Pitts, *Heidegger*, 79.

[11] Idem, 78.

[12] Joan Stambaugh, 'Heidegger, Taoism, and the Question of Metaphysics', in: Parkes, *Heidegger and Asian thought*, 85.

To be sure, as I pointed out in the previous chapter, the will to will plays a central role in both poets' personae. There is also a countercurrent, however, a resistance to the resistance of self-dissolution in Wordsworth and Whitman, that is best exemplified by their orientation towards nature. For Wordsworth, the 'perception of an alien and lifeless nature [...] in the mind of the perceiver is a result of the fall of man, and constitutes the essential nature of evil itself', as M.H. Abrams argued.[13] Whitman, too, believed that 'true evil is the negation of his proper union with nature'.[14] Both poets attempted to bridge the gap, to span the gulf between the natural world 'out there' and the inner world of human consciousness, thereby healing the Cartesian schism between mind and matter and achieving the union of seemingly disparate entities. But they also attempted to commingle the natural and the spiritual in an unprecedented way. In *The Visionary Company* Harold Bloom said 'the most defiant humanism in Wordsworth salutes the immediate possibility of this earthly paradise *naturalizing* itself in the here and now', – an observation one could also make of Whitman as well.[15]

II

By the end of the 18th century, as Basil Willey observed, 'the sacredness of nature was, to those affected by this tradition, almost a first datum of consciousness'.[16] Thomas Paine's Deism founded religion on nature instead of Scripture, 'eliminating at a stroke the authority of the Bible'.[17] Wordsworth did not have to construct his belief that human beings could overcome their estrangement from nature out of thin air, therefore, but he did take this orientation to a new level. Much of this tradition was given to him, but he significantly altered it in a way that became distinctly his own. Whitman similarly inherited Emerson's view of oneness with the natural world, much of which he probably gleaned from the latter's essay 'Nature'. But Emerson could not stomach the open celebration of sexuality found in Whitman's 'Children of Adam' poems of the 1856 *Leaves*, which he implored the poet to remove. So Whitman, too, was provided with a discourse on nature he would significantly alter in a way that became distinctly Whitmanesque.

---

13 Abrams, *Natural supernaturalism*, 222.

14 Denise T. Askin, 'Whitman's theory of evil: A clue to his use of paradox', in: *ESQ* 28 (1982), 128.

15 Bloom, *The visionary company*, 126. (emphasis added)

16 Basil Willey, 'On Wordsworth and the Locke tradition, in: M.H. Abrams (Ed.), *English romantic poets*, New York: Oxford University Press, 1975, 121.

17 Donald Marshall, 'Religion and literature after Enlightenment: Schleiermacher and Wordsworth', in: *Christianity and Literature* 50 (2000) no.1, 54.

Just as I reject Wayne Teasdale's assertion that 'Wordsworth was preeminently a nature mystic' in following a 'religion of nature',[18] so do I find problematic R.A. Gilbert's view of Whitman as a nature mystic and a pantheist.[19] To be sure, the natural world for both poets evoked intense religious awe – an emotion informing much of their cosmic rhetoric. But Wordsworth's view of God, as Dombrowski and Gould have pointed out, is best described as panentheistic – the belief that God is both immanent in nature (as in pantheism) and transcendent (as in theism). To call Wordsworth a nature mystic, then, is to miss something in his verse; it is to overlook what the poet believed was beyond nature. The earlier Wordsworth, it could be argued, was clearly more pantheistic. But the point is that the later Wordsworth found himself at odds with such passages, often revising them to be more in keeping with his orthodox Anglicanism and the view that God is beyond this world. So when we say Wordsworth was a nature mystic, to which Wordsworth are we referring? Clearly, there are more than one. Whitman was less troubled by any heretical elements in his verse, as he openly sang hymns of heterodoxy. To my knowledge, however, no 'nature mystic' ever spoke of 'Winds whose soft-tickling genitals rub against me', as Whitman does in 'Song of Myself' (541); no nature mystic ever so openly extolled the 'procreant urge of the world' (44); no nature mystic ever so daringly glorified the erotic and the homoerotic. Moreover, like the later Wordsworth, Whitman also grew increasingly more world/body-denying as he aged, which is at odds with the natural mystical view of God's immanence in the world.

I similarly reject the opposing, demystifying view, which is best represented by Paul DeMan, who saw in Romanticism 'the illusory analogy that considers man and nature as essentially adapted to each other'.[20] According to this view, not only are Wordsworth and Whitman not nature mystics; they actually delude themselves in their belief of the oneness of the natural world. DeMan's argument merely serves to reinforce the Cartesian schism and its consequent sense of alienation. As I pointed out in the third chapter, the cosmos is, in fact, unified – at least in a physical sense. All matter (as well as time and space) emerged at the Big Bang from one central source. What I would like to suggest, rather, is that the orientation towards nature that Wordsworth and Whitman display in their verse nevertheless participates in mystical discourse in overcoming Cartesian dualism. Although such rhetoric falls short of traditional mysticism, it brings both poets as close to the label of 'mystic' as they could possibly come.

'[N]owhere is the influence of Descartes on modernity so pronounced as in the assumption that God and the world are utterly separate', writes Grace

[18] Teasdale, *The mystic heart*, 181.

[19] Gilbert, *The elements of mysticism*, 52.

[20] Qtd. in Bialostosky, *Wordsworth, dialogics, and the practice of criticism*, xv.

Jantzen.[21] Sometimes Wordsworth depicted characters who experienced this schism. His 'Female Vagrant', for instance, is one such example. She is driven off her idyllic land where she tends a flock of sheep after her father refuses to sell their land to the owner of a 'mansion proud' (39). While young, her days 'in transport roll'd', (5) as she is at one with nature, living in a sort of prelapsarian paradise (7). But when her father dies as a result of his own disconnection with his land, and her husband and children perish as a result of disease and famine, she is left alone and ends living 'upon the mercy of the fields, / And oft of cruelty the sky accused' (254-255). Significantly, she says of all of the calamity that befalls her, 'Some mighty *gulf* of separation past / I seemed transported to another world' (emphasis added, 163-164). Her disconnection from the land, which was caused by greed, pride, and war, leaves her a vagrant and hungry wanderer. 'From the sweet thoughts of home, / And from all hope I was forever hurled' (168-169). She falls into disunity, separated from the natural/spiritual union she had enjoyed during childhood. She loses the consciousness of cosmic unity, or what she calls 'thoughtless joy', (7) because of the intense self-consciousness that suffering brings.

In 'Lines: Left upon a Seat in a Yew-tree' Wordsworth depicts the opposite form of self-consciousness and separation, telling the story of 'A favored Being' (16) who, nevertheless, led an 'unfruitful life' (32) because he took too much pride in his own sensibility, in his capacity to appreciate the beauty of nature. His hubris sets him apart from 'The world and human life', (41) as he would often 'sigh, / Inly disturbed, to think that others felt / What he must never feel' (42-43). As the poem closes, Wordsworth takes the opportunity to promulgate (in heavy-handed fashion) his moral that 'pride, / Howe'er disguised in its own majesty, / Is littleness; that he who feels contempt / For any living thing, hath faculties / Which he has never used' (50-54). Wordsworth's 'Yew-seat' poem is one of the most compelling illustrations of his orientation towards nature, for it depicts the evils of Cartesian self-consciousness. 'The man whose eye / Is ever on himself doth look on [...] The least of Nature's works' (55-57). Despite his refined sensibility, therefore, the descent into the ego-self estranges the man from nature, preventing him from bridging the gulf, from transcending the self and perceiving the continuity between consciousness and matter.

In 'Peter Bell', another overtly moral poem (so much so that it was justifiably ridiculed by Shelley), Wordsworth also depicts a character estranged from nature, which 'ne'er could find the way / Into the heart of Peter Bell' (54-55). Peter lives amid the valleys and the streams, 'in the green wood and hollow dell', but 'he never *felt* / The witchery of the soft blue sky', (emphasis added, 52, 74-

[21] Grace M. Jantzen, 'Power, gender, and ecstasy: Mysticism and post/modernity', in: *Literature and Theology* 11 (1997) no.4, 399.

75). Which is to say, like the female vagrant and the subject of the 'Yew-tree' poem, he cannot transcend selfhood and achieve a cosmic fusion with the natural world. The faithful ass and 'a fervent Methodist [...] preaching to no heedless flock', however, serve as transformative catalysts in Peter's consciousness. Because his heart is opened, 'A holy sense pervades his mind', and 'He feels what he for human kind / Had never felt before' (318-320). Significantly, as a result of learning to feel that 'man's heart is a holy thing', 'Nature, through a world of death, / Breathes into him a second breath, / More searching than the breath of spring' (337-340). 'Peter Bell' is Wordsworth at his most heavy-handed. His character rather sickeningly becomes 'a good and honest man' as the poem closes (400), but what is of interest is the poet's dramatic enactment of the ritual of natural union. Peter overcomes the Cartesian schism; he transcends self and, consequently, apprehends a cosmic connection not only to animals and human beings but to the natural world.

Kerry McSweeney has argued that 'when consciousness and the goodly universe are fused [in Wordsworth's poetry] the result is an experience of transport, an expansion of consciousness, a sense of the sublime'.[22] Nowhere is this transport clearer than in a passage found in 'Descriptive Sketches' that Wordsworth later mined when he wrote the Snowdon scene in *The Prelude*. After seeing the strange blue chasm, the speaker declares that such perception is not merely for lofty souls with a special sensibility. Even the simple person, provided he is 'Nature's child', can bridge the gulf between the physical and the spiritual (434). There was a time, says the poet, when primitive man was 'entirely free, alone and wild' (433) – a time when

> An unknown power connects him with the dead:
> For images of other worlds are there;
> Awful the light, and holy is the air.
> Fitfully, and in flashes, through his soul,
> Like sun-lit tempests, troubled transports roll;
> His bosom heaves, his Spirit towers amain,
> Beyond the senses and their little reign.
> And oft, one that dread division hath past by,
> He holds with God himself communion high,
> There where the peal of swelling torrents fills
> The sky-roofed temple of the eternal hills. (454-464)

Michael O'Neil has argued that a 'major impulse in romantic poetry' is 'the wish to get to the other side of sense experience'.[23] Clearly, the above passage shows

---

[22] McSweeney, *The language of the senses*, 41-42.

[23] Michael O'Neil, '"Wholly incommunicable by words": Romantic expressions of the inexpressible', in: *Wordsworth Circle* 31 (2000) no.1, 13-14.

Wordsworth's transcendence of the senses, but what it also shows and what O'Neil seems to overlook, is an anti-Cartesian/prelapsarian fusion of God and nature. The speaker holds high communion with God, but he does so under the sky and amidst the hills. In this moment God is both beyond the senses and also in the world – transcendent-yet-immanent. The blue chasm itself could be read as an emblem of the separation of the natural and the spiritual, of mind and matter, God and human; it is 'That dark mysterious gulf', as the speaker calls it, dividing that which is ultimately unified (415). Once across this barrier, the speaker internalizes images from this world and transmutes them into otherworldly energies, commingling the two in the meeting place of his own heart. Wordsworth believed 'man can experience a corresponding greatness in himself', wrote Mortensen. 'The organ of this greatness is the seeing heart of "that other eye"'.[24] Significantly, the poet says at the end of the passage preceding the Snowdon chasm: 'Nature ever just, to him imparts / Joys only given to uncorrupted hearts' (403-404). The commingling of the two energies is only possible, therefore, in one whose heart is untainted by self-consciousness. It is only possible because 'To her fair works did nature link / The human soul that through me ran' ('Lines Written in Early Spring' 5-6). What is original in Wordsworth's thought 'is the notion that human happiness arises out of cooperation with external nature and man's own inner nature'.[25]

In 'Passage to India' Whitman positioned himself as a poet prophet, a divine figure who could cross a barrier that other individuals had tried but failed to cross:

> After the seas are all cross'd (as they seem already cross'd)
> After the great captains and engineers have accomplished their work,
> After the Noble inventors, after the scientists, the chemist, the geologist, ethnologist,
> Finally shall come the poet worthy of that name,
> The true son of God show, singing his songs. (101-105)

The crossing of which he speaks, however, is not merely the circumnavigation of the physical globe but the transcendence of the metaphysical barrier separating nature and the human mind:

> Then not your deeds only O voyagers, O scientists and inventors, shall be justified,
> All these hearts as of fretted children shall be sooth'd,
> All affection shall be fully responded to, the secret shall be told

[24] Mortensen, *The time of unrememberable being*, 17-18.

[25] W.B. Gallie, 'Is The Prelude a philosophical poem?', in: Wordsworth, Abrams, & Gill, *The Prelude 1799, 1805, 1850*, 671.

> All these separations and gaps shall be taken up and hook'd and link'd together,
> The whole Earth, this cold, impassive, voiceless Earth, shall be completely justified,
> [...] Nature and man shall be *disjoin'd* and diffused no more,
> The true son of God shall absolutely *fuse* them. (emphasis added, 106-10, 114-15)

With his special insight the speaker has wisdom that sees beyond the noble inventors and scientists. What he brings, in fact, will justify the work of such individuals by soothing the broken hearts, linking together all separations and gaps, and fusing nature and man in such a way that the work of science shall be 'gloriously accomplish'd and compacted' (111). Gay Wilson Allen argued that the Quakers were at least partly responsible for Whitman's belief 'that all physical life is dependant upon and sustained by an infinite spiritual realm'.[26] Regardless of its origin, Whitman seems to be consciously attempting to overcome the Cartesian separation. He is the healer of Descartes' injurious wound; he is the new son of God who will unify the severed connection between human consciousness and Mother earth.

He wrote in 'A Song of the Rolling Earth': 'I swear the earth shall surely be complete to him or her who shall be complete, / The earth remains jagged and broken only to him or her who remains jagged and broken' (90-91). The earth's completeness, however, is not merely dependent upon one's perspective; rather, if one is steeped in an isolationist consciousness, the earth will appear jagged and broken. But it will only *appear* as such, for Whitman's earth – all of nature, that is – is complete in itself, regardless of how it is viewed: 'I swear there is no greatness or power that does not emulate those of the earth, / There can be no theory of any account unless it corroborate the theory of the earth, / No politics, song, religion, behavior, or what not, is of account, and unless it compare with the amplitude of the earth' (92-94). The wellspring of all life, nature provides for all things; nothing is of any consequence unless it is somehow connected to the earth, unless it shares in nature's amplitude.

Whitman is thus 'at ease in Nature'. Unlike the Cartesian 'conquerors' of the natural world, he is 'aplomb in the midst of irrational things, / Imbued as they, passive, receptive, silent as they' ('Me Imperturbe' 1-2). In his biography of the poet, Philip Callow notes that from his earliest years Whitman was fond of floating face-up in the sea,[27] an activity in which it is possible that he cultivated his 'passive' orientation towards nature. Such gazing up at the sky, which is reminiscent not only of Wordsworth's 'wise passiveness' but also of Heidegger's *Gelassenheit*, would persist throughout his life, for in it he derived much pleasure. '[T]here

[26] Allen, *A reader's guide to Walt Whitman*, 19.

[27] Philip Callow, *From noon to starry night: A life of Walt Whitman*, Chicago: Elephant, 1992, 188.

is an ecstatic satisfaction in such lazy philosophy, such passive yielding up of one's self to the pure emanation of nature', he wrote in a notebook.[28] In orienting himself in such a way Whitman was able to avoid the jagged, broken consciousness of Western dualism, achieving a reconciliation of what is seemingly at odds. In another notebook entry he made it clear that he was consciously attempting this fusion of the natural and the spiritual:

> Most writers have disclaimed the physical world and they have not over-estimated the other, or soul, but have under-estimated the corporeal. How shall my eye separate the beauty of the blossoming buckwheat field from the stalks and heads of tangible matter? How shall I know what the life is except as I see it in the flesh? I will not praise one without the other or any more than the other'.[29]

Like Wordsworth, then, Whitman attempted in his verse to combat the rigid Western hubris that subordinates matter to spirit – the biblical/Platonic idealism that denigrates and denies the things of this world by privileging those of the transcendent realm. For Whitman, nature and spirit were interdependent, the one drawing sustenance from the other, the latter finding expression through the former. 'The Godhead is in every blade of grass', as Elias Hicks said.[30]

III

Because of this equality between the spiritual and natural worlds, both poets saw nature as being alive, as possessing consciousness. Harry Wilson, consequently, sees the spirit of 'animism' informing much Romantic verse.[31] Considering that some scientists are now seeing the distinction between organic and inorganic as a 'conceptual prejudice', and considering that not only plants but subatomic particles appear to be making decisions and, therefore, seem to have some type of consciousness, Romantics such as Wordsworth and Whitman seem to have presciently anticipated what we are just beginning to understand.[32]

Wordsworth wrote in his 1802 preface to *Lyrical Ballads*: 'The reader will find that personifications of abstract ideas rarely occur in these volumes', a point one must keep in mind when reading his verse.[33] The depiction of a living, natural

---

[28] Qtd. in Chari, *Whitman in the light of Vedantic mysticism*, 57.

[29] Qtd. in Matthiessen, *American Renaissance*, 525.

[30] Qtd. in David S. Reynolds, *Walt Whitman's America: A cultural biography*, New York: Vintage, 1996, 38.

[31] Wilson, *Psychological projection in six Romantic poems*, ix.

[32] Gary Zukav, *The dancing Wu Li masters*, New York: HarperCollins, 2001 (orig. publ. 1979), 51.

[33] Qtd. in Wordsworth, *Selected poems*, 437.

world is not merely a poetic device for Wordsworth; it is not simply an emblem for something else such as the spiritual realm. Although he did often see spirit behind nature, the natural world in his verse has a life of its own. 'Oh there is a blessing in this gentle breeze, / That blows from the green field and from the clouds / And from the sky', he wrote in the opening passage of *The Prelude* (I. 1-3). The blessing in the breeze suggests it is from another world, but it is also alive, 'half conscious of the joy it gives' (I. 4). The speaker, 'a captive' who has just come from 'a house / Of bondage from yon city's walls set free', greets the breeze as though it has human life (I. 6-7), calling it a 'welcome messenger' and a 'welcome friend' (I. 5). Thus freed from his captivity in the city, he shakes off the 'burthen of my own *unnatural* self' and becomes once again part of the natural world (emphasis added, I. 22). 'The earth is all before me', he declares, wondering, 'what sweet stream / Shall with its murmurs lull me to rest?' (I. 15, 14). He is made whole once again, having returned to the unity of a natural scene he sees literally teeming with consciousness.

Particularly in *The Prelude* but also in many other poems, Wordsworth's natural world comes alive with almost physical human consciousness. 'The budding twigs spread out their fan, / To catch the breezy air', he says of a tree in 'Lines Written in Early Spring'. 'And I must think, do all I can, / That there was pleasure there' (17-20). The wind in his poetry frequently has a breath-like quality; the sounds of nature speak to him in a language only he can understand; the clouds are guides who will show him the way; he *feels* the presence of rocks and streams; the sun and moon are gendered as male and female, and so on. Harry Wilson argues that this element of Wordsworth's verse is merely psychological projection, 'the use of external objects to reflect his mental and emotional state'.[34] Harold Bloom, however, claims that 'we make a mistake if we read this as a projection of the [...] conscience upon the world'.[35] In such moments Wordsworth 'belongs more to the universe of elemental forces, of motions and spirits, than he does to ours'.[36]

Daniel Dombrowski has read Wordsworth's living nature as a form of panpsychism, which he defines as 'the view which suggests that every instance of reality is mind-like or at least exhibits some slight ability to feel the difference between itself and the rest of what is'.[37] Panpsychism is not merely a Romantic poetic device, however, for some modern philosophers articulate a similar philosophical position in 'representational' theories of consciousness, which contain the notion that all physical systems have some degree of conscious awareness.

---

[34] Wilson, *Psychological projection in six Romantic poems*, in abstract.
[35] Bloom, *The visionary company*, 147.
[36] Idem, 148.
[37] Daniel Dombrowski, 'Panpsychism', in: *The Wordsworth Circle* 19 (1988) no.1, 38.

The difference between a 'living' and a 'non-living' system is 'the radical increase (an order of magnitude 20 times greater) in the occupation number of the electronic levels' of a photon, according to Danah Zohar.[38] 'But this difference', she points out, 'is one of degree, not of principal'. The 'difference', then, may be merely a human construct; it may be the result of our Cartesian worldview. Such things as rocks and mountain ranges may respond to stimuli in the same way as a plant or a human might but at a significantly slower pace – so slow, in fact, as to render observation of such a response impossible.

In 'Nutting' Wordsworth reports first learning of this panpsychist presence in nature after disturbing 'with crash / And merciless ravage' the sanctity of a shady nook of hazels (44-45). Feeling 'a sense of pain' when he discerns the presence of Being in nature, he cautions his addressee: 'Then, dearest Maiden, move along these shades / In gentleness of heart; with gentle hand / Touch – for there is a spirit in the woods' (52, 54-56). Dombrowski concludes that 'we should not be too harsh on those who have an overly romantic view of trees'. The pathetic fallacy, he argues, 'is no less dangerous than the "prosaic" or "apathetic" fallacy, its opposite. Reality is not as dull as many sober souls imagine'.[39] Wordsworth's spirit in the woods is a corrective to the Cartesian 'apathetic' fallacy that denies life to objects traditionally considered non-living.

In light of the panpsychist argument such poems as 'Three Years She Grew in Sun and Shower' take on new meaning: Nature sees in the child a flower lovelier than any on earth, and thus absorbs her (through death) into itself. 'She shall be mine', says Nature, 'and I will make / A Lady of my own' (5-6). The girl will then be 'in rock and plain, / In earth and heaven, in glade and bower' (9-11). She will be literally alive, 'sportive as the fawn / That wild with glee across the lawn / Or up the mountains springs' (13-15). But she will also be 'the breathing balm, / And hers the silence and the calm / Of mute insensate things' (17-18). Lucy's individual consciousness will be obliterated, but she still will be alive, having merged her consciousness with that of the living cosmos. As Wordsworth says in 'A Slumber Did My Spirit Seal', another Lucy poem, 'No motion has she now, no force; / She neither hears nor sees; / Rolled round and earth's diurnal course, / With rocks, and stones, and trees' (5-8). Lucy's physical death does not prevent her consciousness from becoming one with the rolling earth, a union with nature that gives her immortal life through the cessation of individuality.

Gay Wilson Allen argued that Whitman got many of his ideas concerning the unity of nature, God, and human from the Stoic tradition with which he was familiar. 'In naming the great authors who have influenced him Whitman nearly always included Epictetus, sometimes Marcus Aurelius, and occasionally

---

38 Zohar, *The quantum self*, 223.
39 Dombrowski, 'Panpsychism', 39.

Seneca'.[40] It is possible, however, that Wordsworth also influenced his views, whether directly or indirectly. In one of Whitman's pre-*Leaves of Grass* notebooks there are ideas reminiscent of both the Stoics and Wordsworth: 'The soul or spirit transmits itself into all matter – into rocks, and can live the life of a rock – into the sea, and can feel itself the sea – into the oak, or other tree – into an animal, and feel itself a horse, a fish, or bird – into the earth – into the motions of the suns and stars'.[41] Regardless of the source, Whitman puts forth in the above passage and in much of his poetry a merging with physical nature, itself alive with consciousness. The human soul can transcend its confines of individuality and become one with all things in the natural world because both consist of Being, both participate in the same consciousness.

Whitman's particular spin on the living cosmos is that he describes his merging with it as a sexual act. In verse-chant 21 of 'Song of Myself', for instance, he looks upon Nature as a sexual object, describing it in highly sensual terms:

> Smile O voluptuous cool-breath'd earth!
> Earth of the slumbering and liquid trees!
> Earth of departed sunset – earth of the mountains misty-topt!
> Earth of the vitreous pour of the full moment just tinged with blue!
> Earth of shining and dark mottling the tide of the river!
> Earth of the limpid gray of clouds brighter and clearer for my sake!
> Far-swooping elbow'd earth – rich apple-blossom'd earth! (438-444)

In a moment suggestive of the oceanic, he sees the earth as having a full and sexually attractive figure. The passage is conveyed in a tone of reverence, as a lover speaks of his beloved. He transmutes the sensuous into the sensual, lusting after the earth in its bountiful richness. 'Smile', he adds, 'for your lover *comes*' (emphasis added, 445). In an orgasmic moment he enters an ecstatically erotic state of consciousness in which the plentiful earth leads him to sexual climax. But this is not mere self-gratification, for he claims to give back the sexual charge: 'Prodigal, you have given me love – therefore I to you give love! / O unspeakable passionate love' (446-447). He then directs his erotic energy towards the sea:

> You sea! I resign myself to you also – I guess what you mean,
> I behold from the beach your crooked inviting fingers,
> I believe you refuse to go back without feeling of me,
> We must have a turn together, I undress, hurry me out of sight of the land,
> Cushion me soft, rock me and billowy drowse,
> Dash me with amorous wet, I can repay you. (448-453)

---

[40] Allen, *A reader's guide to Walt Whitman*, 43.

[41] Qtd. in Gay Wilson Allen, 'Walt Whitman and Stoicism', in: Duane MacMillan (Ed.), *The Stoic strain in American literature: Essays in honour of Marston LaFrance*, Toronto: University of Toronto Press, 1979, 55.

After copulating with the earth, he must have a 'turn' with the ocean, which tantalizes him with inviting fingers as the water unevenly washes upon the shore. He believes the sea demands sexual gratification in bestowing upon him such amorous wetness, and feels obligated to repay it with a wetness of his own. The second orgasm leaves the ocean 'breathing broad and convulsive breaths', as though it has reached an orgasm of its own, satisfied yet wanting more in its post-coital desire (455). Whitman's copulation leaves him unified with nature, as he declares, 'I am integral with you' (458). But it is not an entire obliteration of individuality, as was the case with Wordsworth's Lucy, for he is paradoxically 'of one phase and of all phases' (458). He is at once an individual *and* the entire ocean.

Nature for Whitman thus included not only all aspects of the physical universe, great and small, but the physical body and one of its most powerful drives – the sexual instinct. In 'Song of Myself' he dared to venture into waters uncharted by any previous poetic voyager:

> Through me forbidden voices,
> Voices of sexes and lusts, voices veil'd and I remove the veil,
> Voices indecent by me clarified and transfigur'd.
> [...] Copulation is no more rank to me than death is.
> I believe in the flesh and the appetites, [...]
> If I worship one thing more than another it shall be the spread of my own body,
>   or any part of it, [...]
> Firm masculine colter it shall be you! (516-518, 521-522, 527, 530)

In a repressive Victorian era Whitman celebrated not only the sexual act and the fleshly appetites but his own erect penis. Turning orthodox Western religion on its head, he worships the phallus. Not unlike the ancient fertility cults, Walt also sees the penis as the source of life: 'You my rich blood! your milky stream pale strippings of my life!' (532). But unlike the fertility cults, the phallus has more than mere symbolic significance, for a significant element in Whitman's poetry is a eulogy to pleasure itself, a paean to the joys of sexual sensation but divorced from the Christian stipulation that copulation should lead to reproduction.

Roger Asselineau has noted that as Whitman aged and as his body wore out, his mysticism shed its central *physical* basis.[42] Whitman's earlier mysticism is steeped in physicality, or more specifically, sexuality, which in some ways renders it incompatible with the mystical tradition. Mystics in the Christian 'bridal' tradition metaphorically marry Christ and thus often speak of their spiritual experiences in terms that approach the erotic, and which, in fact, may conceal homoerotic impulses. As Borchert points out, Juan de la Cruz frequently uses

[42] Asselineau, *The evolution of Walt Whitman*, 17-18.

sexual imagery to depict mystical experiences.[43] Mystics in the Eastern traditions also employee pseudo-sexual language in their poetry, with which Whitman was familiar. 'My heart must cleave to my Lover', wrote Kabir. 'I must withdraw my veil, and / meet Him with all my body'.[44] But the difference between Whitman and the traditional mystics is that the latter intend erotic imagery strictly as metaphor, whereas Whitman sings the praises of sexuality for its own sake. Ghulam Fayez makes the mistake of overlooking such a difference in his dissertation, claiming that '[i]t is the erotic dimension of the soul or the self which creates such a striking kinship between the poems of Rumi and Whitman'.[45] As R.A. Gilbert notes, many people misconstrue the sensuous imagery in Sufi poetry, reading it as eroticism when, in fact, it is something quite different.[46]

Asselineau also made the mistake of subordinating sex to spirit in the poet, arguing that 'sexuality in Whitman is overshadowed by mysticism'.[47] To be sure, Whitman did use the sexual as an emblem for the spiritual, but he also prided himself on being a poet of sexuality in its own right. In 'A Backward Glance' he claims that *Leaves of Grass* is distinguished by its 'religiousness', (335) but he says it is also 'The song of Sex and Amativeness, and even Animality' (386-387). Whitman does qualify this last statement by claiming that he intends his definition of sex 'to be lifted into a different light and atmosphere', (389) which is to say, he intended to elevate the sexual to sacred status: 'From the night a moment I emerging, flitting out, / Celebrate you *act divine* and you children prepared for, / And you stalwart loins' (emphasis added, 'From Pent-up Aching Rivers' 55-57). Sex was not only a symbol of the spiritual for Whitman; it was a form of spiritual energy. David Reynolds, consequently, has argued that 'sexual passion is never far from religious vision' in *Leaves of Grass*.[48] Harold Aspiz similarly notes that the sexual urge and the urge to transcend coexist in Whitman. Aspiz, however, subordinates the sexual to the spiritual in a way the poet would not have appreciated. 'Sexuality in Whitman's poems', argues Aspiz, 'is not usually an end in itself, for the sexual state is anterior to and generally less sustained than the transcendent state. In fact, most depictions of the sexual arousal in *Leaves of Grass* are structured to culminate in a state of spiritual and visionary elevation'.[49]

---

43 Borchert, *Mysticism*, 365.

44 Kabir, *Songs of Kabir* (trans. Rabindranath Tagore), York, ME: Weiser, 1998 (orig. publ. 1915), I. 131.

45 Fayez, *Mystic ideas and images in Jalal al-Din Rumi and Walt Whitman*, vii.

46 Gilbert, *The elements of mysticism*, 20.

47 Asselineau, *The evolution of Walt Whitman*, 6.

48 Reynolds, *Walt Whitman's America*, 234.

49 Harold Aspiz, 'Sexuality and the language of transcendence', in: *Walt Whitman Review* 5 (1987) no.2, 1.

While I do not disagree with the idea that sexual arousal often leads to spiritual elevation in Whitman, I would caution against any separation of the two, against any kind of dichotomizing that denies the validity of one and privileges the other. Freud and Jung represent between themselves such a split; whereas the former thought the sex drive the deepest part of the psyche, the latter argued that the religious drive was the deepest.[50] Whitman transcended both of these great thinkers in commingling the two drives. 'Sex contains all', he wrote in 'A Woman Waits for Me'. 'All hopes, benefactions, bestowals, all the passions, loves, beauties, the life of the earth, / All the governments, the judges, gods, follow'd persons of the earth, / These are contain'd in sex as parts of itself and justifications of itself' (3, 6-8). Sexual energy for Whitman was very real indeed. Critics who attempt to deny or subordinate it in their readings of *Leaves* are thus actually saying more about their own Euro/American bias than they are about the poet.

Whitman, therefore, raises the song of sex to an ecstatic/spiritual pitch, but he never forgets his subject matter; he never transmutes the physical into the spiritual but unifies the two. In his dissertation on Whitman, Manohar Wankhade likens the poet's sexual celebration to Tantrism, a tradition born out of Vedanta and Mahayana Buddhism. At the heart of Tantra is a world-affirming attitude, and sex is considered to be the central principle of creation.[51] Wankhade argues that 'sex in Whitman is vital to [the poet's] growth and therefore pivotal in any evaluation of him' – an irrefutable point.[52] In 'One Hour to Madness and Joy' Whitman claims to 'drink the mystic deliria deeper than any other man', but he is not talking strictly about partaking of spirit in a traditional mystical sense; rather, he is compelled to imbibe the sacred elixir because of his 'savage and tender achings' – his powerful sexual drive (4, 5). Such lines as 'Urge and urge and urge, / Always the procreant urge of the world', ('Song of Myself' 44-45) have led the authors of *Start with the Sun* to conclude that Whitman sees the world as a 'sexual pantheist' because for him it is 'infused by creative sexual vitality'.[53] Sex thus played a pivotal role in Whitman's poetic, which is why he resisted Emerson's coercive efforts to have the blasphemous 'Children of Adam' sequence expurgated from the 1856 edition of *Leaves*. His poems of sex were, as he put it in *Specimen Days*, 'more precious than gold' (191). Whitman needed sex to talk about spirituality just as much as he needed spirituality to talk about sex. As he wrote in 'I Sing the Body Electric', 'O I say these are not the parts and poems of the body only, but of the soul, / O I now say these are the soul' (163-164). He recognized the inseparability of the two.

---

[50] Borchert, *Mysticism*, 321.

[51] Manohar Namdeo Wankhade, *Walt Whitman and Tantrism: A comparative study* (Diss. University of Florida, Gainesville, Florida, 1965), 7.

[52] Wankhade, *Walt Whitman and Tantrism*, 9.

[53] Miller, Shapiro, & Slote, *Start with the Sun*, 25.

Wordsworth, however, wrote in a different time and a different place – a context in which it would have been inappropriate to discuss sexuality in such an open, celebratory manner. But he might have been more daring. In *Natural Supernaturalism* M.H. Abrams argued that 'it was a matter of jocular remark in Wordsworth's day, as it is in ours, that he was a conspicuously asexual poet'.[54] Wordsworth goes out of his way, so to speak, to avoid the erotic. Occasionally, his poetry will spring to life with sexual vitality: his hazel trees in 'Nutting', for instance, are 'Tall and erect, with tempting clusters hung, / A virgin scene!' (20-21). For the most part, however, he does not sing of sexuality in any overt manner. Yet, if he does not have sex with nature like Whitman does, he nevertheless shares an unprecedented degree of *intimacy* with it. His apostrophe to nature in *The Recluse* is a case in point:

> Embrace me then, ye Hills, and close me in;
> Now in the clear and open day I feel
> Your guardianship; I take it to my heart;
> 'Tis like the solemn shelter of the night.
> But I would call thee beautiful, for mild
> And soft, and day, and beautiful thou art,
> Dear Valley, having in thy face a smile
> Though peaceful, full of gladness. (110-117)

He sees in nature a place of refuge, and wants to be held – metaphorically hugged – by the hills, which provide him with a sense of peace and security. Beautiful, soft, and gay in its near-human sense of being, the valley, too, smiles at him in gladness. He depicts all of the natural world in such pseudo-erotic terms, a rhetoric culminating in cosmic unity, or what he calls 'A blended holiness of earth and sky' (144). Stuart Sperry, one of the few critics who recognized the erotic in Wordsworth's verse, has argued that there is 'a quality of transfused sexuality that informs so much of his description of landscape'.[55]

This intimate embrace of nature subverts the Western Platonic tradition, which sees natural objects merely as emblems, as imperfect manifestations of ideal forms. In *The Perennial Philosophy* Aldous Huxley decried the Platonic tradition of denigrating the things of the natural world. 'Plato seems to have made an enormous mistake, the grotesque mistake of separating being from becoming. He could never, poor fellow, have seen [...] a bunch of flowers shining with their own inner light [...] he could never have perceived objects in nature as they

[54] Abrams, *Natural supernaturalism*, 143.

[55] Stuart Sperry, 'Wordsworth and the grounds of human consciousness', In: Beverly Taylor & Robert Bain (Eds.), *The cast of consciousness: Concepts of the mind in British and American Romanticism*, Westport, CT: Greenwood, 1987, 69.

existed in their own right'.[56] Wordsworth corrects Plato's error by revering objects of nature not for what they can do but for what they are. He loves nature for its own sake, the way in which a lover loves his beloved. Mary Wedd has observed that the imaginative transmutation of reality in Wordsworth 'rests upon observation and does not consist in throwing a cloud of idealism around objects vaguely seen and imperfectly understood'.[57] In his Taoist reading of the poet, Wu similarly argues that 'Wordsworth's sublime moments are not a revelation of the transcendent lying beyond the pale reality of nature or within the mind, but an awareness of what resides in the very heart of nature as it is'.[58] Wordsworth was in many ways not an idealist.

While such readings do a great deal of justice to the poet, one must exercise caution in seeing him as being *solely* grounded in this world (no pun intended). Wordsworth loved nature in an almost human way, and such sentiments often led him to the spiritual, which is perhaps why Philip Rule claimed, 'it then must follow that sexuality remains an ever-present force, even in transcendental moments' in Wordsworth's verse.[59] In Book Sixth of *The Prelude* he has one such moment, which is revealed through his recollection of Lake Maggiore in Locarno:

> [...] Like a breeze
> Or sunbeam over your domain I passed
> In motion without pause; but ye have left
> Your beauty with me, an impassioned sight
> Of colors and of forms, whose power is sweet
> And gracious, almost, might I dare to say,
> As virtue is, or goodness – sweet as love,
> Or the remembrance of a noble indeed,
> Or gentlest visitations of pure thought
> When God, the giver of all joy is thanked
> Religiously in silent blessedness –
> Sweet as this last itself, for such it is. (675-687)

But his understanding of the spiritual commingles the transcendent and the natural. In elevating the beauty of nature to the Christian virtue of goodness, and in likening his love for the natural world to the state of reverence one cultivates during prayer, he borders on heresy, which is perhaps why he might 'dare to say' such things. He knows he is being radical in kicking over the Western fence

[56] Huxley, *The perennial philosophy*, 18.

[57] Mary Wedd, 'The conjunction of the matter-of-fact and the visionary in the 1805 Prelude', in: *Charles Lamb Bulletin* 104 (1998), 172.

[58] Wu, *The Wordsworthian imagination*, 28.

[59] Rule, 'The gendered imagination in religion and literature', 65.

between the physical and the spiritual, as Tagore said of Kabir's mysticism.[60] The point is, however, that Wordsworth saw a flower as being inherently beautiful in its physicality, but he also saw in such beauty an intimation of the transcendent realm.

IV

Because of these seemingly contradictory elements (the one denies the world while the other embraces it), critics have pointed to a 'deeply paradoxical or problematic character of Wordsworth's dealings with Nature', as Geoffrey Hartman put it.[61] Harold Bloom was perhaps the first to argue for what he saw as an 'unresolved antagonism between poetry and nature' in Wordsworth.[62] According to such a view, imagination may have nothing to do with the natural world at all; it leads to the transcendence or negation of nature, a process Hartman calls, using mystical discourse himself, a 'via naturaliter negativa'.[63] Following the lead of Bloom and Hartman, Klaus Mortensen argued that 'there is a determined and intense effort in Wordsworth's work to maintain the relationship between consciousness and nature as something other than a projection, as depending on a more fundamental inequality than metaphorical likeness'.[64] Medhusudan Pati has likewise suggested that 'nature and mystic imagination might not, after all, have any essential connection' in his verse.[65]

Such criticism, however, never transcends Western dualism. Wordsworth might indeed have had an unresolved antagonism towards nature, but such a conflict stemmed from his own Western enculturation. It has nothing to do with his *perceptions* of the natural world when they are unmediated by any ideology, for in such moments Wordsworth subverts even himself. His antagonism became clearer as he aged and as he reshaped his poetry; most of the post-1815 verse reflects such ideological conflict. But in many of the foregoing passages, most of which appeared in his earlier, pre-1807 poetry, the 'perceiving' speaker transgresses the line of demarcation that designates nature as 'other'. Perhaps because of this transgression, Herbert Lindenberger argued that 'it is difficult to distinguish between the literal and metaphorical level in Wordsworth, for the literal

[60] *Songs of Kabir*, 21.

[61] Geoffrey Hartman, 'A poet's progress: Wordsworth and the *via naturaliter negativa*' (1962), in: Wordsworth, Abrams, & Gill, *The Prelude 1799, 1805, 1850*, 598.

[62] Bloom, *The visionary company*, 145.

[63] Hartman, 'A poet's progress', 599.

[64] Mortensen, *The time of unrememberable being*, 18.

[65] Pati, 'Wordsworth: An Indian view', 69.

becomes figurative and then literal again'.[66] Wordsworth does have an ambivalent attitude towards nature, therefore, but he has countless moments in which imagination and nature appear so harmonized as to render them indistinguishable from one another, despite both himself and Western modes of ideation.

To be sure, Wordsworth's confidence in the natural world was seriously shaken by the death of his brother John. His poem 'Elegiac Stanzas' suggests a moment of near total disillusionment with his spiritualized view of nature, which he calls 'the fond illusion of my heart' (29). John's death leaves him bereft of optimism; it leaves him without 'the gleam, / The light that never was, on land or sea' (15). He can no longer view the objects of nature (particularly the ocean, since John drowned) through a 'visionary' lens. 'A power is gone, which nothing can restore; / A deep distress hath humanize my Soul' (35-36). To say such disillusionment is representative of all of his poetry, however, is a misreading, for the revisions in *The Prelude* of 1850 do not reflect such bitterness. John L. Mahoney has argued that even from his earliest years Wordsworth's poetry contains images of 'skewed light, of brightness touched by shadings of darkness'.[67] To read 'Elegiac Stanzas' as representative of some kind of dark pessimism underlying Wordsworth's orientation towards nature, therefore, is to read only half of the story. There is both dark and light; and if the light is tinged with blackness so is the darkness mitigated by a visionary glow.

Whitman, too, paradoxically both celebrated nature and saw beyond it. Critics have observed a world-denying tendency in him as he aged. Roger Asselineau, for instance, noted that the 1871-72 edition of *Leaves* shows the poet 'tired of life and of its perpetual struggles. [Whitman] would have liked to escape from his body and launch himself with his soul in search of God, a God almost transcendent to the creation, but in whom he could lose himself and find rest and peace'.[68] George Hutchinson also sees in the same edition a decline in Whitman's socially-conscious, ecstatic poetry.[69] According to such critics, Whitman's otherworldly yearnings dominate his verse and signal the decline of his art. Although I do not dispute such an argument, I would point out that there was from the beginning a world-denying element in his poetry. In 'Starting From Paumanok', the introductory poem in the 1860 edition, he speaks of the 'real body' and how it 'will elude the hands of the corpse-cleaners' (181, 182). In 'A Song of Joys', which appeared in the same edition, he claims to discharge his 'excrementitious body to be burn'd, or rendered to powder, or buried, / My real body doubtless

[66] Herbert Lindenberger, 'Images of interaction in The Prelude' (1963), in: Wordsworth, Abrams, & Gill, *The Prelude 1799, 1805, 1850*, 643.

[67] Mahoney, *William Wordsworth*, 30.

[68] Asselineau, *The evolution of Walt Whitman*, 189.

[69] Hutchinson, *The ecstatic Whitman*, 173.

left to me for other spheres / My voided body nothing more to me' (141-143). Even in the earliest 1855 edition of 'Song of Myself' there are references to the poet's belief in reincarnation, a concept that renders the body a mere shell: 'I pass death with the dying, and birth with the new-wash'd babe and am not contained between my hat and boots' (124). In 'O Living Always, Always Dying' (1860) he also yearns 'to disengage myself from those corpses of me, which I turned and look at where I cast them, / To pass on, and leave the corpses behind' (5-6). Whitman celebrated matter and the body, but he was no materialist. 'Are souls drown'd and destroy'd' when the body dies? he asked in 'Thought'. 'Is only matter triumphant?' (9-10). More conservative scholars such as David Keubrich have seized upon the world-denying element in Whitman as proof that he 'depreciates the natural world'.[70] Equally misguided are those who support *only* the other transcendent impulse. The truth, of course, lies somewhere in the middle. As McSweeney has claimed, Whitman's 'purpose was to affirm not an eternal supernatural world but an endless trans-natural world'.[71]

'Without nature', writes Harry Wilson, 'there is no Romantic movement', as artists such as Wordsworth and Whitman saw in the natural world an indivisibility – a wholeness – they could no longer find in civilization.[72] Nature provided both poets with a moral/spiritual education that enabled them to view the world in a radical, non-Western way. Merleau-Ponty has argued that 'to ignore the complex intertwining between pre-theoretical lived experience and conceptual judgement leads to the error of the mind/body opposition'.[73] Wordsworth and Whitman overcame this manmade construction in their dealings with the natural world. Nature taught them to *be*; it taught them to experience the world and (consequently) themselves in a pre-judgmental mode of consciousness that transcended rationalist dualism. As Whitman wrote in *Specimen Days*:

> One lesson from affiliating a tree – perhaps the greatest moral lesson anyhow from Earth, rocks, animals, is that same lesson of inherency, of *what is*, without the least regard to what the looker on (the critic) supposes or says, or whether he likes or dislikes. What worse – what more general malady pervades each and all of us, our literature, education, attitude toward each other, (even toward ourselves,) than a morbid trouble about *seems* [...] (90)

But this 'untellable lesson', as he points out later in the same work, points beyond to God and to spirit, 'infinitely beyond anything from art, books, sermons, or from science, old or new' (119). Nature's lesson is beyond ordinary knowledge,

70 Keubrich, 'Whitman's new theism', 17-18.
71 McSweeney, *The language of the senses*, 127.
72 Wilson, *Psychological projection in six Romantic poems*, in abstract.
73 Merleau-Ponty, 'Preface to "Phenomenology of Perception"', 77.

which left both poets, consequently, without a discourse to account for such natural wisdom. To fill in this gap they put forth in their verse an epistemology of their own. Wordsworth wrote in Book Fifth of *The Prelude*: 'This verse is dedicated to Nature's self / And things that teach as Nature teaches' (230-231). His cosmic poetry is the equivalent of the untellable lesson of the natural world. Whitman, too, claimed to be bringing in his poetry a form of knowing comparable to nature's abundant wisdom. 'Now I re-examine philosophies and religions', he wrote in 'Song of the Open Road'. 'They may prove well in lecture-rooms, yet not prove at all under the spacious clouds and along the landscape and flowing currents' (83-84). In the next chapter I will discuss the cosmic epistemology both poets created in response to the inadequacy of conventional knowledge as a means for apprehending for this natural/soul wisdom.

Chapter VI

COSMIC EPISTEMOLOGY

The Darkness of Enlightenment, the Effulgence of *Agnosia*[1]

'[...] Ye dreamers, then,
Forgers of lawless tales, we bless you then –
Imposters, drivellers, dotards, as the ape
Philosophy will call you – then we feel
With what, and how great might ye are in league,
Who make our wish our power, our thought a deed,
An empire, a possession'
(Wordsworth)

'Beyond thy lectures learn'd professor,
Beyond thy telescope or spectroscope observer keen, beyond all mathematics,
Beyond the doctor's surgery, anatomy, beyond the chemist with his chemistry [...]'
(Whitman)

I

When the Japanese physicist Yukawa was asked how he had conceived of mesons (particles that hold an atomic nucleus together) when so many great Western physicists had not thought of such an idea, he replied, 'You see, we in the East have not been corrupted by Aristotle'.[2] Apparently, Yukawa had arrived at his conclusion of the existence of mesons by means other than ratiocination. In the Western mindset such intuition is too frequently downplayed, having become a subjugated way of knowing in what Michel Foucault has called the totalitarian hierarchy of knowledges.

The repression of these alternative epistemologies reached its zenith in Enlightenment discourse. The age of reason served to pull the West out of its

---

[1] This chapter was previously published under the title 'The darkness of Enlightenment, the effulgence of *agnosia*: Epistemology in Wordsworth and Whitman', in: *Journal of Indian Philosophy and Religion* 9 (2004), 1-32.

[2] Qtd. in John Hitchcock, *Healing our worldview*, West Chester, Penn: Chrysalis, 1999, 66.

dark age, offering the promise of demystification and carrying the illuminating torch of learning and rationality. All aspects of human life could be apprehended, according to such a doctrine. Both human nature and the objective world finally could be explained in a coherent, logical manner via Enlightenment discourse. But as the Romantics found out, and as William James later remarked, 'rationalism only accounts for the superficial aspects of consciousness'.[3] There are much deeper reservoirs of the human soul, such as the ecstasies of deeply felt sentiments, than one's reasoning capacity allowed for. Becoming entangled in the details of the pursuit of knowledge, 'we lose sight of how much of our lives actually flows in a nonrational manner'.[4] For Wordsworth and many other Romantics, the Enlightenment actually represented the Fall of mankind. Enlightenment was tantamount to dissection, a fragmentation of what should remain whole, as M.H. Abrams has pointed out.[5] To move from ignorance into knowledge, according to many Romantics, is to *descend* from a higher innocence to a lower level of knowing; it is to move from the special insight of 'agnosia' (unknowing) into the ironic darkness of Enlightenment and human knowledge.[6]

Many mystical traditions similarly downplay ordinary thought and privilege the wisdom of *agnosia*. The 'Mundaka' Upanishad, for instance, distinguishes between 'two types of wisdom, the higher and the lower'; whereas the latter involves logic and language, the former is beyond all thought, the type of knowledge that can only be described in a discourse that does violence to reason (75). Mystics, much like their Romantic brethren, exalt feeling and imagination above the intellect, and, consequently, embrace a form of anti-intellectualism that is at odds with reason. 'Put thy cleverness away', Kabir wrote, arguing that only in love could one come to true wisdom.[7] As Annemarie Schimmel has pointed out, in the Sufi tradition 'to break the inkpots and to tear the books was considered by some mystics the first step' towards embracing immediate knowledge as opposed to legalistic scholarship.[8]

I do not mean to suggest that Wordsworth and Whitman were mystics in the traditional sense, but the anti-intellectual strain in their verse is preeminent among the Romantic writers. Largely a backlash to the Enlightenment view of human beings 'as entities to be measured and maneuvered', the Romantic privileging of states of feeling over the intellect was an attempt to prevent the reification that

---

[3] James, *The varieties of religious experience*, 73.

[4] Hitchcock, *Healing our worldview*, 67.

[5] Abrams, *Natural supernaturalism*, 219.

[6] Barnstone, *The poetics of ecstasy*, 14.

[7] *Songs of Kabir*, 104.

[8] Annemarie Schimmel, *The mystical dimensions of Islam*, Chapel Hill, NC: University of North Carolina, 1975, 17.

accompanied the Western philosophical/scientific tradition.[9] Although Marxists blame capitalist ideology for such dehumanization, the reification of human beings has its roots firmly planted in Western soil, stretching back well before the exploitation of factory workers in the 19th century. The rise of the bourgeoisie, in fact, was merely the culmination of the underlying Western ideology that objectifies not only nature but the subjective human psyche.

To combat this objectification Wordsworth and Whitman attempted to offer in their verse an alternative mode of knowing, an epistemology unlike anything in the Western philosophical tradition. Giles Deleuze has argued that there are 'alternative modes of ideation that cannot pass through concepts'.[10] Such was the 'epistemology' Wordsworth and Whitman created in their poetry. Unlike philosophers in the Western tradition, however, Wordsworth and Whitman often dissolved the boundaries erected by rationalism, breaking the shackles of reason and freeing themselves from the tyranny of the West's oppressive fetishizing of intellectualism. Both poets brought to a new level the Romantic notion that Cartesian dualism could be transcended by apprehending in a new 'cosmic' way – by conception through intuition rather than ratiocination. The subjective truths of Romanticism could be discerned only through a deeper delving into the heart, the wellspring of intuitive knowledge.

II

Simon Critchley has argued that Nietzschean nihilism caused philosophers to look for non-philosophic discourses that might respond to the resulting crisis in the gap between knowledge and wisdom.[11] Although I do not dispute such a claim, I would point out that this gap existed before Nietzsche in Enlightenment discourse, which Romantics such as Wordsworth and Whitman perceived as devoid of true wisdom. But Critchley's point is well taken, for philosophers such as Heidegger sought solace in the 'meditative thoughtfulness of poetic creation'.[12] Heidegger believed his life's work had been to free us 'from the poison we always carry with us – from the power of 2000 years of philosophical systems, doctrines, and educational systems', as Otto Poggeler observes.[13] Heidegger's way of

[9] J.L. Mehta, 'Heidegger and Vedanta: Reflections on a questionable theme', in: Parkes, *Heidegger and Asian thought*, 22.

[10] Giles Deleuze, 'What is philosophy?', in: Kearney & Rainwater, *The Continental philosophy reader*, 408.

[11] Critchley, *Continental philosophy*, 87.

[12] Ibidem.

[13] Otto Poggeler, 'West-East dialogue: Heidegger and Lau-tze', in: Parkes, *Heidegger and Asian thought*, 58.

knowing has nothing to do with the usurpation of the objects of knowledge, as is typical among Western philosophers. Heidegger's way, which I believe was made possible largely by Romanticism, is a way of thinking 'but not representational thinking'.[14] In other words, Heidegger's epistemology is a reorientation towards reality in which one does not apprehend the mystery of being in a logical sense, but rather finds the 'answer' in the immediacy of a direct relationship to the world. As Mehta argues, 'the experience of thinking [in Heidegger] appropriates the precious element of immediacy in all mysticism'.[15] Such immediacy allows one to overcome the 'technological' attitude (*Gestell*) of Western thought, which carries the illusion of true cognition. But as Karl Jaspers argued, 'cognition of a thing is not cognition of being'.[16] Scientism (the belief that all things can be known through the scientific method) merely produces knowledge of objectified things; it never yields the wisdom of being, which can be obtained only indirectly through such a medium as poetry. Heidegger believed the lyric mode was a more legitimate way of knowing than strict rationalism, seeing in the form both a way to overcome the self-centeredness of the thinking subject of Cartesian philosophy and *Gestell*, both of which precluded the possibility of recognizing the splendour of the world, of Being.[17]

Verse, therefore, is not merely the medium of dreamy Romantics who wanted to shut out the realities of the world and live in a fanciful realm of their own creation. As a way of knowing it yields 'a perspective and dimension on reality that we don't get from any other approach to reality', as Northrop Frye argued.[18] W.B. Gallie has asserted that *The Prelude* is a philosophical poem 'because in it Wordsworth grapples with philosophical problems and because he tries to answer these problems in a way which would be possible only in poetry'.[19] Harold Bloom similarly claimed that Wordsworth's 'Intimations' ode 'only plays at being a logic of concepts – we do it wrong to treat it as thought dressed in images'.[20] The poem, he further argued, 'plays at discursiveness only to mock the limitations of the discursive'.[21] Whitman, too, is a philosophical poet whose verse plays with the rules of rationalism. *Leaves of Grass* is rife with moments of discursive mockery, moments in which the poetic persona explores traditional philosophical

---

[14] Stambaugh, 'Heidegger, Taoism, and the Question of Metaphysics', 85.

[15] Mehta, 'Heidegger and Vedanta', 35.

[16] Karl Jaspers, *Philosophy of existence*, Philadelphia: Pennsylvania University Press, 1971, 59.

[17] Lemay & Pitts, *Heidegger*, 81.

[18] Northrop Frye, *The educated imagination*, Bloomington, IN: Indiana University Press, 1967, 102.

[19] Gallie, 'Is The Prelude a philosophical poem?', 664.

[20] Bloom, *The visionary company*, 173.

[21] Ibidem.

themes but in a way that subordinates reason to intuition. Both poets, in fact, are among the West's greatest philosophers, but they are not recognized as such because they wrote in a devalued medium too often dismissed as imaginative and thus illegitimate.

Interestingly, both poets are rooted in the Enlightenment cult of reason. Wordsworth's positioning of himself as an untutored child of nature, for instance, was pure poetic convention. As John Purkis points out, the poet 'was more bookish and intellectual than many of his fellow-students' at Cambridge, and his two earliest publications, 'An Evening Walk' and 'Descriptive Sketches' were 'aimed at an educated public, and are, if anything, too clever, and give too much evidence of extensive reading'.[22] 'Wordsworth had to *learn* to be simple', as Purkis adds.[23] None of Wordsworth's contemporaries saw him as ill-educated. A common critical complaint in his day was that he was an 'intellectual poet who wrote *deliberately* like a simpleton'.[24] In addition to attending Cambridge, one of the premier schools of his day, Wordsworth also spent four years at Hawkshead Grammar School, which was at the highest point of its reputation when he arrived there in 1782. Even before entering Hawkshead the poet enjoyed the resources of his father's library, which was extensive. At a very early age he was able to repeat large portions of Shakespeare, Milton, and Spenser, which he memorized.[25] By the time he arrived at Cambridge, he was an intelligent and highly educated man, so much so that he was 'in advance of his fellow-students in the basic requirements for the first years work'. He was consequently awarded an academic scholarship for placing first in his class on an examination.[26] Widely read and highly capable, Wordsworth, therefore, was actually one of the intellectual elite.

His earliest extant poem, 'Lines Written As a School Exercise at Hawkshead', is a paean to Enlightenment ideology, for in it he celebrates 'The Power of Education' (6) and the 'rigid precepts' (7) that lead to the 'bright paths of fair majestic Truth' (12). Wordsworth praises the advances of science and knowledge, which 'with joy saw Superstition fly / Before the lustre of Religion's eye' (43-44). He sings the praises of education's release from the thralldom of the religious orders: 'No jarring monks, to gloomy cell confined, / With mazy rules perplex the weary mind; / No shadowy forms entice the soul aside, / Secure she walks, Philosophy her guide' (49-52). As a 'noble' institution, Hawkshead teaches 'The golden precepts of the classic page; / To lead the mind to those Elysian plains / Where, throned in gold, immortal Science reigns' (68-70). Hawkshead is an

---

22 John Purkis, *A preface to Wordsworth*, New York: Longman, 1970, 14-15.
23 Purkis, *A preface to Wordsworth*, 15.
24 Idem, 13.
25 Mahoney, *William Wordsworth*, 6.
26 Purkis, *A preface to Wordsworth*, 14.

embodiment of the Enlightenment notion that the mystery of existence could be discerned through the advancement of knowledge:

Fair to the view is sacred Truth displayed,
In all the majesty of light arrayed,
To teach, on rapid wings, the curious soul
To roam from heaven to heaven, from pole to pole,
From thence to search the mystic cause of things,
And follow Nature to her secret springs. (71-76)

Nothing could be more rationalist than the notion of a curious soul – a 'meddling intellect', as he would later call it, pursuing the objective truths of nature to their secret springs. The image of the majestic light of learning illuminating the mystic cause of things is clearly rooted in the Western tradition of intellectual dissection, of penetration of what should be left virgin, and of apprehending Being through the mind. Basil Willey has argued that the poet also owed to science and the advancement of learning the 'repudiation of concrete mythology. Wordsworth says there must be no abstractions, no symbols, no myths to stand between the mind and its objects' (113). A product of his age, then, Wordsworth was an initiate in the cult of reason and from his earliest years demonstrated at least a partial complicity with the Enlightenment program.

Whitman, too, was in one respect a byproduct of Enlightenment ideology. To be sure, his formal education paled in comparison to Wordsworth's. He spent a mere six years in a Brooklyn public school where instruction was 'confined mainly to arithmetic, geography, reading, and writing', and where one teacher with the assistance of student monitors instructed up to 300 pupils.[27] Whitman's informal education, however, was quite substantial, as he made frequent use of the newly available public libraries, acquainting himself with a variety of subjects such as German, Greek, and Roman philosophy, astronomy, politics, spirituality, physiology, and many others. Whitman was very familiar with poets from all of the world's traditions, and as an inhabitant of New York City he frequently attended public lectures on a variety of literary topics. As Karl Malone has pointed out, the poet made frequent use of the half a dozen or so British magazines then in circulation from which he was able to glean ideas on art theory and trends in literature.[28] As a newspaper writer and editor who worked for a variety of dailies and weeklies, Whitman was exposed not only to world affairs but also to a significant number of reviews of scholarly works on a plethora of subjects, some of which he wrote himself. Those closest to him knew the poet as an avid reader who read randomly and without discipline but voraciously and

---

[27] Allen, *The solitary singer*, 10.
[28] Malone, *Parallels to Hindu and Taoist thought in Walt Whitman*, 16.

with a hunger that was never quelled. Even in his old age Whitman was a gluttonous reader whose few worldly possessions consisted primarily of books.

In the Enlightenment spirit Whitman intoned, 'I accept Reality and dare not question it, / Materialism first and last imbuing' ('Song of Myself' 483-484). He also praised the scientific advances of his day:

Hurrah for positive science! long live exact demonstration!
Fetch stonecrop mixt with cedar and branches of lilac,
This is the lexicographer, this the chemist, this made a grammar of the old cartouches,
These Mariners put the ship through dangerous unknown seas,
This is the geologist, thus works with the scalpel, and this is a mathematician.
Gentlemen, to you the first honors always! (485-490)

Science and Enlightenment 'progress' did not disturb him, as Asselineau points out, because they rendered the world more wonderful than ever. 'Science thus became a springboard for the imagination of the poet who sought to reach the soul and the secret life of things beyond inert material appearances'.[29] Much like the early Wordsworth who sought through knowledge to get at the mystic cause of things, so did Whitman see in the steady march of science a tool for unlocking the many secrets of existence. Such enthusiasm led Vernon Parrington to see Whitman as the 'completest embodiment of the Enlightenment' in an era when the influence of the age of reason began to wane.[30]

However much both poets were complicit in Enlightenment ideology, they also found themselves at odds with its limiting doctrines. As Wordsworth came of poetic age it became apparent that he saw the light of learning in a different way. In 'Expostulation and Reply', for instance, he puts a new spin on en*light*enment. In the second stanza he presents the typical view of the light of learning as savior of the human race:

'Why, William, on that old grey stone,
Thus for the length of half a day,
Why, William, sit you thus alone,
And dream your time away?
'Where are your books? – that light bequeathed
To Beings else forlorn and blind!
Up! Up! and drink the spirit breathed
From dead men to their kind. (1-8)

---

[29] Asselineau, *The evolution of Walt Whitman*, 43.

[30] Vernon Louis Parrington, 'Afterglow of the Enlightenment', in: Bradley & Blodgett, *Leaves of Grass*, 855.

Matthew, the poet's interlocutor, clearly represents the Western prejudice against any form of dreamy idleness, against any form of knowing other than that which can be gleaned from books. He also represents *Gestell*, Heidegger's 'technological attitude', which objectifies the natural world: 'You look round on your Mother Earth, / As if she for no purpose bore you', as if one must incessantly be *doing* in order to *be* (9-10). And yet, his imperative contains the seeds of its own demise, for the light of learning is ironically the spirit of the dead breathed to their own kind, that is, spiritually dead people; it is opposed to the living cosmos Wordsworth is apprehending in his dreamy idleness. The poet's response represents a significant subversion of the Enlightenment tradition:

> 'The eye – it cannot choose but see;
> We cannot bid the ear be still;
> Our bodies feel, where'er they be,
> Against or with our will.
> 'Nor less I deem that there are Powers
> Which of themselves our minds impress;
> That we can feed this mind of ours
> In a wise passiveness.
> 'Think you, 'mid all this mighty sum
> Of things forever speaking,
> That nothing of itself will come,
> But we must still be seeking? (17-28)

In relinquishing the conscious will to the sway of the senses and what the body feels, the poet cultivates what is tantamount to Zen emptiness, or *sunyata*, as John Rudy has observed. Having let go of the incessant desires of the ever-seeking ego, Wordsworth has overcome the technological attitude and cultivated a state of being unavailable to one who merely reads books to unlock the mystery. His 'wise passiveness' bears a resemblance to some mystical states, passivity being one of the defining characteristics of expansion of consciousness experiences, as William James and others have demonstrated. If not full-fledged mysticism, Wordsworth's state of mind is nonetheless a melting of the conscious will, and it is a way of knowing, a wisdom, in contrast to what one obtains from thick tomes. It is available, in fact, only when one spends time away from books, as the poet does in sitting alone and dreaming his time away. This wise passiveness nourishes the mind more than intellectual knowledge, which, in fact, constricts consciousness in a way that prevents such passive expansion.

In 'The Tables Turned', a companion poem to 'Expostulation and Reply', Wordsworth gives Matthew (probably William Hazlitt who was fond of metaphysics, as Christopher Ricks points out) the imperative: 'Up! Up! my Friend, and quit your books; / Or surely you'll grow double' (1-2). In this poem, however, Wordsworth expands his notion of natural wisdom in contrast to intellectual knowledge: 'Books! 'tis a dull and endless strife: / Come, hear the woodland linnet, / How sweet his music! on my life, / There's more of wisdom in it' (9-12). One can learn more from 'The sun' and its 'freshening lustre mellow' (6) than from the 'toil and trouble' of rigorous study (4). 'Come forth into the *light* of things, / Let Nature be your Teacher', he says, reappropriating the premier symbol of the age of reason and turning on its head enlightenment notions of pedagogy (emphasis added, 15-16). He immortalizes these ideas in two of his most well known passages:

> One impulse from a vernal wood
> May teach you more of man,
> Of moral evil and of good,
> Than all the sages can.
> Sweet is lore which Nature brings;
> Our meddling intellect
> Mis-shapes the beauteous forms of things: –
> We murder to dissect. (21-28)

Reason, elevated to almost divine status by enlightenment thinkers, is here depicted as meddlesome, as interfering with the wisdom of nature, and as causing division of what should remain whole. In attempting to get at the mystic source of things through the inquisitive mind, rational man distorts and destroys the beauty that is itself the source, ironically rendering inaccessible the pathways he seeks to traverse. Wordsworth's closing stanza, though clearly hyperbolic, dismisses *intellectual* study altogether: 'Enough of Science and of Art; / Close up those barren leaves; / Come forth, and bring with you a heart / That watches and receives' (29-32). It is important to point out that he is not dismissing expanding one's perceptions and enlarging one's mind but offering an alternative for doing so. The wise passiveness of 'Expostulation and Reply' is here suggested in his imperative to leave the books and become open to wisdom with a passive heart that receives the type of knowledge that can only be had ironically when one ceases to strive for it.

A significant element in *Leaves of Grass* likewise runs against the grain of Enlightenment discourse. Just after he exclaims 'Hurrah for positive science' and 'Gentlemen, to you the first honors always!' Whitman also raises himself above such mundane knowledge: 'Your facts are useful, and yet they are not my dwelling, / I but enter by them to an area of my dwelling' (485, 490, 491-492). He acknowledges his complicity in Enlightenment ideology, but he also is careful to distinguish himself from its limitations. The light of learning shines bright, but it can never penetrate the mystic depths of the soul. 'Are you so given up to literature, science, art, amours? / These ostensible realities…' he asks in 'Starting From Paumanok' (115-116). Ordinary knowledge is useful, but ultimately it is not real wisdom for the poet.

One of Whitman's dilettantish interests was in the findings of astronomy, as he attended lectures and became enthralled by the expansive possibilities this field of study seemed to offer. In 'When I Heard the Learned Astronomer', however, he makes clear his attitude towards the type of knowledge it yielded:

When I heard the learn'd astronomer,
When the proofs, the figures, were ranged in columns before me,
When I was shown the charts and diagrams, to add, divide, and measure them,
When I sitting heard the astronomer where he lectured with much applause in
 the lecture-room,
How soon unaccountable I became tired and sick,
Till rising and gliding I wander'd off by myself,
In the mystical moist night-air, and from time to time,
Look'd up in perfect silence at the stars. (1-8)

He is entirely unimpressed by the contents of the astronomer's lecture, which leaves him feeling as though there must be more, as though the magnitude of the universe cannot be reduced to so many figures, charts, and diagrams. Despite the audience's laudatory reception, he does not feel the astronomer has properly accounted for the sense of awe and wonder he feels when he gazes in solitary 'wise passiveness' at the night sky. The knowledge the astronomer offers comes up short, merely scratching the surface and offering a superficial explanation that fails to capture the magnitude of the poet's own deeper perceptions of the cosmos. He feels the discrepancy so much that it makes him tired and sick, but his faith in his own understanding of the universe is restored when he ventures out into the mystical night. Significantly, however, he is not reassured by any logical counterargument but by the mere silence of the Milky Way.

Whitman's own counterargument, his alternative to scientific knowledge, is his verse and the persona he creates in it. But in 'Song of Myself' he is careful to point out that to properly apprehend the wisdom he is offering one must seek it in alternative places:

If you would understand me go to the heights or water-shore,
The nearest gnat is an explanation, and a drop or motion of waves a key,
The maul; the oar, the hand-saw, second my words.
No shutter'd room or school can commune with me,
But roughs and little children better than they. (1252-1256)

Clearly, it is not to be found in schools and books but in life itself – in activity and experience, as the oar and the hand-saw suggest. Being cannot be taught but only encountered. Whitman's explanation is thus found in the natural world in grand objects (mountains and oceans) and in lowly ones (insects). What he offers in his verse is so fundamental as to be beyond the awareness of ordinary consciousness. But the roughs and children, who do not have the interference of learning and who do not have cluttered minds full of rational answers to what is fundamentally an irrational mystery, can understand the poet well. Children and those who are not hampered by an overabundance of mental knowledge are usually quite phenomenological because they tend to have a 'more innocent eye', as Donald Palmer observes.[31] They can more directly perceive without the filter of preconceived judgement, bias, and the mental clutter of acquired knowledge. For this reason the Taoists attempted to recover childhood consciousness. The ancient Chinese ideogram for the sage and the child, in fact, were the same. Lau-tse, the reputed author of the *Tao Te Ching*, was thus known as 'the Old Boy'.[32]

Whitman may have gotten the idea of the divine child consciousness from his English predecessor, for Wordsworth had a fascination for children, or more specifically, he was fascinated by 'the special kind of insight they possess – the unrefined knowledge, the sense of kinship and closeness to God, [and] the lack of impatience with discontinuities', as John Mahoney points out. The child's state of consciousness represents 'a state of singular blessedness', as it is 'close to nature, uncontaminated by the workings of sophisticated thinking, in tune with the presence of divine power in the world'.[33] Children were more attuned to the cosmic for Wordsworth, as they possessed the unknowledge (agnosia) he attempted to convey in his verse. 'Our simple childhood sits upon a throne', he wrote in Book Fifth of *The Prelude*, 'That hath more power than all the elements' (508-509). The gnosis of adult consciousness is a poor substitute for the agnosia of childhood. 'Ah, is there one who ever has been young / And needs a monitory voice to tame / The pride of virtue and of intellect?' he asks in Book Second (19-21). To be sure, nearly all who have moved from the innocence of child consciousness to the weary weight of adult experience need to some degree a reminder that knowledge gained is predicated upon insight lost. His poetry thus serves such an end, as it is at least a partial glimpse of a state of being no longer available to most adults.

Wordsworth, consequently, went so far as to lament the loss of child consciousness that intellectual study causes. In Book Fifth of *The Prelude*, which is subtitled 'Books', he declares his sympathy for the human race 'not for woes / Which thou endur'st' but 'for those palms achieved [sic] / Through length of time, by study and hard thought, / The honors of thy high endowments; there / My sadness finds its fuel' (5-9). Once again he turns Enlightenment doctrine on its head, seeing the process of rigorous study and intellectual attainment as

---

[31] Donald Palmer, *Structuralism and poststructuralism*, New York: Writers & Readers, 1999, 36.

[32] Smith, *The world's religions*, 196.

[33] Mahoney, *William Wordsworth*, 75.

the source of man's woes. He does not advocate that children be deprived entirely of books, for he does praise imaginative works of great writers such as Milton, Shakespeare, and Spenser, as well as folklore, fairy tales, and mythology. He does point out, however, that all learning should lead to 'Knowledge not purchased with the loss of power!' (V. 425). Which is to say, a child's education should consist of reading in imaginative books, which enhance such power, and the lessons of nature, as both serve to foster rather than to detract from cosmic perception. Both serve to create a different breed:

> A race of real children, not too wise,
> Too learned, or too good, but wanton, fresh,
> And bandied up and down by love and hate;
> Fierce, Moody, patient, venturous, modest, shy,
> Mad at their sports like withered leaves in winds;
> Though doing wrong and suffering, and full oft
> Bending beneath our life's mysterious weight
> Of pain and fear, yet still in happiness
> Not yielding to the happiest upon the earth.
> Simplicity in habit, truth in speech,
> Be these the daily strengtheners of their minds! (411-425)

He contrasts this ideal race of children with the child prodigy, which he calls a 'monster birth / Engendered by these too industrious times' (295-296). In the acquisition of intellectual knowledge the prodigy is 'no child, / But a dwarf man' (294-295). He has been robbed of the wisdom of youth and thus become 'The noontide shadow of a man complete; / A worshiper of worldly seemliness' (297-298). Unlike the wanton and fresh children of the ideal race who live free and happy, the prodigy in his tremendous learning is 'fenced round, nay armed, for ought we know, / In panoply complete', and 'His discourse moves slow, / Massy and ponderous as a prison door' (314-315, 320-321). He is imprisoned by his weighty learning and complexity, and although he has profound thoughts and refined intellectual skills, he does not benefit from the lessons of nature: 'Meanwhile old Grandame Earth is grieved to find / The playthings which for love designed for him / Unthought of – in their woodland beds the flowers / Weep, and the river-sides are all forlorn' (346-349). Though full of intellectual acquisitions, the prodigy's life is empty: 'Now this is hollow, 'tis a life of lies / From the beginning, and in lies must end' (350-351). The prodigy is the tragic culmination of Enlightenment ideology, according to the poet, for in gaining knowledge he loses his humanity, and he deprives himself of life's most valuable lesson.

In 'We Are Seven' Wordsworth contrasts childhood insight with adult knowledge, but he does so in an ironic way, portraying 'ignorance' on two different levels. Paulino Lim has argued that the poem resembles a 'mondo' – 'a dialogue between a Zen master and student designed to frustrate the latter's logical mind so that he can answer from the deeper levels of his intuition'.[34] But the question remains, who is the student and who is the teacher? As the poem closes the speaker is aware of the child's ignorance, as he claims that his efforts to convince her that death has reduced the number of her family from seven to five are futile: '"Twas throwing words away; for still / The little Maid would have her will, / And said, "Nay, we are seven!"' (67-69). In light of Wordsworth's attitude towards childhood consciousness as it appears in *The Prelude*, it seems reasonable to read the speaker's dismissal of the maid's obstinacy with a sense of dramatic irony: The poem reveals not her ignorance but his own. Reason is here pitted against intuition and of course wins the argument on purely logical grounds, for simple math says that seven minus two equals five. But the child has a cosmic sense of connectedness to her deceased siblings that transcends the speaker's annoying adherence to rationality. She communes with them in a way he fails to comprehend. Just as his knowledge reveals her ignorance, so does she have an insight his logic cannot embrace.

Whitman did not mourn the loss of childhood consciousness, as his persona seems to possess the type of cosmic consciousness for which Wordsworth repeatedly expresses nostalgia. This difference is a crucial one, for where the one looks lamentingly upon the past, the other accepts the passage of time 'and sees the overall goodness in the scheme'.[35] But Whitman is not without his disgust for human knowledge, seeing in animals the kind of wisdom Wordsworth saw in children. 'Oxen that rattle the yoke and chain or halt in the leafy shade, what is that you express in your eyes?' he asks in 'Song of Myself'. 'It seems to me more than all the print I have read in my life' (235-236). Reminiscent of Wordsworth's Peter Bell, who says to the loyal ass he encounters in the woods, 'When shall I be as good as thou? / Oh! would, poor beast, that I had now / A heart but half as good as thine', (363-365), Whitman's persona sees insight and wisdom in creatures in which others see only brute animal stupidity:

> The wild gander leads his flock through the cool night,
> *Ya-honk* he says, and sounds it down to me like an invitation,
> The pert may suppose it meaningless, but I listening close,
> Find its purpose and place up there toward the wintry sky.
> The sharp-hoof'd moose of the north, the cat on the house-sill, the chickadee, the
> prairie-dog,
> The litter of the grunting sow as they tug at her teats,
> The brute of the turkey-hen and she with her half-spread wings,
> I see in them and myself the same old law. (245-252)

---

[34] Paulino Lim, 'Zen and Wordsworth', in: *The Wordsworth Circle* 7 (1976), 50.

[35] Paul Ferlazzo, 'Dylan Thomas and Walt Whitman: Birth, death, and time', in: *Walt Whitman Review* 23 (1977), 137.

In the seemingly inarticulate honking of geese Whitman hears meaningful language, and in all other animals, large and small, he perceives the law of cosmic unity, which says that all creatures, human or otherwise, are interconnected. The interference of reason prevents such insight in the 'pert', whose knowledge allows them to subordinate nature and the Earth's animals, which thus prevents the perception, as Wordsworth put it, 'That in the *unreasoning* progress of the world / A wiser spirit is at work for us' (emphasis added, *Prelude* V. 384-385). Reason fills the mind with information that blinds, according to Whitman. The light of learning casts a very dark shadow, and only when it is turned off, only when the mind is emptied, does true illumination occur.

III

Mystics refer to such a process of unreasoning as the *via negativa*, 'which brings the mind to God by emptying it of all images'.[36] Although neither poet employed this via negativa for traditionally religious purposes, both Wordsworth and Whitman privileged unreason over rationality because it rendered access to what Foucault would call in *Madness and Civilization* 'the Dionysian scream of frenzy and ecstasy in the soul of human beings'.[37] Whereas agnosia leads to the perception of cosmic unity, knowledge reduces the whole; it *abs-tracts* from experience, as Paul Strathern notes in his discussion of Derrida. Interestingly, 'the original Latin meaning of abstract is 'to draw' (*traction* has the same root) 'out of' or 'away from' (as in absent)'.[38] Thought, then, leads to ignorance, and agnosia leads to wisdom. Robert Barth has argued that in Wordsworth 'thought and thought alone can cross the boundary between sensory knowledge and the transcendent reality of spirit. Thought is the gift that sets the human person apart from the natural world'.[39] Clearly, such a comment is off the mark, for thought is responsible for the *schism* between human beings and nature, and it is thought, consequently, that prevents one from crossing the boundary between the physical and the spiritual.

Much like Wordsworth's 'unknown modes of being', which William Empson has argued is a 'knowing beyond knowing', Whitman's agnosia transgresses

[36] John Holmes, *William Blake's place in the mystical tradition* (Diss. Kent State University, Kent, Ohio, 1985), 8.

[37] Michel Foucault, *Madness and civilization* (trans. Richard Howard), New York: Random House, 1965 (orig. publ. 1961), 73.

[38] Paul Strathern, *Derrida*, Chicago: Dee, 2000, 36.

[39] Robert Barth, 'Wordsworth and Hopkins: In pursuit of transcendence', in: *Renascence: Essays on Value in Literature* 48 (1996), no.3, 182.

Enlightenment convention.[40] In 'Song of Myself' he forcefully declares, 'What is known I strip away, / I launch all men and women forward with me into the Unknown' (1135-1136). In the first stanza of the same poem he claims to put 'Creeds and schools in abeyance' so he may 'speak at every hazard, / Nature without check with original energy' (10, 12-13). Knowledge imprisons the irrational aspects of human nature, subordinating to reason the Dionysian scream, or what Whitman called his 'barbaric yawp' (1333). Those who approach his verse with a rationalist mindset will remain forever ignorant of his intent:

> For these leaves and me you will not understand,
> They will elude you at first and still more afterward, I will certainly elude you,
> Even while you should think you had unquestionably caught me, behold!
> Already you see I have escaped you.
> For it is not for what I have put into it that I have written this book,
> Nor is it by reading it you will acquire it... ('Whoever You Are Holding Me Now in Hand' 28-33)

Whitman's wisdom can be acquired not by reading any book, not even his *Leaves*, but in direct experience alone. He wrote in 'Song of the Open Road':

> Here is the test of wisdom,
> Wisdom is not finally tested in schools,
> Wisdom cannot be pass'd from one having it to another not having it,
> Wisdom is of the soul, is not susceptible of proof, is its own proof,
> Applies to all stages and objects and qualities and is content,
> Is the certainty of the reality and immortality of things, and the excellence of things;
> Something there is in the flow of the sight of things that provokes it out of the soul. (76-82)

That 'something' is found in unlearning, in stripping away the illusion of objective truth, which is why the poet's leaves will elude those who fixedly hold to the dictates of reason. Yet, however contradictorily, his book is a record of his wisdom. 'Shut not your doors to me proud libraries', he says in a poem by the same name, 'For that which was lacking on all your well-fill'd shelves, yet needed most, I bring' (1-2). *Leaves of Grass* is 'A book separate, not link'd with the rest nor felt by the intellect', a highly subversive tome in which 'untold latencies' will come forth and 'thrill to every page' (5-6). His book is needed most because it is alive, an organic extension of the natural energy it speaks without reservation. It cannot be felt by the intellect because the mind does not feel; only the receptive heart in wise passiveness may catch a glimmer of its resplendence.

---

[40] William Empson, 'Sense in *The Prelude*', in: Wordsworth, Abrams, & Gill, *The Prelude 1799, 1805, 1850*, 626.

Wordsworth, conceivably the source of Whitman's iconoclastic destruction of the rationalist search for objective truth, similarly believed that 'all the meditations of mankind, / Yea, all the adamantine holds of truth / By reason built' implode in the face of the 'living presence' of nature (*Prelude* V. 37-39, 33). Truth for Wordsworth was merely a construction, an artificial edifice erected by humankind's need to dominate what it ultimately cannot. When he arrived at Cambridge, consequently, he claimed to approach his studies with something less than the enthusiasm that should have accompanied such a gifted student: 'To books, our daily fare prescribed, I turned / With sickly appetite' (III. 524-525). His first impression of the school is that it seemed 'To have an eddy's force, and sucked us in / More eagerly at every step we took' (III. 13-14). Because 'other passions had been mine, / More fervent, making me less prompt perhaps / To indoor study than was wise or well, / Or suited to my years', he graduated from Oxford disappointingly without distinction (368-371). Considering, however, that the root of the word education is '*e-ducere*, literally, to lead forth, or to bring out something which is potentially present', as Erich Fromm observed, Wordsworth's time at Oxford was highly successful because it taught him that wisdom could not be found in books.[41] It effected in him a desire for agnosia. He is careful to qualify his dismissal of the type of knowledge Oxford had to offer, claiming, 'Not that I slighted books – that were to lack / All sense' (367-368). Like his later American counterpart, however, Wordsworth found more value in the experiential lessons of the natural world than he did in the mental baggage with which Oxford tried to saddle him. He (or his poetic persona) would learn more from a simple butterfly, a daisy, or some bird than he would from the university's logic consciousness.

When he did embrace logic for a time at Cambridge, Wordsworth experienced a loss of the cosmic vision, having become subservient to the 'mechanical materialism and utilitarianism' that dominated the school.[42] His intellectual training instilled in him 'the love / Of sitting thus in judgement', but it also interrupted 'my deeper feelings', as he put it (XI. 121-123). The dissection of logic cuts him off from the sentiments of his own heart. Like the Taoist image of the uncarved block (*p'u*), which says that to apprehend the simplicity of Being one must leave things in their original wholeness, Wordsworth is here lamenting having caused a cleavage in his own psyche. Logic consciousness causes him to become a slave to the senses, particularly to vision:

The state to which I now allude was one
In which the eye was master of the heart,

---

[41] Erich Fromm, *The art of loving*, New York: Continuum, 1956, 112.
[42] Mahoney, *William Wordsworth*, 18.

When that which is in every stage of life
The most despotic of our senses gained
Such strength in me as often held my mind
In absolute dominion. (XI. 128-133)

Vision here is by no means the visionary, as the poet sees a vast difference between the two. 'Nature is a great deal more than its component physical objects', as Abrams points out, 'and that to which the mind becomes enslaved is the material thing which is the residuum of nature after it has been filtered through the merely physical eye'.[43] Sight, therefore, is the polar opposite of insight. Although he celebrates the things of the physical world, it is important to remember that all such things have a transcendent aspect as well, without which the material counterpart is devoid of life. Having become enslaved by the despotism of physical sight, the poet loses his cosmic vision. Because he sees purely with physical eyes, he is blind to the visionary gleam. Once again, Enlightenment has led to darkness.

Upon his disillusionment with the French Revolution, which had devolved into the Terror under Robespierre, Wordsworth also fell under the sway of logic, finding solace in Godwinian rationalism. Here, too, he claims to have 'cut off my heart / From all the sources of her former strength', as a result of embracing Godwin's theories (XI. 79-80). He calls himself 'A bigot to a new idolatry', who, by 'Some charm of logic' and 'syllogistic words', became convinced that the human race is not connected after all (77, 84, 83): '[E]ven so did I unsoul [...] Those mysteries of passion which have made [...] One brotherhood of all the human race' (83, 85, 89). Through logic he has carved the block, which results in division, multiplicity, and disunion. He has lost, however temporarily, his cosmic vision, so much so that even the work of poets 'withered in my esteem' (94). He no longer privileges the great imaginative power of the human soul, having become the footservant of a tyrannous master under whose dominion he is subjugated.

Confusingly, Wordsworth says that *reason* is responsible for the cosmic perception of one brotherhood of the human race. His term, however, is not synonymous with our contemporary definitions of reason and rationality. Just as intellectual meant 'spiritual' for Wordsworth, so did reason mean something altogether different. Heavily influenced by Milton, who understood reason to be both logic and intuition, as Glimm points out, the term for Wordsworth meant the imagination, or a degree thereof.[44] The Wordsworthian imagination, according to

[43] Abrams, *Natural supernaturalism*, 369.

[44] Glimm, *Five essays on mystical experience in the works of Wordsworth, Coleridge, and Shelley*, 28.

the poet himself, is reason in its 'most exalted mood'.[45] Both logic and rationality, therefore, were aspects of the imagination but more diminutive versions of it. In Book Tenth Wordsworth speaks of the possibilities resulting when reason 'Is not sequestered – what a change is here' (428). Reason encaged is merely logic, whereas reason liberated from the confines of rationality rises to the height of what the poet repeatedly calls the glorious imaginative Power, or what I have termed the cosmic in this study.

Whitman does not ever report having fallen under the sway of logic, perhaps because he learned from Wordsworth of the resulting constriction of consciousness. The American Bard is 'aplomb in the midst of irrational things, / Imbued as they, passive, receptive, silent as they' ('Me Imperturbe' 2-3). 'Logic and sermons never convince', he adds in 'Song of Myself'. 'The damp of the night drives deeper into my soul' (653-654). Glenn Cummings has argued that Whitman's anti-intellectualism is the result of his exposure from an early age to the radical Quaker preacher, Elias Hicks.[46] Gay Wilson Allen, on the other hand, demonstrated the similarities between Epicurus' Stoic attitude towards knowledge and Whitman's.[47] While I do not disagree with either possible influence, I would add that in all probability Wordsworth also contributed to Whitman's prejudice against logic and his privileging of wisdom and insight. The parallels are too striking to be ignored. Although this cosmic anti-intellectualism can be found to a degree among nearly all English Romantics, both British and American, Wordsworth and Whitman are its premier ambassadors.

---

[45] Gravil, 'Wordsworth's ontology of love in "The Prelude"', 240.

[46] Glenn Cummings, 'Placing the impalpable: Walt Whitman and Elias Hicks', in: *Modern Language Studies* 28 (1998) no.2, 77.

[47] Allen, 'Walt Whitman and Stoicism', 47.

Chapter VII

'BREATHINGS FOR INCOMMUNICABLE POWERS'

Anti-Language and the Silence of Cosmic Sound

'Music is the language of being, of the will hidden within individuals'
(Nietzsche)

'Every individual is at once the beneficiary and the victim of the linguistic tradition into which he has been born'
(Aldous Huxley)

I

Many poststructuralist critics, arguing that there is no consciousness that precedes or stands apart from language, discount the notion of poetry as expression. In his famous essay, 'The Death of the Author', Roland Barthes argued that the text 'traces the field without origin – or which, at least, has no other origin than language itself, language which ceaselessly calls into question all origins'.[1] The inner emotional thing a writer attempts to convey via a given literary form is merely 'itself a ready formed dictionary, its words only explainable via other words'.[2] Jacques Derrida has similarly argued that the Romantic notion of expressing consciousness in imaginative voicings is fantastically deceived.[3] According to these thinkers, there is no such thing as pure perception, because language is a conceptual framework that creates experience; it is not merely the byproduct of experience.[4] Language constitutes reality, it does not just record it or label it, according to Ferdinand de Saussure, upon whose work poststructuralist thinkers heavily draw. Language not only precedes but constitutes being.

[1] Roland Barthes, 'The Death of the Author' (1977, trans. S. Heath), in: Newton, *Twentieth-century literary theory*, 122.

[2] Barthes, 'The Death of the Author', 122.

[3] Kiefer, *Figurations of poetic voice in Whitman and Wordsworth*, 3.

[4] Lois Tyson, *Critical theory today*, New York: Garland, 1999, 250.

There is no Cartesian self standing behind language who perceives and then expresses perception through a linguistic medium. Just as the Persian mystic Hafiz said, 'what we speak becomes the house we live in', so did Martin Heidegger conclude, 'language is the house of Being'.[5]

Such statements, however, are often misinterpreted or taken to untenable extremes, as Zen scholar Tetsuaki Kotoh observes. Refuting Hans Georg Gadamer's theory of the linguisticality of human experience, which he claims is based on an erroneous interpretation of Heidegger's comment, Kotoh argues that 'Being constitutes the origin of language', and to assert the primacy of language, therefore, 'is a mistake'.[6] In claiming that language is the house of Being, Heidegger was not reducing human experience and the mystery of existence to the limitations of linguistic structures but merely pointing to the limitations of the expression of Being. Language, moreover, cannot capture the mere nothingness of our lives, the pure nihilism that is 'disconnected from language and floats by itself'.[7] Language is thus an echo of the 'soundless voice of Being', according to both Heidegger and Eastern mystics. 'Philosophy should not consider language as ultimate and regulate everything in accordance with language', Kotoh concludes. 'It should step in the circle of language and experience, which are vitally and intensely tied together, and listen belongingly (*Gehoren*) to the sound of silence, which constantly emanates from the depths of the indescribable, and continue to let this be the source of one's own language'.[8]

Although I do acknowledge that much perception is indeed colored by conception in that to perceive is to interpret, the two activities being closely connected, I would resist the dismissal of consciousness outside of language as merely Cartesian, for to do so is to put the cart before the horse, as Kotoh's study compelling argues. I would also resist such a dismissal because of the findings in modern brain research. According to researcher Richard Restak, there is indeed such a phenomenon as unmediated direct perception:

> [A]longside our verbal system, there may reside any number of mental units that can exist, can have memories, values, and emotions, and all of these can be expressed through any of a variety of response systems. What makes this whole process so eerie is that these systems may not be in touch with the verbal system at all but rather, have their own existence outside of the areas of our brain responsible for our language and our logic.[9]

---

[5] Martin Heidegger, *Basic writings* (trans. Joan Stambaugh; ed. David Farrell Krell), New York: Harper Collins, 1993 (orig. publ. 1962), 281 & 217.

[6] Tetsuaki Kotoh, 'Language and silence: Self-inquiry in Heidegger and Zen', in: Parkes, *Heidegger and Asian thought*, 208.

[7] Kotoh, 'Language and silence', 205.

[8] Idem, 211.

[9] Richard Restak, *The brain*, New York: Bantam, 1984, 257.

In his research on the two hemispheres of the human brain, Restak has discovered that whereas the left hemisphere contains the capacity not just for language but all kinds of symbolic representation, the right hemisphere 'seems to deal with representations that mirror reality more directly, those large chunks of experience that don't employ language'.[10] The right hemisphere, for instance, is responsible for recognition of faces, whereas the left hemisphere is responsible for the memory of names. The inability to put a name with a face would be an example of perception unmediated by language: the right brain directly perceives and recognizes the face before the left brain can recall the name. Direct perception, therefore, involves the right hemisphere, whereas perception colored and thus determined by conception primarily engages the left hemisphere. Such research calls into question Derrida's famous dictum, 'there is nothing outside of the text', as it clearly shows the opposite to be true. Perception can be independent of language, just as knowledge and memory can exist outside of the linguistic structures too often attributed with their origination.

Mystics often report perceptions that are said to be beyond language. One of the defining characteristics of mystical consciousness, according to William James, Evelyn Underhill, and many others, is its ineffability. 'There is a private chamber in the soul which no tongue can speak', as Hafiz put it.[11] Transcending linguistic utterance, mystical consciousness is not unlike 'the real' in Lacanian thought, which is the primordial experience of whatever is prior to any attempts to represent it in any system of symbols. When one attempts to represent 'the real', it 'is lost to us forever'.[12] Wordsworth's poetry is rife with moments of ineffability, with attempts at uttering the unutterable. One such example is found in 'Home at Grasmere', the only section he completed of his abortive philosophical poem, *The Recluse*:

'Tis, but *I cannot name it*, 'tis the sense
Of majesty, and beauty, and repose,
A blended holiness of earth and sky,
Something that makes this individual Spot,
This small Abiding-place of many Men,
A termination, and a last retreat,
A Centre, come from wheresoe'er you will,
A Whole without dependence or defect,
Made for itself, and happy in itself,
Perfect Contentment, Unity entire. (emphasis added, 142-151)

---

[10] Restak, *The brain*, 250.

[11] Hafiz, *The gift* (trans. Daniel Ladinsky), New York: Penguin, 1999, 81.

[12] Palmer, *Structuralism and poststructuralism*, 82.

'There is no word for what he wants to say', as Mary Wedd argues, so he employs the rhetoric of the mystics to describe the monistic sense of oneness, contentment, and stillness that accompanies the collapse of the boundary between the terrestrial and the celestial, the two having become commingled in a blended holiness.[13] Although he conveys a sense of the stillness he feels, and although he quite effectively through suggestion articulates the harmony of the scene he has internalized, he is also at a loss to name this majestic, cosmic emotion. 'It is not that Wordsworth is vague', writes Michael O'Neil. 'It is more that his words mime the effort to express the inexpressible'.[14] He can merely hint at it through symbols of union and peace.

'It lies far hidden from the reach of words', Wordsworth wrote in Book Third of *The Prelude*. 'Points have we all of us within our souls / Where all stand single; this I feel, and make / Breathings for incommunicable powers' (187-190). He admits that his own verse is a weak and ineffectual instrument for the communication of the contents of the heart's private chamber. As Francis Ferguson points out, however, 'consciousness of the inadequacy of words and the deficiencies of language becomes in itself a fidelity to the initial passion'.[15] By acknowledging his inability to express the inexpressible, Wordsworth is thus in a roundabout way achieving some form of expression that borders on the *via negativa* of the mystics, which asserts by denial.

Whitman was similarly conscious of accessing this private inner chamber: 'There is that in me – I do not know what it is – but I know it is in me', he wrote in 'Song of Myself'. 'I do not know it – it is without name – it is a word unsaid, / It is not in any dictionary, utterance, symbol' (1309, 1311-1312). Such a theme recurs throughout *Leaves of Grass*. 'I swear to you there are divine things more beautiful than words can tell', he confidently declared in 'Song of the Open Road' (119). Like Wordsworth, he asserts by recurrent denial:

> There is something that comes to one now and perpetually,
> It is not what is printed, preach'd, discussed, it eludes discussion and print,
> It is not to be put in a book, it is not in this book,
> It is for you whoever you are, it is no farther from you than and your hearing and
> sight are far from you,
> It is hinted by nearest, commonest, readiest, it is ever provoked by them.
> You may read in many languages, yet read nothing about it,
> You may read the President's message and read nothing about it there,

[13] Mary R. Wedd, 'Wordsworth's "Spots of Time"', in: *Literature and Belief* 10 (1990), 55.

[14] O'Neil, '"Wholly incommunicable by words"', 16.

[15] Francis Ferguson, *Wordsworth: Language as counter-spirit*, New Haven: Yale University Press, 1977, 14.

> Nothing in the reports from the State department or Treasury department, or in
>   the daily papers or weekly papers,
> Or in the senses for revenue returns, prices current, or any accounts of stock.
> ('A Song for Occupations' 44-52)

Whitman subverts not only the Enlightenment notion of the capacity for language to express objective truth but also the modern idea that language contains all reality. The poet's 'something' can be expressed by no language and thus must be described in terms of nothing; from the perspective of limited human awareness it can only be negated, never positively stated. Significantly, however, 'it' is as close as the two primary senses can discern; Whitman's something is as close to consciousness as Being itself, which is to say, it is so close as to be imperceptible from the perspective of limited, normal awareness.

'I swear I began to see little or nothing in audible words', Whitman wrote in 'A Song of the Rolling Earth'. 'I swear I see what is better then to tell the best, / It is always to leave the best untold' (90, 103-104). Just as Wordsworth cannot name the cosmic emotion the scene at Grasmere evokes in him, so is Whitman at a loss to speak what he feels is the more substantial truth:

> When I undertake to tell the best I find I cannot,
> My tongue is ineffectual on its pivots,
> My breath will not be obedient to its organs,
> I become a dumb man. (104-107)

Such an admission is startling coming from a celebrated poet, particularly a writer such as Whitman who had a sense that he was doing something very original in literature. He believed, as he wrote in the same poem, that 'All merges toward the presentation of the unspoken meanings of the earth, / Toward him who sings the songs of the body and of the truths of the earth, / Toward him who makes the dictionaries of words that print cannot touch' (99-101). He believed the type of poetry he was writing mirrored the 'language' of the earth, that those who write cosmic poetry conveyed a truth beyond audible words. But ultimately even the premier voice – that is, his own – is 'ineffectual on its pivots'. When charged with the task of conveying the best the earth has to offer, he submissively acknowledges his lack of articulatory power. By such a standard he is merely dumb, a view of himself he would hold to the end of his life. In 'The Unexpress'd', one of the last poems he wrote before he died, he acknowledged his failure to adequately express what he has hinted at throughout his poetic career: 'After the countless songs [...] / Still something not yet told in poesy's voice or print – something lacking, / (Who knows? the best yet unexpress'd and lacking)' (8-10).

Whitman's problem here, to be sure, is that unknowing cannot be understood as knowledge; the untold, consequently, cannot be told. 'The central difficulty of thinking about language is that a language-less control against which to measure language is unthinkable'.[16] Just as psychoanalytic theorists encounter the problem of attempting to describe the unconscious in terms of the conscious, so 'the unknowable is forever condemned to being described in terms of the known'.[17] It is a mistake, however, to deny that a particular passage is mystical on the grounds that mysticism is ineffable, as Harold Bloom does in his discussion of 'Tintern Abbey' in *The Visionary Company.*[18] 'The experience of the mystics may be unintelligible', as John Holmes observes, 'but the mystics themselves are notoriously garrulous'.[19] There would be no such discipline as mystical studies, in fact, if there were no literary 'expressions' of the inexpressible. Mystical visions 'are not *wholly* ineffable, for if they were then the artist would be unable to give them final expression and there would be no part to which we could respond'.[20]

II

One way in which both poets expressed the ineffable was by the silencing of all language. In 'Personal Talk' Wordsworth makes clear his preference for silence over idle chatter: 'I am not one who much or oft delight / To season my fireside with personal talk, / Of friends, who live within an easy walk, / Or neighbors, daily, weekly, in my sight' (1-4). He prefers his wise passiveness, a meditative state of no-thought, to the gregariousness of prattling neighbors:

> Better than such discourse doth silence long,
> Long, barren silence, square with my desire;
> To sit without emotion, hope, or aim,
> In the loved presence of my cottage-fire,
> And listen to the flapping of the flame,
> Or kettle whispering its faint undersong. (9-14)

Detractors might simply view such a passage as an example of Wordsworth's characteristic introversion, as a manifestation of his inclination to avoid the clamour of human contact in favor of the tranquility of his cottage in the country. The state of mind he suggests, however, is more reminiscent of the emptiness Zenists cultivate through meditative practices than it is of an anti-social psyche.

---

[16] Ferguson, *Wordsworth*, 1.

[17] Francoise Meltzer, 'Unconscious', in: Lentricchia & McLaughlin, *Critical terms for literary study*, 149.

[18] Bloom, *The visionary company*, 134.

[19] Holmes, *William Blake's place in the mystical tradition*, 7.

[20] Gilbert, *The elements of mysticism*, 51. (emphasis added)

Significantly, he claims to prefer silence to language but then goes on to describe his enjoyment of listening to two commonplace household sounds, the fire and the kettle. One listens to such sounds, however, in a different manner; whereas listening to language is a left-brain activity, passively listening to the flapping of the flame and the kettle's whisper involves the direct perception of the right hemisphere. The silence he longs for thus involves the cessation of mental noise, the stilling of the seemingly ever-present left-brain clatter. He longs for the cessation of filtered perception, which is the only way one may directly commune with the unutterable.

In 'Composed upon an Evening of Extraordinary Splendour and Beauty' he achieves such communion. In a moment of absolute stillness – 'this silent spectacle', as he calls it – instills in him a restored sense of the 'modulated echoes' of divinity he heard throughout his youth (19, 10). 'No sound is uttered, – but a deep / And solemn harmony pervades / The hollow vale from steep to steep, / And penetrates the glades' (21-24). This holy moment of silence leaves him with the perception of 'An intermingling of Heaven's pomp' with the ground on which 'British shepherds tread!' (39-40). Once again, Wordsworth has dissolved the boundary between the celestial and the terrestrial. In a Promethean moment he has stolen the celestial light of the gods and brought it to the common shepherd. Ironically, although the spectacle is silent, the speaker says that a weary traveler might 'attune his soul to meet the dower / Bestowed on this transcendent hour' (59-60). Which is to say, the traveler may attune his soul to silence; he may still his mental clatter and listen to the sound of cosmic nothingness, which is, in fact, a sound but which can only be described through negation, as no-sound.

Sometimes Whitman embraces the opposite impulse, finding in the Dionysian scream a more appropriate outlet for the expression of the inexpressible: 'I too am not a bit tamed, I too am untranslatable, / I sound my barbaric yawp over the roofs of the world' ('Song of Myself' 1332-1333). Unlike Wordsworth, Whitman (or at least one of the personae in his poetry) vents primal rage; his speaker is attuned to the wild, the primitive, and the irrational aspects of the human psyche. There are more moments, however, when he embraces silence as an alternative to language, as a way to explain the mystery of being. In 'By Blue Ontario's Shore', for example, he puts forth his view of the ideal poet: 'In the dispute on God and eternity he is silent, / He sees eternity less like a play with a prologue and a denouement, / He sees eternity in men and women, he does not see men and women as dreams or dots' (151-153). The ideal poet, that is, Walt himself, knows it is futile to attempt to articulate rational answers to the great religio-philosophical questions, and he sees Being in beings, which is to say, he does not attempt to comprehend human existence intellectually, for to do so would reduce the great mystery of identity to so many dreams or dots. Only silence can do justice to such questions, a point he also makes in 'When I Heard the Learn'd

Astronomer'. The question here, however, is the great mystery of the universe, which the astronomer's formulas, charts, and diagrams fail to answer. Despite much applause, the lecturer makes the poet so 'tired and sick' that he must wander off by himself 'In the mystical moist night-air' to renew in himself the sense of awe and wonder that satisfies the questioning mind (5, 7). Only when he 'Look'd up in perfect *silence* at the stars' is he reassured; only then is he able to still the noise of mental questioning – the noise of left-brain linguistic clatter – and understand the mystery through the clarity of soundlessness (emphasis added, 8).

In 'Who Learns My Lesson Complete', one of the original untitled poems in the 1855 *Leaves of Grass*, the poet claims to hear the unheard: 'I lie abstracted and hear beautiful tales of things and the reasons of things, / They are so beautiful I nudge myself to listen' (10-11). He hears the stories behind things, which tell of mysterious causal reasons. As he is quick to point out in the next line, however, he cannot translate the language he hears: 'I cannot say to any person what I hear – I cannot say to myself – it is very wonderful' (12). Only through the metaphor of sound can he describe this beautiful language, which is ultimately neither any language nor any sound at all but a mystical intuition that has no linguistic equivalent.

'A Song of the Rolling Earth' is Whitman's premier expression of such an idea. 'Were you thinking that those were the words, those upright lines? those curves, angles, dots?' he rhetorically asks as the poem opens. His answer makes clear his attitude towards ordinary human language: 'No, those are not the words, the substantial words are in the ground and sea, / They are in the air, they are in you' (2, 3-4). True words, according to the poet, are 'those inaudible words of the earth', which cosmically connect consciousness and nature (15): 'Air, soil, water, fire – those are words, / I myself am a word with them – my qualities interpenetrate with theirs' (10-11). The 'workmanship of souls' is accomplished by the 'eloquent dumb great mother' – the soundless sound of the earth, whose cosmic energies express the truths of Being in a cryptic inaudible language that nevertheless makes human language seem like the inarticulate grunting of beasts (15, 41).

Whitman's belief that 'the hearing [has] another hearing, and the voice another voice' has its parallel in much mystical discourse ('Assurances' 7). Kabir, for instance, said of the ethereal realms, 'There the whole sky is filled with sound, and there that music is made without fingers and without strings'.[21] He calls this sound 'Unstruck Music', because it is *like* music of the physical world but a thousand times more subtle and beautiful. Because it is beyond linguistic description, 'the wise man is speechless, for this truth may never be found in Vadas or

[21] *Songs of Kabir*, XVII. 65.

in books'.[22] It is possible that Whitman was influenced by such mystical texts, as he was familiar at least with some of them by the time he wrote the first edition of *Leaves of Grass*. It is also possible, however, that Wordsworth was a partial influence, for he, too, speaks of 'inner' sounds:

> Have not we too? – yes, we have
> Answers, and we know not whence;
> Echoes from beyond the grave,
> Recognized intelligence!
> Such rebounds our inward ear
> Catches sometimes from afar –
> Listen, ponder, hold them dear;
> For of God, – of God they are. ('Yes, it was the mountain Echo' 13-20)

The echo is the outward replica of the inward sound, the silence of God, a hint of which can be discerned by the astute auditor. As the poet says, however, it is 'Like – but oh, so different!' from the original. Because it is a translation of sorts, much is lost, which is why one can only catch an intimation of it from afar. In the Wordsworthian poetic one can hear better, in fact, when the physical ear does not interfere with mystical perception. In Book Second of *The Prelude* he speaks of a time of 'bliss ineffable' – a time when the 'sentiment of being spread / O'er all that moves, and all that seemeth still / O'er all that is lost beyond the reach of human thought / and human knowledge' (400, 401-404). In such a state of consciousness he sees in all things 'one life, and felt that it was joy; / One song they sang, and it was audible' (411-412). But this song was 'Most the audible then when the fleshly ear, / O'ercome by grosser prelude of that strain, / Forgot its functions and slept undisturbed' (416-418). One can hear cosmic silence better if the physical ear does not filter out the nothingness, for the inward ear is better equipped to hear the unstruck music.

In 'The Poetics of Prophesy' Geoffrey Hartman attempted to account for Wordsworth's rushing sound as depicted in his famous Snowden vision, arguing that although the text behind the sound cannot be specified, it is 'most probably the word within the word, the Word that was in the Beginning [Jn 1:1], and which uttered as from chaos, "Let there be light"'.[23] Since it is doubtful that Wordsworth had read any of the Eastern mystical poets, Hartman's historicism seems plausible. What I would caution against, however, is too readily associating Wordsworth's (and Whitman's) use of sound and silence with the Judeo-Christian tradition, for in doing so it is easy to overlook the ways in which it disturbs the foundations of Western thought.

[22] Idem, XVII. 63.

[23] Hartman, 'The poetics of prophesy', 38.

In 'Symbolic Discourse: Mystical Writing As Anti-Language' Ming-yu Tseng discusses the ways in which language can serve as a type of ideological resistance, citing the use of koans in Zen Buddhism as an example of the 'violation of the logic of signs'.[24] Anti-languages are generally created by anti-societies such as the Elizabethan underworld, Polish prisons, and Calcutta gangster communities as a conscious alternative to a given power structure. The term, however, can also be applied to some linguistic uses in poetry and fiction, for anti-languages serve to create and maintain an alternative reality, as Tseng argues.[25] What I would like to propose is that the use of sound and silence in Wordsworth and Whitman qualifies as an anti-language in that, like the Zen literary form, the Haiku, it wages war against left-brain logic and linguistic structures by subverting traditional Western modes of articulation. As the above discussion shows, both poets mute the noise of ordinary language to perceive alternative sounds; such stillness creates a new mode of consciousness, a different way of experiencing physical reality.

III

As J.L. Mehta points out in his comparative discussion of Heidegger and Vedanta, Eastern languages such as Sanskrit, Japanese, and Chinese are highly conducive to non-representational modes of utterance.[26] Much like Heidegger, Wordsworth and Whitman attempted to express non-representational thought in a language not very conducive to such an endeavor. The English language simply does not have the capacity to convey this mode of thought. Both poets, consequently, turned to alternatives – to 'anti-language' – in order to convey the non-representational. Just as Westerners are frequently frustrated by the seemingly nonsensical statements of Zen, so do they often dismiss this anti-language in Wordsworth and Whitman as the Romantic denial of sociopolitical realities.

One of the ways in which both poets create this alternative language is through paradox, which, in mystical discourse requires of the reader something other than affirmation or denial, suggesting 'a polarity different from either affirmation or negation – something like the third, indeterminate possibility of three-valued logic'.[27] Mystical paradox should not be confused with dialectic, the difference

---

[24] Ming-yu Tseng, 'Symbolic discourse: Mystical writing as anti-language', in: *Language and Literature* 6 (1997) no.3, 188.

[25] Tseng, 'Symbolic discourse', 4.

[26] Mehta, 'Heidegger and Vedanta, 27.

[27] Joseph Keller, 'The function of paradox in mystical discourse', in: *Studia Mystica* 6 (1983) no.3, 4.

being that in the latter opposites are united through 'mediation in larger and more complex integrations', whereas in the former logical oppositions are asserted simultaneously and nullify each other, 'thus affirming non-opposition'.[28] Mystical paradox 'cancels out conventional analytic possibility and subliminally evokes a unifying awareness through nonpolar thought'.[29] Mystical paradox signifies 'a different kind of existence, a kinetic curve freed from conceptual stasis'.[30] As I have demonstrated in previous chapters, mystical rhetoric paradoxically entails 'an embrace/repulse of the world, a dissolution/integration of the self, and repression/exultation of the senses, a human/divine state of being, a hatred/love of reason'.[31]

In his famous essay 'The Language of Paradox' Cleanth Brooks has demonstrated that all poets tend to be disruptive in violating the denotative meanings of words. 'Even the most direct and simple poet is forced into paradoxes far more often than we think, if we are sufficiently alive to what he is doing'.[32] If all poets are radical in such a respect, it would seem that Wordsworth and Whitman are not so subversive after all. It is important to note, however, that they are radical not for their use of paradox, which is a once-sharp tool of the poetic trade worn dull by untold years of use, but for what they render through paradoxical forms: Both poets wage a war not against the meanings of words but against the value of language itself. 'Wordsworth's revolt against poetic conventions', as David Sampson, quoting Roger Sharrock, argues, stemmed 'from a distrust of language and a desire to preserve actual experience',[33] an observation that also can be extended to Whitman:

> Have you practic'd so long to learn to read?
> Have you felt so proud to get at the meaning of poems?
> Stop this day and night with me and you shall possess the origin of all poems,
> You shall possess the good of the earth and sun, (there are millions of suns left,)
> You shall no longer take things at second or third hand, nor look through the eyes
> of the dead, nor feed on the spectres in books,
> You shall not look through my eyes either, nor take things from me,
> You shall listen to all sides and filter them from your self. ('Song of Myself' 31-37)

---

[28] Chari, *Whitman in the light of Vedantic mysticism*, 51.

[29] Idem, 6.

[30] James Winchell, 'Semantics of the unspeakable: Six sentences by Simone Weil', in: Leonard, *Trajectories of mysticism in theory and literature*, 74.

[31] Holmes, *William Blake's place in the mystical tradition*, 5.

[32] Cleanth Brooks, 'The language of paradox' (1942), in: Arthur Clements (Ed.), *John Donne's poetry*, New York: Norton, 1992, 196.

[33] David Sampson, 'Wordsworth and the "Deficiencies of Language"', in: *ELH: A Journal of English Literary History* 51 (1984) no.1, 62.

Both poets employed the paradox of soundless sound as a means to regain the freshness of direct perception, which is distorted by the left-brain language filter.

Cosmic poetry does violence to the interpretive linguistic faculty that not only colors most perceptions but severs subject and object, the result of which creates the Cartesian illusion of a distinction between the perceiver and the perceived. Frances Ferguson faults Wordsworth's 'attempt to make language an object of speculation and investigation'. Because he 'so thoroughly conflates subject with object – and means with ends [...] the possibility of fixed objects of knowledge and fixed knowing subjects disappears'.[34] Although her work is highly sophisticated, I believe Ferguson has missed the point in calling this position 'untenable' as she does.[35] Reading from a strictly dualistic Western perspective, she cannot allow a conflation of subject with object, which is the hallmark of much paradoxical mystical discourse, and which Wordsworth seems to have consciously employed, because it violates the Western conception of reality. Such a conflation, therefore, is a weakness only if one subjects Wordsworth's verse to rationalist philosophical standards, whereas it is a virtue if situated within the context of mystical rhetoric.

Another way in which both poets create this anti-language is by hearing language where others typically hear only noise. In the sounds of nature, for instance, Whitman often discerns meaningful linguistic utterance. In an entry in *Specimen Days* he addresses a brook, 'gurgling ceaselessly – meaning, saying something, of course (if one could only translate it)' (83). He, the insightful cosmic poet, however, will become capable of such a translation:

> Babble on, O brook, with that utterance of thine! I too will express what I have gather'd in my days and progress, native, subterranean, past – and now thee. Spin and wind thy way – I with thee, a little while, at any rate. As I haunt thee so often, season by season, thou reckest not me, (yet why be so certain? who can tell?) – but I will learn from thee, and dwell on thee – receive, copy, print from thee. (83)

The suggestion here, of course, is that the river has consciousness and thus some form of insight to transfer to a receptive listener who reposes in a Wordsworthian wise passiveness. What the poet receives is copy and print, which is to say a different kind of language. The brook babbles nonsensically only from the perspective of normal consciousness. To a receptive heart, there is significant meaning in the stream's audibly flowing water. Although Whitman may have gotten such an idea from Emerson, it was also available to him through Wordsworth, whose verse frequently conveys a similar sense of natural language. In Book Sixth of *The Prelude*, which recounts his first tour of the Alps with Robert Jones, the

---

34 Ferguson, *Wordsworth*, 7.

35 Ibidem.

poet discerns in the mountain scenery a form of wisdom similarly conveyed through a linguistic medium:

> Whate'er in this wide circuit we beheld
> Or heard was fitted to our unripe state
> Of intellect and heart. By simple strains
> Of feeling, the pure breath of real-life,
> We were not left untouched. With such a book
> Before our eyes we could not chuse but read
> A frequent lesson of sound tenderness,
> The universal reason of mankind,
> The truth of young and old. (469-477)

With young and unripe hearts and minds, Wordsworth and Jones are too inexperienced to fully apprehend the full import of the natural beauty. Its magnitude is such, however, that they have no choice but to read the natural book and thus learn its language, which speaks of the tenderness of the heart, of the mind's reason, and of the truths of age. Conveyed in a cosmic natural diction that 'Did sweeten many a meditative hour', its lesson is tailor-made for them (487). It fuses mind and heart, thereby healing the Cartesian schism and giving them the wisdom they lack. It ripens consciousness, which receptively opens like the lotus flower to nature's mystical language.

Another way in which each poet employed anti-language was through music, or, more specifically, through choosing to hear music where others normally hear either noise or nothing at all. William James wrote that 'not conceptual speech but music best conveys mystical truth' – a point that makes the poets' privileging of harmonious sound seem sensible. Since 'music is the language of being', as Nietzsche argued, it is appropriate that Wordsworth and Whitman turned to music as a way to express the mysteries of consciousness. 'That which even a poet finds difficult to express in poetry is expressed in music', as Khan wrote.[36]

The musical influence on Whitman's form is well-known and much discussed. 'Although capable of finely pictorial images, Whitman composed more by ear than by eye, and his ear being attuned to music of the looser, more variable sort, such as the Italian operas, he strung his poems together on a free melodic line and by means of motifs, voices, recapitulations, rests, *crescendi* and *diminuendi*'.[37] The poet in old age told a friend that it would be strange indeed if there were no music at the heart of his poems, 'for more of these were inspired by music than he himself could remember'.[38] Whitman's verse also shares in

[36] Hazrat Inayat Khan, *The mysticism of sound and music*, Boston: Shambala, 1991, 4.
[37] Chase, 'Oneself I sing (1955)', 894.
[38] Matthiessen, *American Renaissance*, 562.

common with music the feature of repetition, which is the foundation of musical expression, and 'which the artist in language scrupulously avoids'.[39] Whitman, however, 'uses words and phrases more as if they were notes of music than any other writer'.[40]

Less discussed and more frequently misunderstood is Whitman's *thematic* use of music as cosmic anti-language. At the close of 'Starting from Paumanok', which appears in the beginning section of *Leaves of Grass*, and which is the first poem in the collection of any substantial length, Whitman establishes this musical theme: 'O something ecstatic and undemonstrable! O music wild!' (268) Just as Nietzsche said that when music was taken out of Greek drama 'the irrational truth of the human condition was obscured', so does Whitman seem to bring back this primal element of consciousness. But he does so often through mystical, unheard music. He claims to 'hear and behold God in every object', which is to say, everyday sounds take on a spiritual relevance. All sounds are thus sacred. In 'Vocalism' he questions his love for the human voice: 'O what is it in me that makes me tremble so at voices?' (13). Vocalism was in one sense 'the divine power to speak words' for Whitman (1). Human language, however, was also a Platonic imitation of the real: 'I see brains and lips closed, tympans and temples unstruck, / Until that comes which has the quality to strike and to unclose, / Until that comes which has the quality to bring forth what lies slumbering forever ready in all words' (19-21). Words subvert themselves in revealing to him what lies dormant beneath – the unsaid, the unutterable, the soundless sound of the cosmos.

The best example of Whitman's musical anti-language is 'The Mystic Trumpeter': 'Hark, some wild trumpeter, some strange musician, / Hovering unseen in air, vibrates capricious tunes to-night' (1-2). The 'bodiless' musician is an 'ecstatic ghost', whose music 'Gives out to no one's ears but mine, but freely gives to mine, / That I may thee translate' (6, 9, 11-12). Clearly, the speaker is not hearing ordinary sound at all but employing sound figuratively to signify something else; namely, audible mystical insight. Because, as John Hollander has pointed out, 'there is a lack in our language for an auditory equivalent of the word visionary', Whitman transmutes the aural into the ocular to form a synesthetic mystical sense.[41] Despite that he receives the audible wisdom for the purposes of translation, he will never accurately do so because there is no equivalent in the physical world. Every representation, moreover, exacts a cost in the

[39] Basil De Selincourt, 'The form: Constructive principles (1965)', in: Bradley & Blodgett, *Leaves of Grass*, 828.

[40] De Selincourt, 'The form', 829.

[41] John Hollander, 'The music of silence', in: *Prose* 7 (1973), 86.

form of lost immediacy, as W.J.T. Mitchell observes.[42] Only through poetry and its 'bridging properties of metaphor' will he be able to come close.[43]

When Whitman thus writes of 'That music always round me, unceasing, unbeginning' in a poem by the same name, he is not only referring to the operatic performances he frequently attended but also soundless inner music – the 'transparent base shuddering lusciously under and through the universe', as he put it (1, 5). Such music is ever present, 'yet long untaught I did not hear' (1). It takes a cultivated cosmic sensibility to discern the musical subtleties of mystical sound, but once developed it leaves the poet wanting more from the musical performances he loved to attend:

> Have not you [...] while listening to the well-played music of some band like Maretzek's, felt an overwhelming desire for measureless sound – a sublime orchestra of myriad orchestras – a colossal volume of harmony, in which the thunder might roll in its proper place; and above it, the vast, pure Tenor – identity of the Creative Power itself – rising through the universe, until the boundless and *unspeakable* capacities of that mystery, the human soul, should be filled to the uttermost, and the problem of human cravingness be satisfied and destroyed.[44]

Music was for Whitman, as it was for Khan, only a miniature of that which our 'intelligence has grasped from that music or harmony of the whole universe which is working behind us. The music of the universe is the background of the little picture which we call music'.[45] According to such mystical discourse there is a silent origin of all reality, which the Sufis call *Dhat* (zat), that nevertheless manifests as vibrations emitting cosmic sound.[46] Whitman wanted to be immersed in this cosmic music:

> I want the chanted Hymn whose tremendous sentiment shall uncage in my breast a thousand wide-winged strengths and unknown ardors and terrible ecstasies – putting me through the flights of all the passions – dilating me beyond time and air [...] And awakening me again to know [...] The most positive wonder in the world, and that's what we call life.[47]

Ordinary operatic music leads to divine music. Whitman surrenders his consciousness to the inner vibrations of cosmic sound so he may become a more vocal instrument of the ultimate silence at the heart of reality. He wants this wave

[42] W.J.T. Mitchell, 'Representation', in: Lentricchia & McLaughlin, *Critical terms for literary study*, 14.
[43] Frye, *The educated imagination*, 53.
[44] Hutchinson, *The ecstatic Whitman*, 41. Emphasis added.
[45] Khan, *The mysticism of sound and music*, 11.
[46] Idem, 120.
[47] Qtd. in Chari, *Whitman in the light of Vedantic mysticism*, 68.

of sound to carry him beyond the physical universe and even time itself so he may spiritually awaken and know the mystery of the unknown.

IV

William Meher has argued for a radical breach in the Romantic tradition between the old world and the new, claiming that Americans defined themselves by the eye, not by the ear. Whereas the English 'demonstrate a hyperverbal bias', the Americans 'insist on hypervisuality'.[48] John Gatta similarly argued that Whitman privileges the visual over all else, citing verse-chant 5 of 'Song of Myself' as a reworking of Emerson's famous 'transparent eyeball' section in the first chapter of 'Nature'.[49] It would be senseless to deny Whitman's use of light in *Leaves of Grass*. In 'To You', a representative poem, he likens himself to one of the Luminist painters of his day, as David Reynolds and Steven Adams have shown. He sees a divine halo emanating from his models: 'Painters have painted their swarming groups and the centre-figure of all, / From the head of the centre-figure spreading a nimbus of gold-color'd light'. In his leveling, democratic gesture, however, Whitman attributes divine light to all people, not exclusively to a revered saint or holy figure: 'But I paint myriads of heads, but paint no head without its nimbus of gold-color'd light, / From my hand from the brain of every man and woman it streams, effulgently flowing forever' (18-21).

To say Whitman's poetry is 'hypervisual', however, fails to acknowledge a statement Whitman makes in 'Song of Myself': 'My voice goes after what my eyes cannot reach, / With the twirl of my tongue I encompass worlds and volumes of worlds' (564-555). It fails to acknowledge the recurring passages throughout his poetry and prose in which he hears 'rare music' in the midnight flight of birds passing through the air or a 'musical composition' in the droning of bees (*Specimen Days* 84, 85). Most important, to say Whitman's verse is hypervisual also completely overlooks the many poems in *Leaves of Grass* in which the poet privileges hearing over seeing to better discern cosmic music.

In 'The Ecstatic Eye: Wordsworth and 18th-century Modes of Seeing' Robert Ross argues that the Romantics embraced Newton's *Optics* as a metaphor, for they 'saw microscopically and telescopically with their natural eyes', which is to say, they saw very differently than did the average 19th-century person.[50] While I do

---

[48] William Meher, 'Whitman vs. Wordsworth: The fundamental aesthetic difference', in: *Journal of American Culture* 20 (1997) no.1, 75.

[49] John Gatta, 'Whitman's re-vision of Emersonian ecstasy in "Song of Myself"', in: Joann P. Krieg, (Ed.), *Walt Whitman: Here and now*, Westport, CT: Greenwood, 174.

[50] Robert Ross, *The ecstatic eye: Wordsworth and eighteenth-century modes of seeing* (Diss. Cornell University, Ithaca, New York, 1969), 14.

not dispute such a claim, I would object to Ross's assertion that Wordsworth's 'experience is *primarily* visual', as well as his general statement that 'the most important sense for the production of poetry is sight'.[51] Ross makes the same mistake in his reading of Wordsworth that Meher and Gatta do in their reading of Whitman: He concludes that because visual images outnumber the auditory, sight is thus the privileged sense. M.H. Abrams has similarly argued that Wordsworth is 'preeminently a poet of the luminous moment', claiming that such moments are the key to Wordsworth's literary mystery.[52]

It is important to remember that even in the most auditory of poets visual images should outnumber auditory images since sight is the predominant human sense. To say Wordsworth privileged sight over sound, moreover, is to forget that 'as the industrial and urban background noises began to claim the audible universe in the nineteenth century, acoustical silences, moments of soundlessness, came to be auditory epiphanies'.[53] The foregoing sections of this chapter should make clear just how important silence and soundlessness were to the poet. Ross also never mentions Wordsworth's near preoccupation with the tyranny of physical eyesight: 'Whose mind is but the mind of his own eyes', he wrote in 'Personal Talk', 'He is a Slave; the meanest we can meet!' (27-28) In Book Eleventh of *The Prelude* he speaks of an ebb in the development of his imagination 'In which the eye was master of the heart' (171). In such an attenuated state of consciousness he is held in thrall by 'The most despotic of our senses', which gained 'Such strength in me as often held my mind / In Absolute dominion' (173, 174-175). Only when he breaks free from the tyranny of sight does he stand again in nature's presence as 'A sensitive and a *creative* soul' (256).

Wordsworth, like Whitman, is not without his emphasis on vision. Light, in fact, features prominently in his verse. In 'Tintern Abbey', for instance, he perceives 'a sense sublime / Of something far more deeply interfused, / Whose dwelling is the light of setting suns' (95-97). The light he is referring to, however, is nonphysical. The physical sun reflects the *celestial* light, which is so deeply interfused with all of physical reality that it cannot be perceived with the physical eye. Only in its Platonic reflection can one catch a glimpse of its splendour. Although he does not recover the celestial light, as Robert Barth observes, 'he has clearly come to recognize that the light of this world is a reflection of the heavenly light'.[54] Wordsworth often laments the loss of this light, as he does in his famous 'Intimations' ode:

---

[51] Ross, *The ecstatic eye*, 3, viii. (emphasis added)
[52] Abrams, *Natural supernaturalism*, 387 & 389.
[53] Hollander, 'The music of silence', 84.
[54] Barth, 'Wordsworth and Hopkins', 183.

> There was a time when meadow, grove and stream,
> The earth, and every common sight,
> To me did seem
> Appareled in celestial light,
> The glory and the freshness of a dream. (1-5)

Lionel Trilling compellingly argued that what the poet is lamenting is not the loss of his poetic power but the loss of the 'special light' of nonphysical insight.[55] He is lamenting the blinding of the inner eye, which too often loses its ability to see as the child becomes the adult. Wordsworth's poetry is in many respects a dirge sung over the dispossession of this faculty: 'Whither is fled the visionary gleam? / Where is it now, the glory and the dream', he asks time and again in his verse, longing to see Whitman's divine nimbus (56-57).

Despite this ocular focus, Kerry McSweeney has argued that the poet 'overcame the eye's dominance by replacing sight with sound or by shifting the emphasis from sight to sound'.[56] Unlike Whitman, Wordsworth was not moved by vocal and instrumental music, as Brian Morris has claimed, but he did privilege sound in a way that was unprecedented in English poetry and quite possibly served as a direct influence on his younger American counterpart.[57] It is no coincidence, therefore, that the protagonist of 'Michael' can hear what others cannot:

> Hence had he learned the meaning of all winds,
> Of blasts of every tone; and, oftentimes,
> When others heeded not, he heard the South
> Make subterraneous music, like the noise
> Of bagpipers on distant Highland hills. (48-52)

Michael, the ideal rustic who is untutored, unlearned, and thus unencumbered by the weight of knowledge, can hear the unstruck music; he has the cosmic auditory sense to be able to discern the subtleties of soundless sound. Not only shepherds are attuned to cosmic sound, however, for the poet/persona of the prologue of 'Peter Bell' also hears unstruck music. After he searches the stars for a fitting poetic subject, he returns to the earth, which he realizes has a music of its own: 'How tunefully the forests ring! / To hear the earth's soft murmuring / Thus could I hang for ever!' (71-75) Prior to his celestial journey the poet, like the masses of people on the earth, had lost the faculty for discerning audible wisdom. But his little boat (a symbol for the vehicle of poetry) instructs and thus reassures him:

[55] Lionel Trilling, 'The immortality ode' (1942), in: Abrams, *English romantic poets*, 155.
[56] McSweeney, *The language of the senses*, 51.
[57] Brian Morris, 'Mr. Wordsworth's ear', in: *Wordsworth Circle* 10 (1979), 113.

No wonder if you quite forgot
What on the earth is doing.
There was a time when all mankind
Did listen with a faith sincere
To tuneful tongues in mystery versed;
Then Poets fearlessly rehearsed
The wonders of a wild career. (119-125)

His celestial sojourn has harmonized him with the earth's 'subterraneous' music, and, consequently, he proceeds to tell the earthly story of Peter Bell – one who is not in accord with such music: Even though 'through water, earth, and air, / The soul of happy sound was spread', Peter is deaf to the beautiful, secret music that permeates his rustic home (66-67). Because the poet hears the soundless sound, however, he develops the tuneful tongue that enables him to speak of mysterious things to which most are deaf. In cultivating his cosmic listening skills, the poet becomes a linguistic musician who plays the unstruck harmonies.

The poet in 'Peter Bell' is more than a mere persona, for his auditory powers carry over into other poems as well. The persona is thus Wordsworth himself, who depicts countless rivers that make 'ceaseless music' (*Prelude* I. 279); who hears 'a thousand blended notes, / While in a grove I sate reclined' ('Lines Written in Early Spring' 1-2); who hears in nature the 'still, sad music of humanity' ('Tintern Abbey' 91); whose 'every passing zephyr whispers joy' ('Descriptive Sketches' 16); who finds 'In every babbling brook [...] a friend' (26); who mistakes the sound of the wind for 'the panting of my dog' (*Prelude* IV. 178); and whose cuckoo is 'No bird, but an invisible thing, / A voice, a mystery' that yields the consciousness of 'That golden time again' ('To the Cuckoo' 15-16, 28). Wordsworth's use of sound is his alternative to ordinary language in that it enables him suggest what cannot be said; it empowers his voice to articulate 'the mind's / Internal echo of the imperfect sound' (*Prelude* I. 64-65).

He was so mesmerized by sounds that he would often walk amidst thunderstorms and tempests so he could feel 'whate'er there is of power in sound / To breathe an elevated mood' in which his altered consciousness would enable him, like Whitman, to hear 'The ghostly language of the ancient earth' (*Prelude* II. 324-325, 328). In such moods he would then 'drink the visionary power' – the source of poetic imagination (330). In his verse Wordsworth repeatedly longs for the transmutation of nature's music into his own voice. The opening passage of Book Eleventh of *The Prelude*, the turning point in which he discusses how his impaired imagination is restored, is one such example: To the breezes, brooks, and groves that provide a 'ministry' for mankind, he pays his tribute: 'Oh, that I had a music and a voice / Harmonious as your own, that I might tell / What ye have done for me' (15, 20-22). Yet, such a transference need not ever take place, for human consciousness, as Wordsworth states in the opening book of *The Prelude*, possesses a musical quality in its own right:

> The mind of man is framed even like the breath
> And harmony of music. There is a dark
> Invisible workmanship that reconciles
> Discordant elements, and makes them move
> In one society. Ah me, that all
> The terrors, all the early miseries,
> Regrets, vexations, lassitudes, that all
> The thoughts and feelings which have been infused
> Into my mind, should ever have made up
> The calm existence that is the mine when I
> Am worthy of myself. (351-361)

Only when imagination is impaired – that is, only when logic and language serve to filter out cosmic sound – does amnesia cause the poet to forget that he, too, has this musical voice, that he, too, has the tuneful power of harmony and mystery. When it is intact, the imagination allows him to hear the oxymoronic 'idle voice' of the 'secret Power' that reigns in Nature ('Descriptive Sketches' 354, 346). It gives him the cosmic auditory perception that 'All motions, sounds, and voices, far and nigh, / Blend in a music of tranquility' (362-363).

V

I raise the linguistic issues in this chapter primarily because Wordsworth rejected the notion that all mental processes are processes of language, as many brain researchers have demonstrated. Whitman, too, believed in a consciousness existing outside of the linguistic structures he himself used for its expression. Both writers, moreover, engaged the poetic medium as a means for the affective expression of normal emotions and states of mind but with a conscious sense of the difficulties of doing so. Wordsworth, for instance, wrote in a prose work:

> Words, a Poet's words, more particularly, ought to be weighed in the balance of feeling, and not measured by the space which they occupy upon paper. For the Reader cannot be too often reminded that Poetry is passion: it is the history or science of feelings; now every man must know that an attempt is rarely made to communicate impassioned feelings without something of an accompanying consciousness of the inadequateness of our own powers, or the deficiencies of language.[58]

[58] Qtd. in Ferguson, *Wordsworth*, 12.

In addition to being poets of passion, Wordsworth and Whitman also attempted to convey unusual modes of being such as ecstatic expansion and consciousness dilation. As cosmic poets they intimated through their poetry the rapture of cosmic consciousness, a task significantly more difficult than the expression of normal emotions, which was a challenge in its own right. So it is excusable for two of the most verbally skilled poets in the English language to fail in this regard. Wordsworth and Whitman, despite their tremendous powers of eloquence, simply could not articulate in ordinary language a mode of consciousness that countless individuals before them also could not convey. This accounts not only for their literal dumbness when trying to express the subtleties of the cosmic feeling but also for their turning to anti-language as an alternative mode of expression.

Chapter VIII

'GANGS OF KOSMOS AND PROPHETS EN MASSE'

Cosmic Poetics[1]

'[V]isionary power
Attends upon the motions of the winds
Embodied in the mystery of words'
(Wordsworth)

'We too take ship O soul,
Joyous we too launch out on trackless seas,
Fearless for unknown shores on waves of ecstasy to sail,
Amid the wafting winds [...]
Caroling free, singing our song of God'
(Whitman)

I

As I made clear in the previous chapter, one of the characteristics of mystical states, according to William James, Evelyn Underhill, and other experts in the field of mysticism, is their ineffability. Beyond language and all verbal expression, the 'higher' wisdom of the mystics is unutterable and cannot be conveyed but only suggested by means of alternative communication such as 'anti-languages'. Ultimately, mystical consciousness must be experienced to be understood.

Much mystical language and many linguistic forms, however, can be used to transform consciousness. Language is not merely the instrument through which the mystic attempts (but ultimately fails) to convey the experience, for as Steven Katz points out, it can also be used to induce mystical consciousness.[2] The

[1] This chapter appeared under the title '"Gangs of Kosmos and prophets en masse": The cosmic poetics of Wordsworth and Whitman', in: *Romanticism: The Journal of Romantic Culture and Criticism* 10 (2004) no.1, 95-112.

[2] Steven T. Katz, *Mysticism and language*, New York: Oxford University Press, 1992, 6.

clearest example of this 'locomotive power'[3] of language is the Zen koan, an irrational paradox intended to 'perplex the logical faculties' so consciousness can transcend the confines of limited normal awareness.[4] Although the mystical experience itself is wordless, 'words can be the spring board for a leap into the infinite'.[5]

One of the many points of similarity between Wordsworth and Whitman is found in their poetics and their orientation towards language, which, they believed, could be an instrument of consciousness change. Both writers embraced the Romantic 'poetics of prophecy' and thus saw verse as a kind of divine proclamation but of a different, secular order. Neither poet merely proclaimed himself a heavenly instrument to be heard, however, for Wordsworth and Whitman anticipated the effects their verse would have on the reader. Both were conscious of the interplay of rhythm and sound and the impact of these on the reader, which, as Lewitt points out, can have a clear and observable effect on brain waves, altering consciousness in a manner that prose and the language of intellectual abstraction fail to achieve.[6]

Gary Simon has argued that Whitman's theory of poetry is radically opposed to Wordsworth's, seeing in latter's comment that 'the appropriate business of poetry [...] is to treat of things not as they *are* but as they *seem* to exist to the *senses* and to the *passions*' the polar opposite of Whitman's poetics, which is 'constructed around the organic principles of nature and her symbols of spirit'.[7] Simon's distinction, however, while superficially accurate, is misleading in two respects: First, it attributes subjectivity to Wordsworth only, whereas Whitman, too, puts forth his own version of the egotistical sublime. Second, it attributes organicism to Whitman only, whereas both poets subscribed to the notion that 'form takes its origin from within and that poetic experience will find its own natural rhythms in the act of expression'.[8] Wordsworth claimed in his 1802 'Preface' that good poets possess the 'organic sensibility' to an unusual degree (434). Such an idea came from Coleridge, who influenced Wordsworth directly through frequent (almost daily) discussions and Whitman indirectly through Emerson and others. In short, Simon's contrast belies a deeper, subtler affinity between the two poets: their jointly-held theory that poetry is a vehicle for cosmically expanding consciousness, as well as the reader's active role in this process.

---

[3] Katz, *Mysticism and language*, 13.

[4] Schimmel, *The mystical dimensions of Islam*, 13.

[5] Fil Lewitt, 'Wordless words and the evolution of poetry', in: *Kyoto Journal* 29 (1995), 143.

[6] Lewitt, 'Wordless words and the evolution of poetry', 143.

[7] Simon, 'Craft, theory and the artist's milieu', 64.

[8] Ibidem.

II

The Russian formalist Victor Shklovsky argued that human perception becomes habitualized after it repeatedly perceives an object. As 'perception becomes habitual, it becomes automatic',[9] so much so that perceiving an object for the hundredth time seems like a radically different experience than it does for the first. Fresh sensation and habitualized perception of the same object can seem like perception of different objects entirely. 'With admirable economy we learn to see only so much as is needful for our purposes' by putting 'mental tags on things in a mental catalog'. Consequently, the percipient sees 'not the things themselves but the tags only'.[10] The function of art, according to Shklovsky, is to free perception from the tyranny of this automatism of perception.[11] Good art thus 'creates a "vision" of the object instead of serving as a means for knowing it'.[12] The purpose of poetry, one can reasonably deduce from such a theory, is not so much to convey knowledge but to alter consciousness.

Wordsworth anticipated this theory by at least 100 years. Given his Romantic milieu, however, he did not want merely to free habitualized perception but also to instill in his reader 'a mystic discovery of meaning in an otherwise meaningless universe of appearances'.[13] According to Coleridge in *Biographia Literaria*, Wordsworth's specific task in *Lyrical Ballads* was

> to give the charm of novelty to things of every day, and to excite a feeling analogous to the supernatural, by awakening the mind's attention from the lethargy of custom and directing it to the loveliness and the wonders of the world before us; an inexhaustible treasure, but for which, in consequence of the film of familiarity and selfish solicitude, we have eyes yet see not, ears that hear not, and hearts that neither feel nor understand.[14]

It was the task of both poets to spread 'the tone, the atmosphere and with it the depth and height of the ideal world, around forms, incidents and situations of which, for the common view, custom had bedimmed all the lustre, had dried up the sparkle and the dewdrops'.[15] With such a technique they would be able to 'carry on the feelings of childhood into the powers of manhood; to combine the child's sense of wonder and novelty with the appearances which every day' are 'rendered familiar'.[16]

---

[9] Victor Shklovsky, 'Art as technique', in: K.M. Newton (Ed.), *Twentieth-century literary theory*, New York: St. Martin's, 1997 (orig. published 1965), 5.

[10] Ross, *The ecstatic eye*, 28.

[11] Idem, 4.

[12] Idem, 5.

[13] Idem, 28.

[14] Coleridge, *Biographia literaria*, 169.

[15] Idem, 48-49.

[16] Idem, 49.

Wordsworth articulated this theory in his 1802 'Preface', where he claims the principal poetic object in *Lyrical Ballads* 'was to choose incidents and situations from common life in a selection of language really used by men and at the same time to throw over them a certain coloring of the imagination whereby ordinary things should be presented to the mind in an unusual way' (433). When he claimed in the 1815 'Preface' that the appropriate business of poetry is to treat things not as they are but as they appear, he did so not with the intention of trying to deny the validity of the objective world but merely to render such ordinary things unusually, which is to say, to render objects in their original freshness as opposed to adding to the mental tags one places on them for convenience' sake. To reduce Wordsworth's poetics to the effort of rendering what seems, as Simon does, is to neglect the context in which the comment was made.

Rendering the commonplace in an entirely new light, Whitman likewise anticipated Shklovsky's estrangement theory. Objects previously overlooked as too ordinary to warrant any kind of status are in *Leaves of Grass* cast in a Wordsworthian celestial hue. Weeds, pebbles, abandoned buildings, docks, prostitutes, and the like are rendered sacred by Whitman, who sees in all things a oneness, an interconnectedness that transcends all division and distinction. Whitman nowhere explicitly states his adherence to Wordsworth's poetic endeavor to present ordinary situations in an unusual way, as he was in all probability too conscious of the direct influence to acknowledge it. He did, however, acknowledge finding inspiration in Millet's idea that 'one must be able to make use of the trivial for the expression of the sublime', as Stephen Adams points out.[17] It seems highly improbable that Whitman was unaware of Wordsworth's frequent practice of seeing 'inherent sublime in the common', which Abrams has claimed supplanted the epic tradition in its celebration of the 'grandiose low'.[18]

Whitman thoroughly embraced this poetic, which Adams says is part of the Romantic redefinition of the sublime, taking it to an even higher level in his use of what are commonly referred to as 'catalogues'. Nearly all of his poems contain lists of commonplace objects and scenes, the depiction of which may seem tedious to the untrained observer. It is important to remember, however, that these 'enumerations', as Gay Wilson Allen called them, 'are the means by which the poet "incarnates" the life and scenes of his country. And they are more than catalogues, accumulations, for each image is sharply focused'.[19] William Bevis has argued that Emerson's aphorisms should not be read with an analytical mind because they are intended to jolt the reader by their 'constantly fresh and surprising assertions into a kind of ecstasy'.[20] Whitman's enumerations I believe should be read in such

[17] Stephen Adams, 'The luminist Walt Whitman', in: *American Poetry* 2 (1985) no.2, 9.
[18] Abrams, *Natural supernaturalism*, 392.
[19] Allen, *The solitary singer*, 177.
[20] Bevis, 'Emerson', 55.

a way, as it seems safe to assume he was conscious of this aspect of Emerson's form. Like the Zen Haiku, Whitman's poems of seemingly endless lists of things were intended to transform consciousness by their freshness, their ability to serenade the impressionable imagination. William Stein has argued that Emerson attempted 'to curb the roboting of impression and expression by displaying the untrammeled flights of his own imagination', which accounts (at least in part) for Whitman's own mystical rendering of ordinary things in *Leaves of Grass*.[21] Just as Emerson believed the artist's job was to elevate the reader's consciousness to that of his own (because 'servitude to literality entails a surrender to the animal functions of perception',) so did Whitman through his catalogues attempt to jolt the reader out of the bondage of automated perception.[22] Whitman's catalogue technique was 'intended to induce a special state of awareness through which the poet engages the reader' – to bring him, by means of repetition, rhythm, and parallelism, to what George Hutchinson has called a 'dizzying gyre'.[23]

What is of special significance here is the inscription of the reader in the poetic form, which, in fact, is incomplete without the imaginative power the reader supplies. In *Start with the Sun* Miller, Shapiro, and Slote claimed that cosmic poetry 'realizes its latent order in the emotional reconstruction provided by the responding and "participating" reader'.[24] A necessary component in cosmic poetics, the reader, not the writer, breathes the spirit of life into the text. Or perhaps it is better to say they co-create the text together. Wordsworth's poetry was meant 'to serve as a corrective, to purify the hearts of its readers by awakening them to wonder', as well as 'leading them to see for themselves the strangeness and beauty of the world around them'.[25] By rendering the ordinary world in a supernatural light, Wordsworth hoped to reenchant his disillusioned readers, most of whom had been indoctrinated by 200 years of hubristic scientism, which said that all truly valuable knowledge must be ascertained through reason alone.[26] The Enlightenment cult of reason resulted in the destruction of any sense of awe and wonder towards the natural world, and many 19th-century people were left feeling as though something was missing, as though science had failed to account for what was most precious – a sense of humankind's mysterious and inexplicable existence in the world. This sense of wonder was lost, and Wordsworth, among others, took it upon himself to instill once again in his readers an apprehension of the great mystery. As John Rudy has claimed,

---

[21] William Stein, 'Emerson's "History": The rhetoric of cosmic consciousness', in: *ESQ* 69 (1972), 201.

[22] Stein, 'Emerson's "History"', 204.

[23] Hutchinson, *The ecstatic Whitman*, 71.

[24] Miller, Shapiro, & Slote, *Start with the Sun*, 53.

[25] Hopkins, 'The mystical dimensions of Wordsworth's poetry', 55.

[26] Carroll Terrell, 'The reenchantment of the word', in: *Rendezvous* 22 (1986) no.1, 66.

'Wordsworth wants literally to redeem his readers, to buy [sic] them back to a lost divinity'.[27] He considered this lost state of consciousness semi-divine in that, like Aristotle, he believed wonder is similar to some forms of religious experience, as Joe Kenneth Jackson observes.[28]

Because wonder 'causes the mind to be liberated from habit, familiarity, custom and dogma', Wordsworth frequently depicts scenes in which characters experience it.[29] In doing so he induces in the reader a similar sense of wonder through sympathetic identification. 'The reader identifies with the character and shares the experience'.[30] Much like phenomenological 'reductions' that 'slacken the intentional threads which attach us to the world', as Merleau-Ponty observed, the experience of wonder in Wordsworth's poetry can destabilize the reader's consciousness and bring about an awareness that borders on spiritual awakening.[31] Or such was his intention. In the post-revolution age of demoralization, according to M.H. Abrams, Wordsworth attempted to inaugurate 'a revolutionary mode of imaginative perception which accomplishes nothing less than the "creation" of a new world', which is to say, a new state of consciousness.[32]

As the premier Romantic in the American tradition, Whitman likewise intended his art to be a means to morally awaken his readers, as Denise Askin has argued.[33] 'I say the profoundest service that poems or any other writings can do for the reader is not merely to satisfy the intellect, or supply something polish'd and interesting, nor even to depict great passions, or persons or events', he wrote in 'A Backward Glance O'er Travel'd Roads'. The purpose of poetry, rather, was to fill the reader 'with vigorous and clean manliness, religiousness, and give him *good heart* as a radical possession and habit' (332-336). Perhaps following Keats's dictum – 'we distrust literature that has a palpable design upon us' – Whitman claimed the poet's moral impact on the reader should be subtle: 'Without effort and without exposing in the least how it is done, the greatest poet brings the spirit of any or all events and passions and scenes and persons, some more and some less, to bear on your individual character as you hear or read' (247-250). Because of such passages Gay Wilson Allen concluded, 'it is now abundantly obvious that Walt Whitman's greatest ambition was to be a moral leader, but he hoped to initiate and exert this leadership through his poems'.[34]

---

[27] Rudy, *Wordsworth and the Zen mind*, 199.
[28] Jackson, *Wonder and defamiliarization in Wordsworth*, 8.
[29] Idem, vii.
[30] Idem, viii.
[31] Merleau-Ponty, 'Preface to "Phenomenology of Perception"', 84.
[32] Abrams, *Natural supernaturalism*, 338.
[33] Askin, 'Whitman's theory of evil', 129.
[34] Qtd. in Bradley & Blodgett, *Leaves of Grass*, 900.

He did so by decentering consciousness so as to effect a greater understanding of the cosmos – knowledge unavailable if one's perceptions are automated. Whitman frequently 'alternates the valence of moral abstractions' in his verse 'from conventional to unconventional', at once subverting and reinforcing prevailing ideologies, but his intention 'at all times is to jolt the reader into a new perspective'.[35] Whitman attempted to awaken his readers, however, by means other than the sympathetic identification of characters who experience wonder in speaking directly to the reader. *Leaves of Grass* is itself in nearly all places a direct address to the reader. Steven Adams and David Reynolds have both demonstrated Whitman's indebtedness to the mid-19th-century American Luminist painters, who, in their effort to engage viewers of their work, often suggested scenes extending beyond the boundaries of the canvas, so a person looking at the painting would be forced to imaginatively create what has not been depicted.[36] Whitman's verse is full of such suggestion; much is often left unsaid so the reader will bring his or her imagination to bear on the text and be jolted out of habitualized perception into a sense of awe and wonder. In 'A Backward Glance O'er Travel'd Roads' he discusses this aspect of his verse:

> The word I myself put primarily for the description of [my poems] as they stand at last, is the word Suggestiveness. I round and finish little, if anything; and could not consistently with my scheme. The reader will always have his or her part to do, just as much as I have had mine. I seek less to state or display any theme or thought, and more to bring you, reader, into the atmosphere of the theme or thought – there to pursue your own flight. (316-322)

Whitman believed, in fact, that the best literature a writer can produce 'does not shine by any luminosity of its own', for the reader provides the true brilliance. 'The actual living light is always curiously from elsewhere – follows unaccountable sources, and is lunar and relative at the best' (126-129).

Because the reader supplies this living light, the poet repeatedly insists the reader cannot passively read but must actively engage the text and supply what is lacking. In 'Roots and Leaves Themselves Alone' Whitman calls his poems 'Love-buds put before you and within you whoever you are, / Buds to be unfolded on the old terms'. Because they are not given in germinated form, however, the reader must complete the process of organic poetic creation: 'If you bring the warmth of the sun to them they will open and bring form, color, perfume, to you, / If you become the aliment and the wet they will become flowers, fruits, tall branches and trees' (7-10). The unstated implication here is that his poems remain forever closed to those who do not bring the requisite

[35] Askin, 'Whitman's theory of evil', 123.
[36] Adams, 'The luminist Walt Whitman', 12.

light. One can read the words from a variety of different perspectives, but without the appropriate amount of sunshine and wetness a reader will never see the flowering of the cosmic dimensions of *Leaves*.

Perhaps taking his cue from Emerson's principle of self-reliance, Whitman insisted the reader must engage life in the same way as he does the text – actively and without an intermediary: 'No friend of mine takes his ease in my chair, / I have no chair, no church, no philosophy', he wrote in 'Song of Myself' (1204-1205). He claimed instead merely to point out the direction in which the reader must venture: 'Not I, nor anyone else can travel that road for you, / You must travel it for yourself' (1210-1211). Whitman insisted 'that there be no theory or school founded out of me', as he wanted his readers to stand on their own principles. 'I charge you to leave all free, as I have left all free' ('Myself and Mine' 28-29). Refusing the aggrandizement often accompanying the stature of great poets, he insisted readers must find the solutions to their own problems. 'You are also asking the questions and I hear you, / I answer that I cannot answer, you must find out for yourself' ('Song of Myself' 1223-1224). *Leaves of Grass*, therefore, is in one sense not the record of any kind of truth whatsoever, for it cannot provide answers to questions if one is passively hoping information will be bestowed upon him.

In another sense, however, *Leaves* is a record of truth in that it frees the reader from such a subjugated, determined position. Whitman uses mystical rhetoric to describe this movement from blindness to vision: 'Long enough have you dream'd contemptible dreams, / Now I wash the gum from your eyes, / You must habit yourself to the dazzle of the light and of every moment of your life' (1228-1230). The form, not the theme, is the liberating element in his verse. Whereas past writers have bestowed light and wisdom on their readers, Whitman teaches how to find illumination and knowledge for oneself. Again using mystical rhetoric, he intones in one of the 'To You' poems: 'O I could sing such grandeurs and glories about you! / You have not known what you are, you have slumber'd upon yourself all your life, / Your eyelids have been the same as closed most of the time' (22-24). His poetry is the stimulus that awakens the reader from the slumber of a forgotten divinity. Like the amnesiac Hindu Prince who wanders his kingdom in rags, or the tiger that is oblivious to its fearsomeness because it has been raised by sheep, the reader can, through Whitman's verse, rouse himself and awaken to the grandeur of his glorious position in the cosmos.

Wordsworth does not speak directly to the reader in his poetry nearly as much as Whitman did, but his poetics took into account the reader as an integral element. In a famous statement in the 1802 'Preface', he declared that 'all good poetry is the spontaneous overflow of powerful feelings', which can be modified and directed by one's thoughts. If the reader, who plays an active role in the poetic process, 'be in a healthful state of association, [he] must necessarily be in some degree enlightened, and his affections ameliorated' by the type of verse Wordsworth was writing (434-435). He intended his poetry as a means to alter the consciousness of his readers 'without the application of gross and violent stimulants' (436). One needs a subtle sensibility – a 'very faint perception of its beauty and dignity' – to be moved by his verse, however, for 'one being is elevated above another in proportion as he possesses this capability' (436). Using a mystical image similar to Whitman's, he claims that through poetry 'Would I arouse the sensual from their sleep / Of Death' ('The Recluse' 813-814).

In discussing the difficulties of creating the taste by which an original poet is to be relished, Wordsworth rhetorically asks: '[D]oes it lie in establishing that dominion over the spirits of Readers by which they are to be humbled and humanized, in order that they may be purified and exalted?' ('1815 Preface' 497). The implied answer is a resounding 'yes', of course, for he believed that habitualized perception had a tendency 'to enslave the mind' and 'Oppress it by the laws of vulgar sense, / And substitute a universe of death', as he put it in Book Thirteenth of *The Prelude* (139-141). It was his function to help free the reader from these shackles, to morally purify and exalt through the unusual depiction of the commonplace.

III

In Book Twelve of *The Prelude* Wordsworth discusses the dawning of a new 'higher power', (363) as he calls it – which is the culmination of his poetic development:

> [...] I remember well
> That in life's everyday appearances
> I seemed about this period to have sight
> Of a new world – a world, too, that was fit
> To be transmitted and made visible
> To other eyes, as having for its base
> That whence our dignity originates. (368-374)

His life's mission is to transmit this vision of a new world to his readers, not only to paint it in words but to alter consciousness in a way that allows other people to see it for themselves. He believed that many individuals, not only gifted poets, are endowed with this cosmic sense – 'The vision and the faculty divine', as he calls it in Book First of *The Excursion* (79). These people are nature's poets, 'endowed with highest gifts' but 'wanting the accomplishment of verse', which was denied them 'through lack / Of Culture and the inspiring aid of books' (77, 80, 82-83). What distinguishes Wordsworth from them, of course, is this inspiring aid of education. He has the articulatory power they do not, an 'internal brightness' given to him 'That must not die, that must not pass away' ('The Recluse' 675, 676). The ability to express this Miltonic inward light is 'shared by none', and the poet must thus 'impart it' and 'spread it wide, / Immortal in the world which is to come' (686, 690-691).

This 'world' yet to come is actually a state of being 'whose presence soothes / Or elevates the mind' (760-761). It is a world

> Of Truth, of Grandeur, Beauty, Love, and Hope,
> And melancholy Fear subdued by Faith;
> Of blessed consolations in distress;
> Of moral strength, and intellectual Power;
> Of joy in the widest commonalty spread; (767-771)

It is, in short, cosmic consciousness – 'the law supreme / Of that intelligence which governs all' (775). As cosmic poet it is his function to record in his verse and instill in his readers this knowledge. As I discussed in chapter six, however, such awareness is beyond 'learning, moral truth, / Or understanding', as Wordsworth says in Book Third of *The Prelude* (91-92). As the beholder of the new world, he is 'otherwise endowed', which is to say, what he brings is the higher wisdom that transcends normal consciousness (93).

The new world is found in 'the Mind of Man', which he also says is 'My haunt, and the main region of my song' ('The Recluse' 794). The human mind is, despite Wordsworth's unprecedented celebration of nature, 'A thousand times more beautiful than the earth', as he claims in the closing stanza of *The Prelude* (XIII. 447). Mind is 'In beauty exalted, as it is itself / Of substance and of fabric more divine' than 'this frame of things' – the material world (451-452, 448). In one of his most seemingly world-denying passages Wordsworth is here attributing a vastness and a power to human consciousness that dwarfs anything external to the self. It is important to remember, however, that nothing in Wordsworth is external to mind. He chants the 'spousal verse' of the 'great consummation' and proclaims 'How exquisitely the individual Mind' to the 'external world is fitted' (810, 811, 816, 818). But he also claims to demonstrate the reverse – how 'The external World is fitted to the mind' (821).

One could argue that because heightened cosmic awareness adds the missing element, nature is subordinated. It is important to remember, however, that Wordsworth believed the imagination has the ability to confer 'additional properties upon an object' by 'abstracting from it some of those which it actually possesses, and thus enabling it to react upon the mind which hath performed the process, like a new existence' ('1815 Preface' 468). It would be more in keeping with Wordsworth's poetics, therefore, to say the vision of the new world rectifies wrong vision; it clarifies the limited (and thus skewed) perspective of normal consciousness. It is merely the movement of consciousness that gets altered, not the object itself. The imagination shapes and creates by 'consolidating numbers into unity, and dissolving and separating unity into number – alternations proceeding from, and governed by, a sublime consciousness of the soul in her own mighty and almost divine powers' (469-470). In other words it does not add what is not already present but alters perspective to show that what seems not to be present actually is, and vice versa. The individual mind, 'as the agent of the one great mind', is 'creator and receiver both / Working but in alliance with the works / Which it beholds' (*The Prelude* II. 75, 272-273). The poet, Wordsworth argued in his 1802 'Preface', 'considers man and nature as essentially adapted to each other, and the mind of man as naturally the mirror of the fairest and most interesting qualities of nature' (444). To say the mind is a thousand times more beautiful than the material world, therefore, is actually to say that it is a thousand times more beautiful than the limited human view of nature, for ultimately mind and nature are one and the same.

The poet, armed with this immense power of Imagination, 'binds together by passion and knowledge the vast empire of human society, as it is spread over the whole earth, and over all time' (444). He unifies all disparate entities, and his instrument – his verse – serves as 'the breath and finer spirit of all knowledge; it is the impassioned expression which is in the countenance of all Science' (444). Scientists seek through their method 'truth as a remote and unknown benefactor', but the poet, 'singing a song in which all human beings join with him, rejoices in the presence of truth as our visible friend and hourly companion' (444). The Romantic poet knows better than to seek truth as an object, for it can be found only in the subjectivity of human consciousness. Only through the 'vision and faculty divine' could one ascertain the ultimate truth – the underlying unity of all reality. To read his poems is one way of arriving at such knowledge, as Wordsworth believed 'they will operate in their degree, to extend the domain of sensibility for the delight, the honor, and the benefit of human nature' ('1815 Preface' 502). The wings of poesy will uplift the reader to untold heights of cosmic understanding.

Whitman's break from Wordsworth and the English tradition was in the method he used for uplifting the reader. Whereas Wordsworth used rhymed and blank verse, Whitman turned to free verse in general and parallelism and repetition in particular, two of the most primitive of poetic techniques. Although Bruce Berquist has done an excellent job of revealing the many biblical echoes, allusions, images, and ideas in *Leaves* in his dissertation on the poet, it is important to remember that Whitman's inspiration for parallelism went beyond the Bible. Similar examples of parallelism and repeated words and phrases can be found in North American Indian songs, chants of the aborigines of Australia, of the pygmies of Africa, and of other peoples without a written language. In *A Reader's Guide to Walt Whitman*, Gay Wilson Allen has argued that Whitman is unlikely to have known of such sources,[37] but in 'Old Chants', a poem he penned a year before his death, Whitman aligns his verse with the ancient chants of 'Egyptian priests, and those of Ethiopia, / The Hindu epics, the creation, Chinese, Persian, / The Biblic books and profits, and deep idyls of the Nazarene', as well as many others: 'The Iliad, Odyssey, plots, doings, wanderings of Eneas, / Hesiod, Eschylus, Sophocles, Merlin, Arthur, / The Cid, Roland at Roncesvalles, the Nibelungen, / The troubadours, minstrels, minnesingers, skalds...' (9-15). Allen says it would have pleased Whitman well to know he was recovering some of the earliest poetic techniques of mankind, but it seems the poet was in fact highly conscious of doing so. 'The primitive poets, their subjects, their style, all assimilate', Whitman wrote in a notebook. 'Very ancient poetry of the Hebrew prophets, of Ossian, of the Hindu singer and ecstatics, of the Greeks, of the American aborigines, the old Persians and the Chinese, and the Scandinavian Sagas, all resemble each other'.[38]

In his 1856 letter to Emerson, Whitman complained of American authors' subservience to the English tradition, which he felt was too weak and ineffectual for American tastes:

> There is no great author; every one has the demeaned himself to some etiquette or some impotence. There is no manhood or life power in poems; there are shoats and geldings more like. Or literature will be dressed up, a fine gentleman, distasteful to our instincts, foreign to our soil. Its neck bends right and left wherever it goes. Its costumes and jewelry prove how little it knows Nature. Its flesh is soft; it shows less and less of the indefinable hard something that is nature.[39]

America demanded a poetry that is 'bold, modern, and all-surrounding and kosmical, as she is herself', as he put it in 'Democratic Vistas'.[40] Clearly, he is not acknowledging the tremendous engagement with nature one finds in Wordsworth's own 'cosmical' poetry. Generally speaking, however, his point is well taken, for the gentile tradition in American letters kept trade relations between England and America 'well lubricated'.[41] But such 'anglophilic servility' also kept American letters enslaved and thus derivative and unoriginal.[42]

In 'Democratic Vistas' Whitman dismissed the English tradition because it lacked the informing spirit of Nature, which he believed, should 'furnish the pervading atmosphere to poems' (in *Specimen Days* 249). Once again misreading or failing to acknowledge Wordsworth, he believed British poets rendered

[37] Allen, *A reader's guide to Walt Whitman*, 169.
[38] Qtd. in Hutchinson, *The ecstatic Whitman*, 47.
[39] Qtd. in Bradley & Blodgett, *Leaves of Grass*, 736.
[40] Walt Whitman, *Specimen Days & Collect*, New York: Dover, 1995 (orig. publ. 1883), 245.
[41] Qtd. in Bradley & Blodgett, *Leaves of Grass*, 710.
[42] Ibidem.

nature as 'smooth walks, trimm'd hedges, poseys and nightingales' at the expense of 'the whole orb, with its geologic history, the kosmos, carrying fire and snow, that rolls through the illimitable areas, light as a feather, though weighing billions of tons' (249-250). He saw English writers as 'a parcel of dandies and ennuyees, dapper little gentleman from abroad, who flood us with their thin sentiment of parlors, parasols, piano-songs, tinkling rhymes, the five-hundredth importation – or whimpering and crying about something, chasing one aborted conceit after another, and forever occupied in dyspeptic amours with dyspeptic women' (242). Harsh words indeed, but they were Whitman's way of claiming a space for himself, for inaugurating a new poetic tradition, and for bringing verse back to its primitive roots of incantation, enchantment, and the more suitable subject matter of humankind's primal grounding in mother Earth.

By taking poetry back to its ancient origins through free verse, repetition, and parallelism, Whitman no doubt subverted the tradition in which Wordsworth occupied a significantly prominent position. His call for the informing spirit of Nature is in some ways a battle cry for a second revolutionary war, as much English poetry had become too gentrified, too polite, and too rarefied for the American sensibility. Raw Nature, however, did furnish the pervading atmosphere of Wordsworth's poems. To be sure, he did not celebrate the erotic as Whitman did, but he nevertheless overcame the Cartesian separation of mind and matter in his engagement with the natural world. More important, nature for Wordsworth was often *sublime* nature – awe-inspiring and overpowering in its scope and grandeur.

Whitman celebrated the eloquent powers of nature, often yearning for a transmutation of natural energy into his poetic voice. He says of the sea, for instance, that he would 'gladly barter' the skills of the greatest bards in history for the 'undulation of one wave, its trick to me transfer', imploring the sea to 'breathe one breath of yours upon my verse, / And leave its odor there' ('Had I the Choice' 6, 7-9). Perhaps not coincidentally Wordsworth also frequently invokes nature as his muse: 'Descend, prophetic Spirit! that inspir'st / The human Soul of universal earth', he commands in 'The Recluse' (836-837). Knowing he is dealing with primitive natural energies, he refers to this soul of the earth as a 'dread Power! / Whose gracious favor is the primal source of all illumination' (853-854). Like Whitman, he also hopes for a transference of this awesome eloquence into his own poetic voice: In Book Twelfth of *The Prelude* he longs for 'An influx' of this energy and hopes 'that a work of mine, / Proceeding from the depth of untaught things, / Enduring and creative, might become / A power like one of Nature's' (309-312). Wordsworth was no dapper little dandy, no ennui who wrote tinkling rhymes of dyspeptic amours; his verse was much more primal and *natural* than Whitman acknowledged.

IV

'America needs, and the world needs', Whitman wrote in 'Democratic Vistas', 'a class of bards who will now and ever, so link and tally the rational being of man, with the ensembles of time and space, and with this vast and multiform show, Nature [...] as to essentially harmonize, satisfy, and put at rest' (253). Despite Whitman's desire to break from the influence of English letters, however, Wordsworth had already inaugurated this new tradition: 'Prophets of Nature, we to them will speak / A lasting inspiration, sanctified / By reason and by truth', he wrote in the last stanza of the last book of the 1805 *Prelude*. '[W]hat we have loved / Others will love, and we may teach them how' (XIII. 442-445). In the first book of *The Prelude* he similarly establishes his role as Nature's minister:

> [...] To the open fields I told
> A prophecy; poetic numbers came
> Spontaneously, and clothed in priestly robe
> My spirit, thus singled out, as it might seem,
> For holy services'. (59-63)

He is the latest in the line of poets inspired by nature's prophetic Spirit, as Abrams noted in *Natural Supernaturalism*,[43] and his poetic enterprise will consist in the redemption of his readers 'by liberating their sensibilities from bondage to social-aesthetic norms and so opening their eyes to his own imaginative vision of a new world, in which men who are equal in the dignity of their common humanity are at home in a nature which, even in its humblest or most trivial aspect, is instinct [sic] with power and grandeur'.[44]

Whitman's positioning of himself as a 'chanter of Adamic songs, / Through the new garden the West' represented a break from the European tradition, but it was made possible by the premier poet of that tradition ('Ages and Ages Returning at Intervals' 4-5). Like Wordsworth, he heartily embraced the poet/prophet role and thus discerned the 'Prophetic spirit of materials shifting and flickering around me', as he says in 'Starting From Paumanok' (136). True to his Quakerism, however, he does not clothe himself in priestly robes. In fact, 'the priest departs, and the divine literatus comes' in Whitman's scheme ('Democratic Vistas' 206). The divine literatus is a member of a superior breed, what he also calls in his 1855 'Preface' 'gangs of kosmos and prophets en masse' who represent all people by teaching them to be their own priest (622). The 'poets of the kosmos' will complete and thus surpass 'The immortal poets of Asia and Europe' who have 'done their work and pass'd to other spheres' ('By Blue Ontario's Shore' 49). Not only

---

43 Abrams, *Natural supernaturalism*, 28.

44 Idem, 392.

will they 'advance through all interpositions and coverings and turmoils and stratagems to first principles' by penetrating the surface and exposing the 'real body and soul' ('1855 Preface' 434). They will also 'mediate to the Modern, to Democracy, interpret yet to them, / God and eidolons' ('Eidolons' 71-72). Although the poet is 'the true son of God', and although because of him 'Nature and Man shall be disjoin'd and diffused no more', he is not superior to any other person and he subordinates no one ('Passage to India' 111, 114). He mediates only for those who insist on believing they need an intermediary for access to the spirit-world. Although his mind is 'lit with the infinite', the poet of the Kosmos is rare only in that he can articulate his vision of the new world.

In 'The Poetics of Prophecy' Geoffrey Hartman claims it is 'sophomoric' to think that poets are prophets, that they have 'something of the audacity and intensity – the strong speech – of Old Testament prophets who claimed that the word of God came to them'.[45] Hartman's conclusion that the only connection between poet and prophet is a fidelity to 'the old language, its pathos, its animism, its fallacious figures' may, in fact, be true. It is important to remember, however, that both poets also draw quite heavily upon mystical rhetoric, which in many ways runs against the grain of this old language.[46] Wordsworth and Whitman, moreover, subvert the Judeo-Christian tradition's subordination of nature, as I argued in chapter 5. To read their poetics in such Christian terms is to overlook the subversive element in their understanding of the poet-prophet.

George Hutchinson has argued that Whitman's poetics of prophesy was inspired by Carlyle,[47] whereas Joan Frances Hallisey[48] and David Keubrich claim Emerson as 'the most important single influence upon Whitman's development as a poet-prophet'.[49] (Keubrich does acknowledge, however, that Whitman's particular version of religious millenialism departs from the main corpus of Emerson's writings.) In his essay in *Specimen Days* on the death of Carlyle, Whitman himself credits his childhood religion as the source: The prophet's function is not merely to predict but 'to reveal and out-pour the God-like suggestions pressing for birth in the soul. This is briefly the doctrine of the Friends or Quakers'.[50] While I do not discount any of these possible sources, I would also suggest Wordsworth as a significant influence. Whitman's failure to mention his English predecessor in this regard is in keeping with his anxiety of influence and suggests

[45] Hartman, 'The poetics of prophesy', 15.

[46] Idem, 39.

[47] Idem, 46.

[48] Joan Frances Hallisey, *Walt Whitman, Hart Crane, and Denise Levertov: Poet/prophets in the tradition of Ralph Waldo Emerson* (Diss. Brown University, Providence, Rhode Island, 1978), 2.

[49] Keubrich, 'Whitman's new theism', 30.

[50] Idem, 169.

there is more of a connection than scholars realize. When Whitman calls for a new class of cosmic Nature bards, he was thus drawing on a discourse inaugurated in part by Wordsworth.

His understanding of the purpose and origin of literature was informed by a Wordsworthian poetic, as well. Just as Wordsworth sings in 'dithyrambic fervour', which he likens to 'A waterspout from heaven', (*The Prelude* VII. 5, 9) so does Whitman, mesmerized by the mystery of consciousness, 'stop and loiter all the time to sing it in ecstatic songs' ('Beginning My Studies' 6). 'The altitude of literature and poetry has always been religion – and always will be', he wrote in a footnote to 'Democratic Vistas' (250). 'The religious tone, the consciousness of mystery, the recognition of the future, of the unknown, of Deity over and under all, and of the divine purpose, are never absent, but indirectly given to all – exhibit literature's real heights and elevations, towering up like the great mountains of the earth' (250). Although Wordsworth warned of people who read poetry for traditionally religious reasons, arguing in his 1815 'Preface' that they are often 'beset with misconceptions and mistakes peculiar to themselves', he nevertheless believed 'poetry is most just to its own divine origin when it administers the comforts and breathes the spirit of religion' (480). Whitman never acknowledged the source, but he embraced it thoroughly:

> Ever since what might be called thought, or the budding of thought, fairly began in my youthful mind, I had had a desire to attempt some worthy record of that entire faith and acceptance ('to justify the ways of God to man' is Milton's well-known and ambitious phrase) which is the foundation of moral America. I felt it all as positively then in my young days as I do now in my old ones; to formulate a poem whose every thought or fact should directly or indirectly be or connive at an implicit belief in the wisdom, health, mystery, beauty of every process, every concrete object, every human or other existence, not only considered from the point of view of all, but of each. ('A Backward Glance' 410-419)

He claims to put forth both a macroscopic and a microscopic perspective – a godlike vision of the totality from which the poet can render the all in each and each in the all.

The scope of his poetic undertaking is no less than Wordsworth's, which is equally as ambitious and Miltonic: 'For I must tread on shadowy ground, must sink / Deep – and, aloft ascending, breath in worlds / To which the heaven of heavens is but a veil' ('The Recluse' 781-783). He even goes on to claim the need for a greater vocal strength than 'Jehovah – with his thunder, and the choir / Of shouting Angels, and the empyreal thrones – / I pass them unalarmed' (786-788). Like Whitman's, his poetic perspective is spiritual in that it is a conduit for heavenly power.

In his moment of poetic awakening as he recounts it in Book Fourth of *The Prelude*, Wordsworth realizes he has become a chosen son: 'I made no vows, but vows / Were then made for me: bond unknown to me / Was given, that I should be – else sinning greatly – / A dedicated spirit' (341-344). His mission, of course, is to be a poet-prophet and to cosmically awaken his readers from their aesthetic slumber. To ignore the call would be a grievous sin, as it would deprive those who need it most – people culturally hypnotized by the Enlightenment cult of reason. Whitman's own poetic awakening, as he describes it in 'Out of the Cradle Endlessly Rocking', is similarly couched in quasi-religious terms. After hearing the mocking-bird's plaintive song of loss, the young poet hears 'meanings which I of all men know' (60). The bird raises its song to an ecstatic pitch, and the boy experiences an awakening that borders on a mystical experience: 'The love in the heart long pent, now loose, now at last tumultuously bursting', the boy also becomes a dedicated spirit (137). 'Now in a moment I know what I am for, I awake, / And already a thousand singers, a thousand songs, clearer, louder and more sorrowful than yours, / A thousand warbling echoes have started to life within me, never to die' (147-149). By awakening to his own poetic calling, he, like Wordsworth, will enlighten the unawakened masses. The poet-prophet will bring what is needed most – a cosmically empowered voice uttering the mysteries of the universe.

V

As I have suggested earlier, the poet-prophet does not merely articulate this mystery but induces it in the reader. In *The Unremarkable Wordsworth* Geoffrey Hartman claims that a Wordsworth poem often has no point. 'As readers we respond to the mystery of his response. That the poem exists at all, that it emerges into answerable style has to be understood together with that style'.[51] The poet, therefore, does not merely convey a given theme to a passive reader. By drawing the reader into the creative process, Wordsworth helps the reader experience what can only be understood on an experiential level. Whitman's poetic, too, is informed by such Wordsworthian ideas. Rebelling against approaches to art that seek to understand the world in a rational sense, he believed aesthetic creations mean something only in the most elusive sense – 'as love does, and religion does, and the best poem; but who shall fathom those meanings?' (*Specimen Days* 198). No one, of course – at least, no one can do so on a purely objective, intellectual level. The 'grandest poetic passages are only to be taken at free removes, as we sometimes look for stars at night, not by gazing directly toward them, but off one side' (199). For Whitman, as for Wordsworth,

[51] Geoffrey Hartman, *The unremarkable Wordsworth*, Minneapolis: University of Minnesota Press, 1989, 209.

aesthetic meaning could be discerned only peripherally, because to seek it objectively in a straightforward manner is to look for what is not present in a text. Because the 'meaning' is the reader's subjective response, and because both poets wanted to lift consciousness beyond the confines of normal awareness, Wordsworth and Whitman consciously crafted verse that renders the world strange, thereby destabilizing consciousness and replacing habitualized perception with a sense of awe, wonder, and mystery. A cosmic poetic creates a 'gang of Kosmos', as every reader is potentially the poet-prophet who co-creates with the artist a vision of the new world.

Chapter IX

WEDDED IN NATURAL MATRIMONY

Cosmic Love[1]

'Publish my name and hang up my picture as that of the tenderest lover,
Who was not proud of his songs, but of the measureless ocean of love within,
and freely pour'd it forth'
(Whitman)

''Mong other consolations, we may find
Some pleasure from this offering of my love'
(Wordsworth)

I

In a fairly recent essay P.M.S. Dawson decries the so-called Romantic denial of history: 'The Romantic poets called upon their readers to imagine the world anew in order to transform it – but the social world would have to be transformed first if the possibilities of imaginative vision were to be available to any but a privileged few'. 'The error is more pardonable', Dawson goes on to say, 'in poets than in political philosophers'.[2] Such criticism evinces an expressly Western perspective: It subordinates poetry to philosophy and subjugates mysticism to reason; it treats poetry as though it were factual statement, and then faults it for not being factual; it insists art should be in the service of political change, and when it is not, it is condemned as bourgeois ideology.

Dawson goes on to warn of the danger in Romanticism of resorting to the visionary mode, which 'may cut the visionary off from the human community'.[3]

---

[1] This chapter was published as 'Wedded in natural matrimony: Cosmic love in Wordsworth and Whitman', in: *Renascence: Essays on Values in Literature* 56 (2004), 161-180.

[2] P.M.S. Dawson, 'Poetry in an age of revolution', in: Stuart Curran (Ed.), *The Cambridge companion to British Romanticism*, New York: Cambridge University Press, 2000, 72.

[3] Dawson, 'Poetry in an age of revolution', 73.

As I hope to show in this chapter, however, such a comment will appear nonsensical, for Wordsworth and Whitman both had very strong connections to the human community, which accounts for one of the reasons why scholars have discerned similarities in their verse. One of the most compelling transatlantic bridges between these poets, in fact, is their positioning of themselves as poets of love. Cosmic rhetoric in their verse culminates in a mystical vision of love as the universal binding force, the cosmic cement that allows all disparate entities to adhere together in a great, everlasting similitude. Love plays such a central role in both poets' verse that it is safe to subordinate all else – even nature – to it. M.H. Abrams, drawing on the calculations of H.J.C. Grierson, has observed that the ratio of the word 'love' to 'nature' in Wordsworth is thirteen to eight.[4] I am unaware of any such lexical analysis in Whitman, but I strongly believe the ratio would be the same if not higher. Love functions in both poets as a formal and thematic wellspring, providing each writer with a rhetoric, a poetics, and a desire to instill the sentiment in the hearts of their readers. This rhetoric of love is a compelling challenge to the critics who read in their work a denial of the most important issues in life, for few can reasonably argue for the importance of anything over love and its healing power.

II

In 'Wordsworth's ontology of love in "The Prelude"', Richard Gravil has noted the importance of love in Wordsworth's poetry, claiming it is the imagination's 'breath of life'.[5] Imaginative power is 'a lonely power, a severe power', but without the informing spirit of love, 'it is no power at all'.[6] Love is the principle of individual growth in Wordsworth's verse, and it is the stay of being.[7] Not only does it organize both perception and intuition; love binds all human beings to nature and God.[8] Love thus makes the many forms of communion possible in Wordsworth's poetry.

The Wanderer in *The Excursion* is an example of Wordsworthian imaginative power without the necessary component of love. As a boy, the Wanderer can discern the loneliness and the severity of Nature, having 'perceived the presence and the power' of its greatness (I. 135). He can perceive the sublime element in overwhelming natural objects such as lakes and mountains, which lay 'Upon his mind like substances, whose presence / Perplexed the bodily sense' (138-139).

[4] Abrams, *Natural supernaturalism*, 295.
[5] Gravil, 'Wordsworth's ontology of love in "The Prelude"', 245.
[6] Ibidem.
[7] Idem, 248.
[8] Ibidem.

But he lacks the central ingredient for true cosmic perception, for 'In his heart, / Where Fear sate thus, a cherished visitant, / Was wanting yet the pure delight of love' (185-187). Without this love he cannot achieve the cosmic union with the natural that leads to a transcendence of nature. Nature, however, sets him up to learn 'Deeply the lesson of love', which he cannot help but learn, having been reared amid such power and beauty (194). Once he comprehends this lesson, which is beyond all intellectual understanding, he can read 'unutterable love' (205) in the 'silent faces' (204) of the oceans, the earth, and the clouds, all of which melt into him and swallow up his sense of individual selfhood. Having achieved this 'still communion' (215), he now transcends nature and experiences in his high state of consciousness a 'visitation from the living God' (212). Nature has led to love, which leads to a glimpse of heavenly power. This cosmic sentiment, which Wordsworth calls 'intellectual love', is a bridge between the terrestrial and the celestial. Love, as Gravil observes, allows for the fullest involvement with the 'living cosmos',[9] and it also purges the self so it may expand beyond its own limiting confines. 'Love makes the ego lose itself in the object it loves', as D.T. Suzuki has put it.[10] The Wanderer lives his life thereafter in 'a just equipoise of love', and although he is a 'lone Enthusiast', he is connected to humanity: 'His heart lay open; and, by nature tuned / And constant disposition of his thoughts / To sympathy with man' (I. 355, 362-64).

Wordsworth's near preoccupation with the downtrodden – beggars, idiots, shepherds, forsaken Indian women, and the like – is informed by this sense of love and sympathy. He is attuned to humanity, cosmically connected to nature and God, despite his retreat into the country, and despite his seemingly antisocial inclinations. In *The Art of Loving* psychologist Erich Fromm claims that man is alone 'inasmuch as he helps another'.[11] To overcome the isolation of the individual's existence in a nihilistic world, one must transcend the confines of selfhood through love for one or more people. Wordsworth's way of overcoming this sense of the isolated self was to reach humanity through his verse, which is his offering of love and solace to the world. His poetry was the means by which he cosmically connected with other human beings. He thus 'poses himself', as Lance Massey has observed, 'as the archetypal "medicine man" who enlightens and teaches and who unifies and heals the schism of Cartesian consciousness.[12]

Not coincidentally, Whitman is likewise the medicine man – the shaman, as George Hutchinson calls him, whose purpose in a society is to heal. Cultures

[9] Idem, 240.

[10] D.T. Suzuki, *Swedenborg: Buddha of the North* (trans. Andrew Bernstein), West Chester, PA: Swedenborg Foundation, 1996, 192.

[11] Fromm, *The art of loving*, 65.

[12] Massey, 'Tintern Abbey's "Tranquil Restoration"', 56.

undergoing stress often spawn charismatic and spiritualistic 'curing cults that can be connected with reform and even develop into full-fledged revitalistic religions', as Hutchinson claims.[13] Whitman's sociopolitical milieu, embroiled as it was in a crisis of disunion between North and South, was therefore conducive to the shamanic persona of *Leaves of Grass*. In 1855 America did not enjoy the same stability it does today, and Whitman's ecstatic poetry was a means to reassure the people of the conflicted states that the powers controlling the world 'are near and can be invoked'.[14]

The authors of *Start with the Sun* similarly identify Whitman as a 'life writer' – one who performs the ritual of union in his art.[15] Life writers help human beings connect with other humans and with God by 'touch[ing] the earth with awareness and love'.[16] Whitman thus offers his poems in the natural image of leaves and also as containing his great love for humanity. In the third poem in *Leaves of Grass* – 'In Cabin'd Ships at Sea' – he likens his book of poems to a cosmic ship 'cleaving the ether', journeying to its delivery point, the hearts of his fellow human beings: 'Bear forth to them folded my love', he commands his book. '[D]ear mariners, for you I fold it here in every leaf' (18, 21). Every poem is infused with his love, which is the underlying purpose of his poetics of union. 'Take my leaves America, take them South and take them North', he says in 'Starting from Paumanok'. 'Surround them East and West, for they would surround you, / And you precedents, connect lovingly with them, for they connect lovingly with you' (45, 47-48). His medicine is love's healing power, which not only makes the fragmented whole but unifies past and present.

Elsewhere he calls his poems 'Love-buds put before you and within you whoever you are' ('Roots and Leaves Themselves Alone' 7). He does not merely bestow love on a passive reader, however, as the latter must nourish the buds: 'If you bring the warmth of the sun to them they will open and bring form, color, perfume to you, / If you become the aliment and the wet they will become flowers, fruits, tall branches and trees' (9-10). By involving the reader in the creative poetic process, Whitman overcomes the isolation of Cartesian consciousness, for love bridges poet to reader and reader to poet. This need for transcendence is one of humankind's most basic needs, as Fromm argued, for psychological health can be achieved only through the type of integration and self-transcendence that love yields.[17] Love causes one to move out of the confines of the isolated *cogito* because the lover identifies no longer with himself alone but with the object of

[13] Hutchinson, *The ecstatic Whitman*, 50.
[14] Idem, 19.
[15] Miller, Shapiro, & Slote, *Start with the Sun*, 229.
[16] Idem, 230.
[17] Fromm, *The art of loving*, 46.

his love. Whitman's poetic, therefore, is an attempt to effect self-transcendence in the reader through the healing properties of love.

Harold Bloom has noted this healing quality of Whitman's verse, claiming to read the poet when he needs 'to assuage grief'.[18] 'I remember one summer, in crisis', writes Bloom, 'being at Nantucket with a friend who was absorbed in fishing, while I read aloud to both of us from Whitman and recovered myself again'.[19] Whitman is indeed the 'caresser of life', as he claims in 'Song of Myself' (232). If read in the right frame of mind, his poetry can offer solace for the grieving and hope for the disenchanted. Interestingly, critics have similarly found Wordsworth's verse a place of refuge in times of emotional turmoil. John Stuart Mill wrote of Wordsworth's poetry as 'a source of inward joy' that helped to alleviate his depression.[20] The poet reassured Mill 'that there was real, permanent happiness in tranquil contemplation'.[21] Mathew Arnold likewise found Wordsworth's verse a source of psychological succor: 'Where will Europe's latter hour / Again find Wordsworth's healing power?' he asked in his *Memorial Verses*.[22] The poet's intention of offering 'blessed consolations in distress' and 'Of joy in widest commonalty spread', as he put it in 'The Recluse', no doubt fell on ears that heard him all too well (769, 771).

Today, however, critics seem to ignore this aspect of Wordsworth's poetry, finding in his work a denial of realities, as opposed to anything valuable. Lance Massey is one of the few critics of recent years to take the poet at his word. In 'Tintern Abbey's "Tranquil Restoration": Toward a Methodology of Healing in an Age of Anxiety' Massey goes outside of poststructural criticism in order to perceive a sense of 'presence, of transcendence' in Wordsworth.[23] But he also acknowledges the riskiness of his venture to write 'appreciatively' of the poet at a time when 'beauty and meaning and transcendence seem to be relics rather than requisites' in the study of literature.[24] If one is to accurately comprehend the Wordsworthian poetic, however, it is necessary to understand the ways in which the poet restores our trust in a seemingly unintelligible world; it is necessary to understand how he achieves a sense of presence in his work, however false a deconstructor could render such an 'illusion' to be. Leon Waldoff claims Wordsworth achieves his healing appeal by substituting feelings of estrangement and emptiness with 'a confident sense of the meaningfulness of existence by connecting the landscape with the quiet of the sky [...] In other words, he heals a

[18] Harold Bloom, *The Western canon*, New York: Riverhead, 1994, 270.
[19] Ibidem.
[20] Qtd. in Massey, 'Tintern Abbey's "Tranquil Restoration"', 1028.
[21] Ibidem.
[22] In Abrams, *Natural supernaturalism*, 134.
[23] Massey, 'Tintern Abbey's "Tranquil Restoration"', 45.
[24] Ibidem.

crippling nostalgia over a lost paradise and restores our basic trust that both the inner world of the self and the outer world of existential reality are interfused with undeniable meaning'.[25] The poet effects his healing, therefore, through cosmic rhetoric and the marriage of humankind and nature.

As such, Wordsworthian nature has human feelings: 'It loves us now, this Vale so beautiful / Begins to love us!' he exclaims of his cherished refuge at Grasmere in 'The Recluse' (179-180). In 'To My Sister' he similarly intones, 'Love, now a universal birth, / From heart to heart is stealing, / From earth to man, from man to earth: / – It is the hour of feeling' (21-24). As in all marriages, there is a reciprocity in the relationship, as human gives love to and receives love from the earth. The two are wedded in natural matrimony by a 'blessed power that rolls / About, below, above' (33-34). This power – nature's spirit – is love itself, and it permeates all things, both physical and spiritual. 'We'll frame the measure of our souls', he tells his sister, which 'shall be tuned to love' (35-36). Once in harmonious resonance the soul's distress can be alleviated:

> [A] slumber seems to steal
> O'er vale, and mountain, and the starless sky.
> Now, in this blank of things, a harmony,
> Home-felt, and home-created, comes to heal
> That grief for which the senses still supply
> Fresh food [...] ('Written in Very Early Youth' 5-10)

Like a lover, nature offers solace and refuge from the cares of the artificial world that causes feelings of isolation and estrangement. The harmonious relationship is home-felt because the soul once enjoyed such union but lost it through the separation of mind and matter that results from prolonged grieving. In returning home to the lost consciousness of a primal state of unity, the poet has overcome the only true Romantic evil – that which drives apart.[26] Since the good is 'equated with the aggregate of what pulls the sundered parts together', Wordsworth embraces the most powerful integrative force known to human experience – love.[27]

Don Johnson has argued that Wordsworth's mother's death caused the poet to transfer some of his most heartfelt sentiments for his mother onto nature.[28] Because he could not accept the finality of the loss, Wordsworth projected onto natural objects his deepest psychological needs and then fulfilled them by communing

[25] Leon Waldoff, 'Wordsworth's healing power: Basic trust in "Tintern Abbey"', in: *University of Hartford Studies in Literature* 4 (1972), 164.

[26] Abrams, *Natural supernaturalism*, 295.

[27] Idem, 294.

[28] Don Johnson, 'The grief behind the spots of time', in: *America Imago* 45 (1988) no.3, 287.

spiritually with the natural world. Whether such a psychological assessment is accurate is open to considerable debate. But even if Johnson is correct and Wordsworthian Nature can be demystified and exposed as a defense mechanism, one can nevertheless read in the poet's verse a tremendous sense of psychological health. The deepest human need, according to Fromm, is the need to overcome separateness, to deal with the anxiety aroused by the knowledge of one's isolation from other people.[29] The human race in its infancy still feels a oneness with nature, as 'the soil, the animals, the plants are still man's world'.[30] But the more human beings emerge from these primary natural bonds, 'the more intense becomes the need to find ways of escaping separateness'.[31] By loving nature Wordsworth may indeed have been playing out his unresolved separation from his mother, but he is also in his own way rectifying that relationship and thus healing a psychic wound. There is nothing pathological in taking consciousness back to the primal bond the human race once shared with nature, for in doing so Wordsworth is healing a wound long in need of medicine.

In 'Wordsworth's ontology of love in "The Prelude"', Richard Gravil has likened the poet's sense of love to Heidegger's 'care', a mode of consciousness in which one 'is engaged as a Being-in-the-World with all that environs him'.[32] The analogy is appropriate, as Heideggerian care provides an alternative to 'Gestell', or the technological attitude, which results in the view of nature as something to be manipulated and exploited for the use of humankind. Through caring for another being, 'we care for it as part of Being as a whole. We recognize all the other things in harmony with the individual being'.[33] Wordsworth's love allows for and leads to his vision of cosmic unity and the interrelation of all phenomena, both physical and spiritual.

Interestingly, the care Heidegger says one must bestow upon another human being, Wordsworth often reserves for nature. He thus loves the sun and moon with feelings analogous 'To patriotic and domestic love', as he says in Book Second of *The Prelude* (195). He loves them not 'as a pledge / And surety of our earthly life' but simply for their aesthetic beauty (185-186). To him the objects of nature are like family members one loves intrinsically and unconditionally. This love he bestows on nature is reflected back as well. In Book Sixth of *The Prelude*, for example, he recalls such a perception while hiking with Dorothy and his future wife, Mary Hutchinson:

[29] Fromm, *The art of loving*, 9.
[30] Idem, 10.
[31] Ibidem.
[32] Gravil, 'Wordsworth's ontology of love in "The Prelude"', 242.
[33] Lemay & Pitts, *Heidegger*, 82.

[...] O'er paths and fields
In to the all that neighborhood, through narrow lanes
Of eglantine, and through the shady woods,
And o'er the Border Beacon and the waste
Of naked pools and common crags that lay
Exposed on the bare fell, was scattered love –
A spirit of pleasure, and youth's golden gleam. (239-245)

One could argue that Wordsworth is merely projecting his feelings of love for Dorothy and Mary onto the landscape and engaging in the simple poetic technique of personification. But such a view would be a misreading of his poetics. As he himself said in his 1802 'Preface', 'personifications of abstract ideas rarely occur in these volumes' (437). Whereas personification involves the attributing of human qualities and sentiments to inanimate objects by a poet who looks on nature as devoid of life, Wordsworth's perception is one of a living cosmos – a natural world teeming with life and consciousness that actually projects its sentiments upon him. The difference is profound, for Wordsworth did not subscribe to the mechanistic worldview, which rendered nature devoid of life. Like his Wanderer in *The Excursion*, therefore, he approaches 'Nature with a humble heart' and views it 'with a superstitious eye of love' (I. 241, 242).

III

As Gay Wilson Allen has observed in 'Walt Whitman and Stoicism', the American poet was influenced deeply by Marcus Aurelius, who believed all parts of nature were in love with each other.[34] Nature for Whitman was thus alive with human emotion and love. His particular spin on this concept, which is informed by Wordsworthian ideas as well, is his merging with the natural in *sexual* union. In verse-chant 21 of 'Song of Myself', for instance, he looks upon Nature as an object of desire, describing it in highly sensual terms:

Smile O voluptuous cool-breath'd earth!
Earth of the slumbering and liquid trees!
Earth of departed sunset – earth of the mountains misty-topt!
Earth of the vitreous pour of the full moment just tinged with blue!
Earth of shining and dark mottling the tide of the river!
Earth of the limpid gray of clouds brighter and clearer for my sake!
Far-swooping elbow'd earth – rich apple-blossom'd earth! (438-444)

He sees the earth as having a full and sexually attractive figure. The passage is conveyed in a tone of reverence, as a lover speaks of his beloved. He transmutes

[34] Allen, 'Walt Whitman and Stoicism', 57.

the sensuous into the sensual, lusting after the earth in its bountiful richness. 'Smile', he adds, 'for your lover *comes*' (emphasis added, 445). In an orgasmic moment he enters an ecstatically erotic state of consciousness in which the plentiful earth leads him to a sexual climax. But this is not mere self-gratification, for he claims to give back the sexual charge: 'Prodigal, you have given me love – therefore I to you give love! / O unspeakable passionate love' (446-447). Having made love with the earth, he then directs his erotic energy towards the sea:

> You sea! I resign myself to you also – I guess what you mean,
> I behold from the beach your crooked inviting fingers,
> I believe you refuse to go back without feeling of me,
> We must have a turn together, I undress, hurry me out of sight of the land,
> Cushion me soft, rock me and billowy drowse,
> Dash me with amorous wet, I can repay you. (448-453)

Now he must have a 'turn' with the ocean, which tantalizes him with inviting fingers as the water unevenly washes upon the shore. He believes the sea demands sexual gratification in bestowing upon him such amorous wetness, and feels obligated to repay it with a wetness of his own. The second orgasm leaves the ocean 'breathing broad and convulsive breaths', as though it has reached orgasm, satisfied yet wanting more in its post-coital moment (455). Whitman's copulation with nature leaves him unified with it, as he declares, 'I am integral with you' (458).

Roger Asselineau has noted that as Whitman aged and as his body wore out, his mysticism shed its central physical basis.[35] Whitman's earlier mysticism is steeped in physicality, or more specifically, sexuality, which in some ways renders it incompatible with the mystical tradition. Mystics in the Christian 'bridal' tradition who metaphorically marry Christ often speak of their spiritual experiences in terms that approach the erotic, and which, in fact, may conceal homoerotic impulses. As Borchert points out, Juan de la Cruz frequently uses sexual imagery to depict mystical experiences.[36] Mystics in the Eastern traditions also employee pseudo-sexual language in their poetry, with which Whitman was familiar. 'My heart must cleave to my Lover', wrote Kabir. 'I must withdraw my veil, and / meet Him with all my body'.[37] But the difference between Whitman and the traditional mystics is the latter *intend* erotic imagery strictly as metaphor, whereas Whitman sings the praises of sexuality for its own sake. Ghulam Fayez makes the mistake of overlooking such a difference in his dissertation, claiming that '[i]t is the erotic dimension of the soul or the self which creates such

---

35 Asselineau, *The evolution of Walt Whitman*, 17-78.
36 Borchert, *Mysticism*, 365.
37 *Songs of Kabir*, I. 131.

a striking kinship between the poems of Rumi and Whitman'.[38] As R.A. Gilbert notes, however, many people misconstrue the sensuous imagery in Sufi poetry, reading it as eroticism when, in fact, it is something quite different.[39]

Asselineau similarly made the mistake of subordinating sex to spirit in the poet, arguing that 'sexuality in Whitman is overshadowed by mysticism'.[40] (6). To be sure, Whitman did use the sexual as an emblem for the spiritual, but he also prided himself on being a poet of sexuality in its own right. In 'A Backward Glance' he claims *Leaves of Grass* is distinguished by its 'religiousness', (335) but he says it is also 'The song of Sex and Amativeness, and even Animality' (386-387). He qualifies this defining characteristic of *Leaves* by claiming that he intends his definition of sex 'to be lifted into a different light and atmosphere', (389) which is to say, he intends to elevate the sexual to sacred status: 'From the night a moment I emerging, flitting out, / Celebrate you *act divine* and you children prepared for, / And you stalwart loins' (emphasis added, 'From Pent-up Aching Rivers' 55-57). Sex was not only a symbol of the spiritual for Whitman; it was a form of spiritual energy. David Reynolds, consequently, has argued that 'sexual passion is never far from religious vision' in *Leaves of Grass* (234).

Harold Aspiz similarly notes that the sexual urge and the urge to transcend coexist in Whitman. Aspiz, however, subordinates the sexual to the spiritual in a way the poet would not have appreciated. 'Sexuality in Whitman's poems', argues Aspiz, 'is not usually an end in itself, for the sexual state is anterior to and generally less sustained than the transcendent state. In fact, most depictions of the sexual arousal in *Leaves of Grass* are structured to culminate in a state of spiritual and visionary elevation'.[41] While I do not disagree with the idea that sexual arousal often leads to spiritual elevation in Whitman, I would caution against any separation of the two, against any kind of dichotomizing that denies the validity of one and privileges the other. Freud and Jung represent between themselves such a split; whereas the former thought the sex drive the deepest part of the psyche, the latter argued that the religious drive was the deepest. Whitman transcended both of these great thinkers in commingling the two drives. 'Sex contains all', he wrote in 'A Woman Waits for Me'. 'All hopes, benefactions, bestowals, all the passions, loves, beauties, the life of the earth, / All the governments, the judges, gods, follow'd persons of the earth, / These are contain'd in sex as parts of itself and justifications of itself' (3, 6-8). Sexual energy for Whitman was very real indeed. Critics who attempt to deny or subordinate it

---

[38] Fayez, *Mystic ideas and images in Jalal al-Din Rumi and Walt Whitman*, vii.

[39] Gilbert, *The elements of mysticism*, 20.

[40] Asselineau, *The evolution of Walt Whitman*, 6.

[41] Aspiz, 'Sexuality and the language of transcendence', 1.

in their readings, therefore, are actually saying more about their own Euro/American bias than they are about the poet.

Whitman raises the erotic song of love to an ecstatic/spiritual pitch, but he never forgets his subject matter; he never transmutes the physical into the spiritual but unifies the two. In his dissertation on Whitman Manohar Wankhade likens the poet's sexual celebration to Tantrism, a tradition born out of Vedanta and Mahayana Buddhism. At the heart of Tantra is a world-affirming attitude, with sex being the central principle of creation (7). Wankhade argues that 'sex in Whitman is vital to [the poet's] growth and therefore pivotal in any evaluation of him' – an irrefutable point (9). In 'One Hour to Madness and Joy' Whitman claims to 'drink the mystic deliria deeper than any other man', but he is not talking strictly about partaking of spirit in a traditional mystical sense; rather, he is compelled to imbibe the sacred elixir because of his 'savage and tender achings', his powerful sexual drive (4, 5). Such lines as 'Urge and urge and urge, / Always the procreant urge of the world', ('Song of Myself' 44-45) have led the authors of *Start with the Sun* to conclude that Whitman sees the world as a 'sexual pantheist' because for him it is 'infused by creative sexual vitality' (25). Sex thus played a pivotal role in Whitman's poetic scheme, which is why he resisted Emerson's coercive efforts to have the blasphemous 'Children of Adam' sequence expurgated from the 1856 edition of *Leaves*. His poems of sex were, as he put it in *Specimen Days*, 'more precious than gold' (191). Whitman needed sex to talk about spirituality just as much as he needed spirituality to talk about sex. As he wrote in 'I Sing the Body Electric', 'O I say these are not the parts and poems of the body only, but of the soul, / O I now say these are the soul' (163-164). He recognized the inseparability of the two.

Nevertheless, George Saintsbury aptly claims it is a mistake to suppose the erotic occupies the chief place in Whitman's poetic, arguing that the poet's ideal of 'robust American love' deserves privileged status over all other forms.[42] As the poet himself says in 'Starting from Paumanok': 'It is a painful thing to love a man or woman to excess, and yet it satisfies, it is great, / But there is something else very great, it makes the whole coincide, / It, magnificent, beyond materials, with continuous hands sweeps and provides for all' (126-128). While I agree with Saintsbury's general idea, I believe it is also important to point out that robust American love consists of many impulses – the erotic, the homoerotic, friendship, intimacy, 'brotherly' love, or love between equals, as Fromm calls it, as well as cosmic love for all things in the entire universe.[43] It would be a mistake, then, to interpret the many forms of love in Whitman as merely symbols for divine

[42] George Saintsbury, 'Leaves of Grass' (1874), in: Bradley & Blodgett, *Leaves of Grass*, 785.
[43] Fromm, *The art of loving*, 43.

love, just as it would also be a mistake to subordinate one form of love to another. Love in *Leaves* can mean *eros, philia,* or *agape* depending on the poet's mood, or it can mean all three at once, which is more frequently the case.

Whitman's sense of love is too often reductively misconstrued by queer theorists as simple homoeroticism. To be sure, there is a homoerotic strain in *Leaves,* particularly in the 'Calamus' poems, but this element is often too overt to be a sublimation of homosexual impulses. In 'Earth, My Likeness', for instance, he clearly speaks of a male athlete who is 'enamour'd of me, and I of him'. In this attraction 'toward him there is something fierce and terrible in me eligible to burst forth' (5, 6). Other examples abound in *Leaves*. The love he more frequently speaks of is a greater love that manifests in the many forms of human attraction, all of which proceed from it. 'Love like the light silently wrapping all' ('Song of the Universal' 52) permeates the universe and makes human life and even death possible ('Starting from Paumanok' 212). His love has a purpose including but ultimately exceeding the erotic. As he says in 'For You O Democracy', itself a 'Calamus' poem:

> Come, I will make the continent indissoluble,
> I will make the most splendid race the sun ever shone upon,
> I will make divine magnetic lands,
> With the love of comrades,
> With the life-long love of comrades. (1-5)

David Keubrich has read this love of comrades as ideal, Platonic love, whereas David Reynolds has claimed such attraction comes from the French utopian socialist Charles Fourier, 'who conceived of an ideal society whose members were bonded by an intrapersonal magnetic pull as powerful as gravity'.[44] Whatever the source, Whitman's 'irrepressible love', as he calls it in 'Starting from Paumanok', is not simply homoerotic desire, for it binds the entire continent in its magnetism (212). In a prose passage from 1876 the poet attempted to clarify his motive for writing his book of poems:

> I also sent out *Leaves of Grass* to arouse and set flowing in men's and women's hearts, young and old, (my present and future readers,) endless streams of living, pulsating love and friendship, directly from them to myself, now and ever. To this terrible, irrepressible yearning, (surely more or less down underneath in most human souls,) this never-satisfied appetite for sympathy, and this boundless offering of sympathy – this universal democratic comradeship – this old, eternal, yet ever-new interchange of adhesiveness, so fitly emblematic of America – I have given in this book, undisguisedly, declaredly, the openest expression.[45]

---

[44] Reynolds, *Walt Whitman's America*, 224.

[45] Qtd. in Allen, *A reader's guide to Walt Whitman*, 41-42.

Generally speaking, Whitman's love is mature, healthy love, which he hoped would serve to awaken boundless sympathy in the hearts of his readers. He also hoped it would lead to interpersonal and political solidarity and convey the insight of cosmic unity. The persona of *Leaves* is thus more 'omnifutuant rather than homo-erotic', as Anthony Burgess claimed.[46] The erotic is present but subsumed by a more expansive, more inclusive cosmic sentiment.

Wordsworthian love is similarly cosmic in proportion. As Whitman's predecessor concludes in Book Thirteenth of *The Prelude*, 'From love, for here / Do we begin and end, all grandeur comes, / All truth and beauty – from pervading love' (149-151). His whole poetic autobiography, he claims, is the story of love, without which there would be neither any story to tell nor any life at all. 'That gone', he emphatically adds, 'we are as dust' (152). Wordsworth's love of nature is not merely that of one who prefers the bucolic quietude of the country to the city's cosmopolitan din. His love for nature has religious overtones, and he thus speaks repeatedly in his verse of 'That spirit of religious love in which / I walked with Nature' (*Prelude* II. 376-377). Like Whitman, who in all likelihood was influenced by his English counterpart, Wordsworth speaks of a 'higher love' than simple communion with nature (*Prelude* XIII. 161). The love one can feel by observing happy creatures living tranquilly amidst nature 'is human merely', as he says (164). The transcendent, higher love 'proceeds / More from the brooding soul, and is divine' (164-165). It 'comes into the heart / With awe and a diffusive sentiment' (162-163). Wordsworth is not simply a nature mystic, as critics sometimes wrongly label him, for his sense of love transcends the immanence of God's presence in the world, and it also includes a profoundly human element.

He is careful to avoid such a category, devoting a whole chapter (Book Eighth) of *The Prelude* to demonstrate how his love of nature led him to the love of humankind. Having been hitherto attuned to the love emanating from mother earth, which causes him to love natural objects, he recalls the precise moment when this sentiment is transmuted into an immense sympathy for human beings: the shepherds at Grasmere Fair, who 'As tender infants are – and yet how great', instill in Wordsworth a sense of nature's immense bounty (54, 55). In a cosmic moment he sees the inextricable ties between the natural and the human. The morning light 'Loves' the shepherds 'as it glistens on the silent rocks' (55-56). The moment not only leads him to the conclusion that 'all things serve them' (55); it also leaves him with a 'deep devotion' to Nature and 'High thoughts of God and man, and love of man' (62, 64). His nature worship has led to and become a deep reverence for humankind:

---

[46] Anthony Burgess, 'The answerer' (1968), in: Bradley & Blodgett, *Leaves of Grass*, 974.

> 'Twas thy power
> That raised the first complacency in me
> And noticeable kindliness of heart,
> Love human to the creature in himself
> As he appeared, a stranger in my path,
> Before my eyes a brother of this world –
> Thou first didst with those motions of delight
> Inspire me. (74-81)

Nature instills in his own heart the insight 'That we have all of us one human heart', as he put it in 'The Old Cumberland Beggar' (153). The common sights of the green earth fasten onto the heart of the growing boy, 'So that we love, not knowing that we love, / And feel, not knowing whence our feeling comes' (*Prelude* VIII. 170-171). As stranger becomes brother, the constituents of the human race no longer seem separate individuals but one consciousness with a multitude of different faces. Consciousness has shifted, and now the poet's aesthetic love of nature becomes cosmic love. When he becomes cognizant of this process he achieves insight, a wisdom beyond all knowing.

IV

Love is the only true path to knowledge in Wordsworth, just as it is for many mystics. One can know through analysis and tearing things apart, the *modus operandi* of the Western world, which results in the reification of nature and human beings 'as entities to be measured and maneuvered'.[47] Although Marxists blame capitalist ideology for such objectification, reification has its roots firmly planted in Western soil, stretching back well before the exploitation of factory workers in the 19th century. The rise of the bourgeoisie, in fact, was merely the culmination of an underlying Western ideology that objectifies not only nature but the subjective human psyche. But as Paul Strathern notes in his discussion of Derrida, knowledge reduces the whole; it *abs-tracts* from experience.[48] Because 'the original Latin meaning of abstract is "to draw" (*traction* has the same root) "out of" or "away from" (as in absent)', deductive reasoning is *reductive* in nature, as it necessarily entails a loss or a diminution of the object of thought.[49]

To know something in its fullest sense, therefore, one must not turn to objectification but to love or something on the order of Heideggerian 'care'. Heidegger's way of knowing has nothing to do with the usurpation of the objects of

---

[47] Mehta, 'Heidegger and Vedanta', 22.
[48] Strathern, *Derrida*, 36.
[49] Ibidem.

knowledge, as is typical among Western philosophers. Heidegger's way, which I believe was made possible in part by Romanticism, is a way of thinking 'but not representational thinking'.[50] In other words, Heidegger's epistemology is a reorientation towards reality in which one does not apprehend the mystery of being in a logical sense, but rather finds the 'answer' in the immediacy of a direct relationship to the world. As Mehta argues, 'the experience of thinking [in Heidegger] appropriates the precious element of immediacy in all mysticism'.[51] Such immediacy allows one to overcome the 'technological' attitude (*Gestell*) of Western thought, which carries the illusion of true cognition. But as Karl Jaspers argued, 'cognition of a thing is not cognition of being'.[52] Scientism (the belief that all things can be known through the scientific method) merely produces knowledge of objectified things; it never yields the wisdom of being, which can be obtained only indirectly through love. Heidegger's care is a more complete way of knowing than strict rationalism, as it is a way to overcome the self-centeredness of the thinking subject of Cartesian philosophy and *Gestell*, both of which preclude the possibility of recognizing the 'splendour of the world, of Being'.[53]

Wordsworthian love, the equivalent of 'care', opens an alternative path to knowledge and makes possible a higher form of knowing. Because love involves union, as Fromm observed, there is no objectification and thus no reduction of the object of love.[54] In loving union, rather, there is a fusion between subject and object, a blurring of the boundary between the two, which opens up avenues of knowledge forever blocked by the thinking isolated *cogito* of Cartesian philosophy. Because Nature has instilled in Wordsworth a recognition of the 'grandeur in the beatings of the heart', he can thus discern the 'soul that art the eternity of thought' – the 'Wisdom and spirit of the universe' (*Prelude* I. 441, 429, 428). Love, and only love, can unlock the mystery whose emblem is nature. As he tells Dorothy in 'To My Sister', 'bring no book', for one moment of loving union with nature 'may give us more / Than years of toiling reason (15, 25-26). Love is the force behind all knowledge and learning, according to Wordsworth. It serves, 'like an awakening breeze', to quicken the 'torpid life' of a newborn infant, who, 'Subjected to the discipline of love', receives 'Along his infant veins' the 'gravitation and filial bond / Of Nature that connect him with the world' (*Prelude* II. 245, 244, 251, 262-264). As a result of the mother's love, the infant's mind expands, and, as the 'agent of the one great mind', he becomes 'creator and receiver both' (II. 272, 273). Microcosm of the macrocosm, the infant has expansive wisdom the likes of which make reason seem to pale in comparison.

---

50 Stambaugh, 'Heidegger, Taoism, and the question of metaphysics', 85.
51 Mehta, 'Heidegger and Vedanta', 35.
52 Jaspers, *Philosophy of existence*, 59.
53 Lemay & Pitts, *Heidegger*, 81.
54 Fromm, *The art of loving*, 28.

Love thus informs Wordsworth's privileging of childhood consciousness over the cares of adulthood. His famous passage in the 'Intimations' Ode indicates why:

> Shades of the prison-house begin to close
> Upon the growing boy,
> But He
> Beholds the light, and whence it flows,
> He sees it in his joy;
> The Youth, who daily farther from the east
> Must travel, still is Nature's Priest,
> And by the vision splendid
> Is on his way attended;
> At length the Man perceives it die away,
> And fade into the light of common day. (67-77)

Children do not have the interference of learning and do not have cluttered minds full of rational answers to what is fundamentally an irrational mystery. Children are usually quite phenomenological because they tend to have a 'more innocent eye', as Donald Palmer observes.[55] They can more directly perceive without the filter of preconceived judgement, bias, and the mental clutter of acquired knowledge. Attuned to love, children have the wisdom of unknowing. For this reason, the ancient Chinese used the same ideogram for the sage and the child.[56] Lau-tse, the reputed author of the *Tao Te Ching*, was known as the 'Old Boy' because he had preserved his childhood wisdom through adulthood. He did not allow the prison-house to grow upon him and never lost sight of the celestial light, which the child-become-adult too often lets die away.

Whitman, perhaps not coincidentally, also saw love as the only traversable route to knowledge. A passage in one of his early notebooks, for instance, sheds light on his orientation towards truth, which he believed one could ascertain only through love:

> All truths lie waiting in all things. – They neither urge the opening of themselves nor resist it. For their birth you need not the obstetric forceps of the surgeon. They unfold to you and emit themselves more fragrant than roses from living buds, whenever you fetch the spring sunshine moistened with summer rain. – But it must be yourself. – It shall be in yourself. – It shall come from your soul. – It shall be love.[57]

True to the Romantic gospel of subjectivity, he did not subscribe to the notion of objective truth, believing in subjective perception and the necessity of love for

---

[55] Palmer, *Structuralism and poststructuralism*, 36.

[56] Smith, *The world's religions*, 196.

[57] Qtd. in Matthiessen, *American Renaissance*, 520.

the completion of knowledge. Truth lies impregnated in all things, but the percipient must supply the necessary ingredient – love – for the completion of the birth. Significantly, one cannot extract truth with obstetric forceps, which is to say the delivery cannot be forced by a meddling intellect that 'murders to dissect', as Wordsworth's line goes. Rather, only gentle love will facilitate knowing; only love will enable one to avoid objectification and thus destruction of the object of knowledge.

Whitman saw love, then, as the source of all truth. Having studied ancient and modern systems of knowledge, he concludes in 'The Base of all Metaphysics' that underneath all of these is simply 'The dear love of man for his comrade, the attraction of friend to friend, / Of the well-married husband and wife, of children and parents, / Of city for city and land for land' (13-15). Love can even help one to see through the terrible doubt of appearances, as he claims in a poem by the same name. The uncertainty 'that we may be deluded' in our belief in the soul and an afterlife can be resolved by simple love: 'To me these and the like of these are curiously answer'd by my lovers, my dear friends' (2, 10). In moving consciousness from the head to the heart he resolves the issue. 'Then I am charged with untold and untellable wisdom, I am silent and I require nothing further' (13). Ironically transcending the confines of the machinery of knowledge – that is, the mind – allows one's ultimate questions to be answered. Real wisdom can be found only through the cessation by love of the incessant churning of the mind's gears, only through the joy of ineffable unknowing.

Whitman's profound sense of love and joy pervades his poetry. He is the premier poet of cheer and optimism and the 'vast elemental sympathy which only the human soul is capable of generating and emits in steady and limitless floods', as he put in 'Song of Joys' (23). This joy comes from the soul and is the basic, primal consciousness underlying all human awareness. Those in touch with this sense of joy are psychologically healthy and look through evil to the all-pervasive good in the cosmos. Those out of touch with it are much in need of the healing that Whitman as 'Kosmos' can bring. In 'The Sleepers' he, the awakened one, thus brings solace to the spiritually slumbering souls who remain oblivious of universal joy in their restless unconsciousness: 'I pass my hands soothingly to and fro a few inches from them, / The restless sink in their beds, they fitfully sleep' (24-25).

In real life as an honorary nurse in the Civil War camps he performed his soothing healing as well, offering cheer more than any actual service. As he wrote in *Specimen Days*, 'In my visits to the hospitals I found it was in the simple matter of personal presence, and emanating ordinary cheer and magnetism, that I succeeded and help'd more than by medical nursing, or delicacies, or gifts of money, or anything else' (38). In his verse he is 'The true son of God' whose arrival will rectify all wrongs:

Then not your deeds only O voyagers, O scientists and inventors, shall be justified,
All these hearts as of fretted children shall be sooth'd.
All affection shall be fully responded to, the secret shall be told,
All these separations and gaps shall be taken up and hook'd and link'd together.
The whole earth, this cold, impassive, voiceless earth, shall be completely justified,
Trinitas divine shall be gloriously accomplish'd and compacted by the true son of God, the poet. (105-111)

Whitman's gospel of joy will complete all knowledge, and it will bring spiritual succor for the weary. It will provide the missing element in all human sentiments and conjoin the disparate. Not only the earth but the trinity in heaven will be complete. The cosmic poetic persona is a divine figure who must give back the sacred energies to which he is privy. To fail to do so would violate the cosmic law of joy, which constantly demands expression. 'Dazzling and tremendous how quick the sun-rise would kill me, / If I could not now and always send sun-rise out of me', as he says in 'Song of Myself' (560-561). Giving, according to Fromm, is the highest expression of potency. 'In the very act of giving', he writes, 'I experience my strength, my wealth, my power. This experience of heightened vitality and potency fills me with joy. I experience myself as overflowing, spending, hence as joyous' (21). Whitman's godlike persona is attributable to the immense sense of empowerment that comes from giving love so freely, which fills him with boundless, inexpressible joy.

William James has called Whitman the 'supreme contemporary example' of healthy-mindedness because he refused to feel and/or express anything but expansive, joyous, happy sentiments.[58] Despite the filth, rats, and sewage of Manhattan streets, the piles of sawed-off limbs at the Civil War camps and hospitals, and his own deteriorating and constipated body as he declined in age, Whitman refused to linger on the unpleasant aspects of life. Scholars from the New Critics onwards have found the poet's optimism 'distressing', as Harold Blodgett put it, as though one should, in keeping with the modern/postmodern temper, dwell on the darkness, as though the light, happy, and cheerful side does not exist.[59] The poet may in fact express cheer in the face of harsher sociopolitical realities, but in doing so he is elevating consciousness in a way not possible if he were to fixate on inequality, war, oppression, and the like. In 'Democratic Vistas' he argued that the benchmark for a 'great literatus' will be 'the absence in him of the idea of the covert, the lurid, the maleficent, the devil, the grim estimates inherited from the Puritans, hell, natural depravity, and the like' (in *Specimen*

[58] James, *The varieties of religious experience*, 84.
[59] Bradley & Blodgett, *Leaves of Grass*, 992.

Days, 248). Critics may call his cheer naive, but in doing so they point out their own failure to grasp a profundity-in-simplicity in the work of uncontestably America's greatest poet, and they also overlook a centrality in his poetics. 'The known universe has one complete lover and that is the greatest poet', as he wrote in 1855 'Preface' (216).

A possible source of Whitman's healthy-mindedness may be found in Wordsworth's verse, in which abounds a sense of 'Diffusing health and sober cheerfulness', as he put it in 'The Recluse' (465). Like Whitman, Wordsworth sees in nature only the good and receives from it an insulation from the cares of the world. 'Nature never did betray / The heart that loved her', he wrote in 'Tintern Abbey' (122-123). But it is important to point out that this relationship does not cause him to ignore or deny the darker side of life but allows him, rather, to see beyond it:

> [Nature] can so inform
> The mind that is within us, so impress
> With quietness and beauty, and so feed
> With lofty thoughts, that neither evil tongues,
> Rash judgements, nor the sneers of selfish men,
> Nor greetings where no kindness is, nor all
> The dreary intercourse of daily life,
> Shall e'er prevail against us, or disturb
> Our cheerful faith, that all which we behold
> Is full of blessings. (125-134)

Wordsworthian love elevates consciousness above the seamy aspects of life and the meanness of self-interested people. It protects the speaker from these harsher evils in mesmerizing him with a sense of solitude and beauty that borders on the sacred. Nature is both the reflection and the fountain of this love, as it gives to and receives from the speaker a pervasive sense of joy. Because the earth is alive 'with a heart / Joyous' and soothes him with its 'sense of touch', the poet sees it almost as a lover (*Prelude* I. 15-16, 89). His apostrophe in 'The Recluse' is a typical example:

> Embrace me then, ye Hills, and close me in;
> Now in the clear and open day I feel
> Your guardianship; I take it to my heart;
> 'Tis like the solemn shelter of the night.
> But I would call thee beautiful, for mild
> And soft, and day, and beautiful thou art,
> Dear Valley, having in thy face a smile
> Though peaceful, full of gladness. (110-117)

He sees in nature a place of refuge, and wants to be figuratively hugged by the hills, which provide him with a sense of peace and security. Beautiful, soft, and gay in its near-human sense of being, the valley, too, smiles at him in gladness. He depicts all of the natural world in such quasi-erotic terms, a rhetoric culminating in a sense of cosmic unity, or what he calls 'A blended holiness of earth and sky' (144). Stuart Sperry, one of the few critics who recognize this aspect of Wordsworth's verse, has argued that there is 'a quality of transfused sexuality that forms [the poet's] landscape'.[60] Wordsworthian joy and healthy-mindedness thus have erotic dimensions. If he does not have sex with nature like Whitman does, he nevertheless shares an unprecedented degree of *intimacy* with it.

Ultimately, however, it was a more expansive sense of love Wordsworth wanted to convey. In 'Nature and the Humanization of the Self In Wordsworth' Geoffrey Hartman attributes the poet's healing power to the 'corporate nature of selfhood' as he depicts it in his verse, as well as the 'quiet yet infinite ties between man and man, or man and nature, without which we could not exist'.[61] M.H. Abrams saw in Wordsworth 'the ancient struggle for the blessedness of reconciliation with an alienated God', which becomes 'the attempt to recover in maturity an earlier stage of integrity with oneself and the outer world, in a mode of consciousness for which the standard name is "joy"'.[62] Or as Francis King put it, love in Wordsworth is an overcoming of the Fall, a post-post-lapsarian return to paradise 'resting on an inner state of undividedness, one consciousness, one light'.[63] Wordsworthian joy leads to a reintegration of the psyche. The self's *atonement* with the cosmos, it heals and makes whole again the fragmentation of Cartesian consciousness.[64]

V

Such healing power in both poets may not have been engaged in the immediate political scene, but it arguably more closely connected them with the human community than any form of sociopolitical praxis. The spiritual sustenance readers have derived from their verse is a compelling refutation of the view of their estrangement from humanity. What underlies such readings is the notion that society determines consciousness. Both poets, however, would have vehemently defended the opposite view – that consciousness determines society. Although

---

60 Sperry, 'Wordsworth and the grounds of human consciousness', 69.

61 Geoffrey Hartman, 'Nature and the humanization of the self in Wordsworth' (1970), in: Abrams, *English romantic poets*, 130.

62 Abrams, *Natural supernaturalism*, 123.

63 Francis King, 'Love and landscape in Wordsworth', in: *The Wordsworth Circle* 18 (1987) no.1, 13.

64 Massey, 'Tintern Abbey's "Tranquil Restoration"', 50.

outward conditions undoubtedly impact inward states of being, viable sociopolitical change results from an alteration in values, from a transformation of consciousness.

For both poets, love provided a way to heal the self, the community, the nation, the earth. It is what binds culture to individual, and individual to culture. Love can heal schisms intrapersonally and interpersonally, and it can unify the disparate and the antithetical. Given that love is the most humane force on the planet, it seems ridiculous, then, to argue that the two premier poets of love in the anglophone tradition were disconnected from the human community. The opposite is true, for both poets are closer to us than we often realize. In showing us how to reconnect with nature and with love of humanity, Wordsworth and Whitman remind us that love is the foundation stone of human life.

Chapter X

ORTHODOX HETERODOXY

The Paradox of Romantic 'Religion'

'Man is fundamentally the desire to be God'
(Jean-Paul Sartre)

'The conflict between right and wrong
Is the sickness of the mind'
(Zen epigram)

'He ask'd me if I enjoy'd religion. I said, 'Perhaps
not, my dear, in the way you mean, and yet, may-be,
it is the same thing'
(Whitman in *Specimen Days*)

I

Wordsworthian scholars are fond of demonstrating the Christian element in his version of Romanticism. In *Natural Supernaturalism* M.H. Abrams noted the 'religio-aesthetic' dimensions of Wordsworth's verse, claiming the poet never breaks free from the 'centuries-old Judeo-Christian culture' in which he wrote.[1] Behind Wordsworth stands Milton, according to Abrams, and behind Milton stands the Bible.[2] In 'The Poetics of Prophesy' Geoffrey Hartman employs Blooms' theory of influence to show the ways in which the poet returns not to the precise verbal content of scripture but to its implicit spirit.[3] Hartman claims that Wordsworth appropriates the Biblical language of the prophets in its 'pathos, its animism, [and] its fallacious figures'.[4]

Many Whitman scholars have similarly demonstrated the influence of the Christian tradition on the American bard. Bruce Allan Bercquist, for example, claims this influence is more pervasive than scholars have recognized, arguing that

[1] Abrams, *Natural supernaturalism*, 397 & 13.
[2] Idem, 32.
[3] Hartman, 'The poetics of prophesy', 36.
[4] Idem, 39.

Whitman is actually within the mainstream of the Western tradition, perhaps as a 'heretic' but within the fold nevertheless.[5] Michael Sowder has argued that Whitman wrote in the midst of an 'antebellum culture of conversion, a Christian culture of religious preaching and writing'.[6] Not only does his 1855 'Preface' resemble the biblical pattern of prophesy and fulfillment, according to Sowder; Whitman also appropriated many cultural and rhetorical practices from Christianity.[7] David Keubrich's excellent study, *Minor Prophesy*, also situates Whitman within the confines of the Judeo-Christian tradition. Keubrich reads Whitman's 'religion' in terms of the prophetic tradition, but he does acknowledge that what distinguishes the poet from the prophet is the former's unabashed celebration of sexuality.

Although such scholarship is sound, it leaves unsaid the markedly heterodox nature of the cosmic rhetoric found in Wordsworth and Whitman. Both poets may indeed be complicit in biblical rhetorical modes, but they also undermine those modes in describing subjective experiences of consciousness transformation. Such 'anti-social' experiences challenge the collective nature of orthodox religions, which often pressure their adherents to conform to uniform standards of worship. The early Quakers and Methodists, whose 'inner light' experiences marginalized them for decades, are a case in point.[8] Orthodoxy in general fosters a deep distrust of intensely subjective, mystical and/or religious experiences. In the Western tradition mystics are often seen as heretics or lunatics, and they frequently have found themselves excommunicated or at odds with the established order.

In his Taoist reading of Wordsworth, Qian-zhi Wu acknowledges that the poet was bred and steeped in the Western tradition and thus 'could not but have frequent recourse to its existing concepts and their accompanying language'.[9] But Wu argues that Wordsworth never seemed 'comfortable or content with the theories or terminology that were available to him'.[10] Wordsworth may have appropriated biblical language, but he was never at ease with the limitations of the Judeo-Christian tradition. Although he grew increasingly more orthodox as he aged and embraced Anglicanism, he was never *unconsciously* at ease as a Christian. Wordsworth often had to revise his poetry to be in keeping with Anglican doctrine. His 1850 version of *The Prelude*, as Harold Bloom observes,

---

[5] Bruce Allan Bercquist, *Walt Whitman and the Bible: Language echoes, images, allusions, and ideas* (Diss. University of Nebraska, Lincoln, 1979), 14.

[6] Michael Sowder, 'Walt Whitman, the apostle', in: *Walt Whitman Quarterly Review* 16 (1999) no.3-4, 202.

[7] Sowder, 'Walt Whitman, the apostle', 206 & 202.

[8] Twitchell, *Romantic horizons*, 23.

[9] Wu, *The Wordsworthian imagination*, 5.

[10] Idem, 6.

shows 'better craftsmanship, but it also sometimes manifests an orthodox sensor at work, straining to correct a private myth into an approach at Anglican dogma'.[11] His earlier pre-1807 poems, particularly 'Tintern Abbey' and the 1805 *Prelude* but many others as well, are steeped in mystical rhetoric, so much so that Wordsworth's later reworking of them shows his uneasiness over the subversive aspects of such language. The many 'Christian' revisions of the 1850 *Prelude*, which Jonathan Wordsworth, Stephen Gill, and M.H. Abrams have also noted, are a clear example of this revision.

Whitman was certainly more at ease with his own cosmic rhetoric, often celebrating the fact that he was destroying orthodox conventions. 'I know my words are weapons full of danger, full of death', he wrote in 'As I Lay with My Head in Your Lap Camerado' (4). He reveled in the instability that results from subverting orthodoxy: 'For I confront peace, security, and all the settled laws, to unsettle them' (5). In destabilizing consciousness, Whitman believed he could awaken the reader out of the slumber of habitualized perception, which prevents the type of insight he was attempting to convey in his poetry. Established patterns of thought and belief are inimical to the cultivation of cosmic consciousness. He thus claimed to 're-examine philosophies and religions', which may 'prove well in lecture-rooms, yet not prove at all under the spacious clouds and along the landscape and flowing currents' ('Song of the Open Road' 83-84). He also declared himself free of all doctrinal and clerical restraints: 'Allons! from all formules [sic]! / From your formules, O bat-eyed and materialistic priests' (129-30). Harsh words from a poet that some critics claim conforms to the Western tradition.

To be sure, Whitman was raised in the Quaker tradition, which eliminated the traditional priestly function and all ritual, embracing instead a radical form of religious egalitarianism.[12] Members of the Quaker congregation themselves can speak, should they be moved to do so, but the central practice centers around silent meditation in which worshippers attempt to connect with what its founder, George Fox, called 'the inner light'.[13] Quakerism is thus radical Protestantism, for nothing – not even the Bible – can stand between a worshipper and the divine. But Whitman's brand of Quakerism was the Hicksite strain, an unorthodox version of Christianity even by Quaker standards. Glenn Cummings astutely observed that the critical past has oversimplified the Christian/Quaker elements in Whitman's verse.[14] Too often, Cummings argues, the influence of Elias Hicks has been underappreciated, for Hicks was a heterodox Quaker isolated from the

[11] Bloom, *The visionary company*, 141.
[12] Freke & Gandy, *The complete guide to world mysticism*, 99.
[13] Ibidem.
[14] Cummings, 'Placing the impalpable', 69.

more traditional version of the denomination.[15] Whitman was profoundly influenced by Hicks, as several critics have argued, but it is worth noting that he never considered himself a Quaker. When asked by Horace Traubel why he never fully accepted Quakerism, he replied, 'I was never made to live inside a fence'.[16] He was too radical even for a subversive faction of a subversive Christian denomination.

Whitman felt dissatisfied with Christian theology, as V.K. Chari has observed, and, despite embracing such mystics as Swedenborg and Behmen, he felt they ultimately failed by 'attaching themselves to the Christian symbol'.[17] Whitman's tone in *Leaves* towards Christ and the Christian God is thus less than celebratory. At one point in 'Song of Myself' he does call for the acceptance of 'the Gospels' and 'him that was crucified, knowing assuredly that he is divine' (1106). But earlier in the same verse-chant he also elevates himself to Christlike status and even predicts his own second-coming: 'Enclosing worship ancient and modern and all between ancient and modern, / Believing I shall come again upon the earth after five thousand years...' (1096-1099). Elsewhere in 'Song of Myself' his tone borders on hostility towards Christ, the church, and its repressive morality:

> I think I could turn and live with the animals, they are so placid and self-contain'd,
> I stand and look at them long and long.
> They do not sweat and whine about their condition,
> They do not lie awake in the dark and weep for their sins,
> They do not make me sick discussing their duty to God,
> [...] Not one kneels to another, nor to his kind that lived thousands of years ago... (684-688, 690)

There is an equivalent here of the Wordsworthian privileging of childhood wisdom over the knowledge of adulthood. In animal consciousness Whitman sees the antithesis of Christian guilt and its sense of obligation. Nor do animals subordinate themselves to any other, let alone to one who lived two millennia ago. Perhaps in the Quaker spirit, Whitman also dismisses all that stands between humans beings and God, including both the most revered Western text and all clergy: 'Bibles may convey and priests expound, but it is exclusively for the noiseless operation of one's isolated self to enter the pure ether of veneration, reach the divine levels, and commune with the unutterable' (*Specimen Days* 234). Whitman's religion thus emphasized the participant: 'We consider bibles and religions divine – I do not say they are not divine, / I say they have all grown out of you, and may grow out of you still, / It is not they who give the life, it is you

[15] Idem, 72.
[16] Idem, 84.
[17] Chari, *Whitman in the light of Vedantic mysticism*, 135.

who give the life' ('A Song for Occupations' 78-80). In a truly heretical gesture, he has stolen fire from the heavens by attributing the source of all holy texts and religions to human origin. In past eras such rhetoric would have gotten him burned at the stake. In the 19th century it clearly would have ruffled many feathers to say the least.

And ruffle feathers it did, which of course only fueled Whitman's subversive spirit. 'My call is the call of battle', he proudly declared in 'Crossing Brooklyn Ferry'. 'I nourish active rebellion' (211-212). In response to the iconoclasm with which many conservatives charged him, he claimed a position of neutrality: 'I hear it was charged against me', he wrote in a poem by the same name, 'that I sought to destroy institutions, / But really I am neither for nor against institutions' (1-2). The supreme poet of contradictions, he is clearly exhibiting his ambivalence towards institutions. It might have been more appropriate if he said he was *at once* for and against them, as the institution he claims to construct sounds close in spirit to Jesus' own reformation of Judaism: 'Without edifices or rules or trustees or any argument', he will inaugurate 'The institution of the dear love of comrades' (6-7). He believed in institutions but also saw the indispensability of the revolutionary spirit, which helped to 'counterbalance the inertness and fossilism making so large a part' of them (*Specimen Days* 221). Whitman believed human institutions tended to 'ossify' consciousness in a way that runs against the spirit of the institution itself (221).

There is a similar impulse in Wordsworth to subvert the rigidity of Christian theology. In his famous sonnet, 'The World Is Too much with Us', for instance, he exclaims, 'Great God! I'd rather be / A pagan suckled in a creed outworn' than get so caught up in the world as to become blind to the effulgence of nature and its immense splendour (9-10). The protagonist in the earlier version of the 'Pedlar' similarly embraces a natural religion:

> [...] He had early learned
> To reverence the Volume which displays
> The mystery, the life which cannot die:
> But in the mountains did he feel his faith.
> There did he see the writing. All things there
> Breathed immortality, revolving life,
> And greatness still revolving: infinite. (242-248)

Although the pedlar learns intellectually from the sacred text of spiritual mysteries, nature completes the lesson by educating the heart. The writing he sees is a language beyond linguistic utterance, for it can be discerned only by the receptive heart, the wellspring of intuitive knowledge. There is a subversion of traditional theology here, for nature's lesson undermines the Bible by bestowing a higher wisdom on the Pedlar.

Klaus Peter Mortensen has astutely observed that Wordsworth's 'removing paradise out into nature' only seems like a breach with the Christian tradition. It is actually in line with 'roots stretching right back to St. Paul', who taught that Nature is the book in which God as creator has depicted both his being and his will.[18] Although I acknowledge Mortensen's excellent observation, I would also point out that Wordsworth may in fact be reading God's book, but his orientation towards the natural world significantly undermines Biblical attitudes towards nature. Unlike many other traditions, particularly those in the East, the Judeo-Christian Bible does not place nature on an equal footing with human beings. 'The Bible is unlike the mythology of other races', notes Bruno Borchert. 'Scant respect is paid to nature and the cosmos. The heavenly bodies are lower creations, and mankind stands apart from them'.[19] Such disrespect is established in the first chapter:

> God said, 'Let the earth bring forth living creatures, according to their various kinds: cattle, creeping things, and wild animals, all according to their various kinds'. So it was; God made wild animals, cattle, and every creeping thing, all according to their various kinds; and he saw that it was good. Then God said, 'Let us make human beings in our image, after our likeness, to have *dominion* over the fish in the see, the birds of the air, the cattle, all wild animals on land, and everything that creeps on the earth.[20]

So there is at the outset of the Western tradition a schism between human beings and the natural world, as though each excluded the other – as though the one subjugated the other. In *The Perennial Philosophy* Aldous Huxley decried such attitudes towards nature:

> [M]an no longer regards Nature as Being in any sense divine and feels perfectly free to behave towards her as an overweening conquerer and tyrant. The spoils of recent technological imperialism have been enormous [...] What is obvious, however, is that the advantages accruing from recent technological advances – or, in Greek phraseology, from recent acts of *hubris* directed against Nature – are generally accompanied by corresponding disadvantages, that gains in one direction entail losses in other directions, and that we never get something except for something.[21]

The world, the cosmos, no longer reveals 'a higher order, a supreme intelligence', writes Michael Gellert. '[I]t is just nature – to be conquered and manipulated for technological, material gain'.[22]

---

[18] Mortensen, *The time of unrememberable being*, 24.
[19] Borchert, *Mysticism*, 117.
[20] Genesis 1:24-26 (emphasis added).
[21] Huxley, *The perennial philosophy*, 79-80.
[22] Gellert, *Modern mysticism*, 204.

Wordsworth's orientation with nature overcomes this technological attitude – *Gestell* as Heidegger called it. The cosmos itself is alive with consciousness in the Wordsworthian poetic. For Wordsworth, the 'perception of an alien and lifeless nature [...] in the mind of the perceiver is a result of the fall of man, and constitutes the essential nature of evil itself', as M.H. Abrams argued.[23] The poet attempted to bridge the gap, to span the gulf between the natural world out there and the inner world of human consciousness, thereby healing the Cartesian schism between mind and matter and achieving the union of seemingly disparate entities. But he also attempted to commingle the natural and the spiritual in an unprecedented way. Harold Bloom has said 'the most defiant humanism in Wordsworth salutes the immediate possibility of this earthly paradise *naturalizing* itself in the here and now' well.[24] The pedlar, then, is at once orthodox and heterodox, for he reads God's book but also elevates nature's status higher than Christian limits would allow. Contrary to the Judeo-Christian version of nature, the pedlar's exists on equal terms with humankind. It does not exist for objectification and exploitation by humans but to convey profound intuitive insight, to overcome the dualism reinforced by Western modes of ideation.

The original draft of 'Peter Bell' also reveals Wordsworth's dissatisfaction with orthodoxy. Whereas Christian theology subordinates human to God and reinforces a sense of the individual soul's otherness, Wordsworth puts forth an ideal 'In which all beings live with God, *themselves* / *Are* God, existing in one mighty whole'.[25] Such extreme pantheism upsets the Christian scheme, as God and human are not merely placed on equal footing but collapsed into an indistinguishable unity. Meister Eckhart preached the same doctrine, which was considered highly heretical and accounted in part for the many problems he had with church authorities.[26] The Sufi mystic al-Hallah was actually tortured and murdered for uttering such ideas.[27] Wordsworth himself suffered no such fate, but Coleridge was so frightened by the lines that he convinced the poet to change them. As his biographer, Rosemary Ashton, observes, Coleridge moved away from pantheism to a more traditionally transcendental vision of God as he aged.[28] Harold Bloom has also noted Coleridge's fear of descending into paganism.[29] Under such an influence, Wordsworth's revised ideal becomes one 'In which all

---

[23] Abrams, *Natural supernaturalism*, 222.
[24] Bloom, *The visionary company*, 126 (emphasis added).
[25] Qtd. in Wordsworth, Abrams, & Gill, *The Prelude 1799, 1805, 1850*, 574.
[26] Ursula King, *Christian mystics*, New York: Simon & Schuster, 1998, 104.
[27] Freke & Gandy, *The complete guide to world mysticism*, 114.
[28] Ashton, *The life of Samuel Taylor Coleridge*, 293.
[29] Bloom, *The visionary company*, 201.

beings live with God, *are lost / In God and Nature*, in one mighty whole…'.[30] Despite his own impulses, Wordsworth's orthodox sensor and Coleridge's influence would not allow such heresy.

Jenny Guest, among others, has noted the increasingly orthodox tone of Wordsworth's poems, particularly those written after 1807 but especially *The Excursion*, in which the Wanderer 'becomes a moralizing mouthpiece for Wordsworth himself'.[31] Even Wordsworth's contemporaries noticed such a trend. In *Don Juan* Byron wrote of 'A drowsy, frowsy poem called *The Excursion*, / Writ in a manner which is my aversion' (III. 847-848). William Hazlitt said that in the poem 'we are talked to death by an arrogant old proser, and buried in a heap of the most perilous stuff and the most dusty philosophy'.[32] Whereas the earlier version of 'The Pedlar' concludes that 'all the grief / The passing shows of being leave behind / Appeared an idle dream that could not live / Where meditation was' (924-27), the wanderer of *The Excursion* puts a particularly Christian spin on the same passage:

> […] all the grief
> That passing shows of Being leave behind,
> Appeared an idle dream, that could maintain,
> Nowhere, dominion o'er the enlightened spirit
> Whose meditative sympathies repose
> Upon the breast of Faith. (I. 950-955)

The 'wise passiveness' of unmediated mystical perception has here given way to a more orthodox reliance upon Christian faith. A personal experience has been reworked into a more appropriately social context.

Nevertheless, *The Excursion* does contain traces of the earlier subversive rhetoric. Although 'The Wanderer' grew up under the principles of the Scottish Church and 'The strong hand of her purity', for instance, his religion appears to the speaker to be 'Self-taught, as of a dreamer in the woods; / Who to the model of his own pure heart / Shaped his belief, as grace divine inspired, / And human reason dictated with awe' (I. 300, 409-412). Here Wordsworth comes close to depicting the Wanderer as a pagan suckled on a creed outworn, as his character transcends the 'unrelenting eye' of the Scottish Church (I. 400). His religion involves his own direct perceptions, which aligns it more with mysticism than any form of orthodoxy. It also involves a mystical intimacy with Nature that would seem to contradict traditional theology. James Glimm has argued that Wordsworth's poetry is not unique in its treatment of mystical experience but

---

[30] Qtd. in Wordsworth, Abrams, & Gill, *The Prelude 1799, 1805, 1850*, 574.

[31] Jenny Guest, 'Wordsworth and the music of humanity', in: *The Critical Review* 20 (1978), 21.

[32] Bloom, *The visionary company*, 193.

because 'the experience comes to us trailing clouds directly from heaven and not dragging the threadbare vestments of institutionalized religion'.[33] I would qualify Glimm's keen perception, however, as it is applicable primarily to the pre-1807 poems. The later Wordsworth labored diligently to alter his rhetoric to be more in keeping with institutionalized religion. Occasionally, the subversive impulse will escape the sensor's unrelenting eye, as in the passage quoted above, but too often Wordsworth softens the rhetoric at the expense of the poetry. Lamenting the 1850 version of *The Prelude*, Frederick Garber has argued that such orthodox intrusions falsify 'an experience in which it has no essential part'.[34] Mysticism and religion are in some respects at odds.

II

Whitman's mysticism in particular runs against the grain of Christian orthodoxy. Whereas Wordsworth toyed with the idea of placing human beings on an equal plane with God but then recoiled from his own rhetoric, Whitman embraced such a notion with unequalled vigor. '[N]othing, not God, is greater to one than oneself is', he boldly declared in 'Song of Myself' (1271). In celebrating himself, Whitman elevates his own status to the divine level and becomes a god. He anticipates his inclusion in the divine pantheon, 'waiting my time to be one of the supremes, / The day getting ready for me when I shall do as much good as the best, and be as prodigious' (1051-1052). He claims to magnify and outbid the achievements of Jehovah, Kronos, Zeus, Hercules, Osiris, Isis, Belus, Brahma, Buddha, and others. In 'A Song of Joys' he celebrates the death of the body and the subsequent deification of the soul, wondering what it will be like 'To be indeed a God!' (150). In 'To Him that Was Crucified' he likens himself to Christ and others before and since who 'labor together transmitting the same charge and succession' (5). In 'Songs of Parting' he intones what it is 'To be this incredible God I am!' (29).

The godlike persona is also found in 'Song of the Open Road', in which the speaker ordains himself 'loos'd of limits and imaginary lines, / Going where I list, my own master total and absolute' (53-54). Thus freed of the restraints of human consciousness he then inhales 'great draughts of space', claiming, 'The east and west are mine, and the north and the south are mine. / I am larger, better than I thought, / I did not know I held so much goodness' (58-61). In 'Song of Myself' he takes such rhetoric to truly heretical extremes:

---

33 Glimm, *Five essays on mystical experience in the works of Wordsworth, Coleridge, and Shelley*, 9.

34 Garber, 'Point of view and the egotistical sublime', 417.

And I said to my spirit *When we become enfolders of those orbs, and the pleasure and knowledge of every thing in them, shall we be fill'd and satisfied then?*
And my spirit said *No, we but level that lift to pass and continue beyond.* (1221-1222)

Which is to say, of course, that when his consciousness encompasses the entire cosmos, he will not be content but must continue expanding and becoming more omnipotent and godlike. Critics who read Whitman in Christian terms tend to overlook such passages, which forcefully challenge orthodox ideas. To claim the poet is a Christian in spite of himself is to read selectively and to force one's interpretation. It is to willfully overlook that Whitman repeatedly expresses ideas for which he would have been persecuted in other epochs.

It is important to remember that he is not exhibiting a form of megalomania in declaring himself God, for all human beings are equally godlike in Whitman's religion. What he possesses over the common person is not an exclusively divine nature but simply a recognition of his own divinity. 'None has begun to think how divine he himself is', as he wrote in 'Starting from Paumanok' (109). His function as poet-god was to awaken other gods through the medium of his verse to the realization that 'as man comes forth, ascends to his place, God disappears, the whole idea of God as presented in the religions disappears'.[35] Human supplants God in Whitman's theology, an idea some critics have likened to the Vedantic concept *tat tvam asi* (thou art that). In Hinduism *atman* (soul) is *brahman* (God), the two being indistinguishable and thus inseparable. 'What do you suppose will satisfy the soul, except to walk free and own no superior?' Whitman rhetorically asks in 'Laws for Creations'. 'What do you suppose I would intimate to you in a hundred ways, but that man or woman is as good as God?' (7-8). Whether or not Whitman consciously reworked this Hindu idea of the soul's equality with the oversoul remains in debate. But in effect he has done so, and the result shakes the foundation of Western theology.

Whitman's conception of God is thus problematic. In some passages he seems to subscribe to theistic notions of the Western God:

O Thou transcendent,
Nameless, the fibre and the breath,
Light of the light, shedding forth iverses, thou centre of them,
Thou mighty centre of the true, the good, the loving,
Thou moral, spiritual fountain... ('Passage to India' 194-198)

In the same poem, however, God is an 'Elder Brother', and the individual soul is the younger brother who 'melts in fondness in his arms' (222, 223). The two are essentially the same, as the soul contains within itself the totality of God –

[35] Chari, *Whitman in the light of Vedantic mysticism*, 135.

an idea running against the grain of the Christian notion of the utter separation of soul and God. In a homoerotically charged moment Whitman also calls God a 'hugging and loving bed-fellow' who sleeps at his side through the night 'and withdraws at the peep of the day with stealthy tread' ('Starting From Paumanok' 60). God is thus a 'Lover divine and perfect Comrade' ('Gods' 1). Here, too, he is challenging traditional theism, for 'God' is not some transcendent abstraction utterly removed from the world but 'the Ideal man, / Fair, able, beautiful, content, and loving, / Complete in body and dilate in spirit' (4-7).

Elsewhere Whitman challenges the monotheistic bedrock upon which the Western traditions have constructed their faiths. 'Did you suppose there could be only one Supreme?' he asks in his 1855 'Preface'. 'We affirm there can be unnumbered Supremes, and that one does not countervail another any more than one eyesight countervails another [...] and that men can be as good or grand only of the consciousness of their supremacy within them' (304-308). His most famous schema, found in 'Chanting the Square Deific', contains four supremes: The 'square' contains both the stern gods of old such as Jehovah and Kronos and the 'cheer-bringing God' – the Christ figure – who offers 'sweet love' and a 'gentle hand' (21, 25, 14). It also interestingly contains a warlike, 'evil' god – 'crafty, despised' and 'full of guile' – as well as 'Santa Spirita', which encompasses both 'Saviour and Satan', pervading all life and existing in the absolute beyond (28, 31, 36, 40). Although this poem is often taken to be Whitman's definitive articulation on God, it seems more likely, considering the many contradictory passages in *Leaves*, that his God changed with his mood and perspective. A statement in verse-chant 48 of 'Song of Myself' perhaps most accurately encapsulates his theology: 'I hear and behold God in every object, yet understand God not in the least, / Nor do I understand who there can be more wonderful than myself' (1281-82). 'God' for Whitman was everywhere – within the self and out there in the world, but to attempt to understand God intellectually was an impossibility that leads to self-contradiction and seeming incoherence. Nevertheless, 'the notion of a deity whose immanent nature courses its way upward through all creation toward its transcendent source remained constant' in his poetry.[36] The poet's God was in nature, in the self, and in the great beyond all at once.

Wordsworth's conceptions of God and soul are not nearly as heterodox, but they are similarly problematic. The individual soul does have the 'godlike power' to create by using the imagination (*Prelude* IV. 156). Much like God, the soul can give shape to the shapeless. The agency he attributes to the individual soul transcends the Christian conception of the soul as standing midway between

---

[36] Keubrich, 'Whitman's new theism', 229.

God and the natural world in the great chain of being. The soul is elevated to a much higher status, and its power approaches, though never eclipses, that of God's. As James Engell has argued, the Romantic concept of the soul in many respects stands 'outside Christian doctrine', as it is seldom allied 'with a specific theology or organized religion'.[37] Wordsworth's conception of the soul is, particularly in the earliest poetry, 'undogmatic, free from doctrinal overlay, and not associated primarily with orthodox religious belief'.[38] '[T]here's not a man / That lives', Wordsworth wrote in Book Third of *The Prelude*, 'who hath not had his god-like hours, / And knows not what majestic sway we have / As natural beings in the strength of Nature' (191-194). Regrettably, this 'majestic sway' becomes simply 'an empire we inherit' when Wordsworth revised the passage for the 1850 version. Perhaps sensing his own attribution to the individual soul of too much God-power, he changed his rhetoric to reflect a more passive, more orthodox conception of the soul's place in the cosmos.

David Rogers has argued that Wordsworth's gradual movement towards orthodoxy began as early as 1797 in his poem, 'Lines Left upon a Seat in a Yew-tree', which is a record of the poet's 'first step toward an adult acceptance of Christianity'.[39] Rogers reaches this conclusion because the virtues Wordsworth recommends in the poem – love and humility – 'are eminently Christian virtues'.[40] In another essay, 'God and Pre-existence in Wordsworth's Immortality Ode', Rogers also claims the God in the Ode 'is unquestionably Christian' because the qualities the poet assigns to It are those of the Christian God of love.[41] Although I do not dispute Rogers' observations entirely, I would suggest they need some qualification. Christians have not cornered the religious market on love and humility, for other traditions have prized such virtues as well. Moreover, Wordsworth's trend towards orthodoxy may indeed have begun as early as 1797, but the movement away from heterodoxy did not occur in a straight line, as there are many passages in the pre-1807 poetry that would render such Christian readings deeply problematic. It might be more appropriate to say that 1797 marks the beginning of the poet's *conflicted* version of Christianity. Consciously, he may have begun to interweave Christian concepts in his verse, but it would take many years before 'the heavy frost' of orthodoxy would encrust his great spirit.[42]

---

[37] James Engell, 'The soul, highest cast of consciousness', in: Taylor & Bain, *The cast of consciousness*, 5 & 3.

[38] Engell, 'The soul, highest cast of consciousness', 13.

[39] David Rogers, 'God and pre-existence in Wordsworth's immortality ode', in: *Durham University Journal* 30 (1969), 88.

[40] Rogers, 'God and pre-existence in Wordsworth's immortality ode', 88.

[41] Idem, 145.

[42] Bloom, *The visionary company*, 195.

R.D. Havens has argued, in contrast to Rogers, that Wordsworth's sense of 'one life in all things', as he depicts it in *The Prelude*, is seldom connected with the Christian deity.[43] The one life is more of 'an impersonal force' not to be confused with orthodox conceptions of God.[44] In 'Wordsworth's ontology of love in "The Prelude"', Richard Gravil has similarly noted that when Wordsworth speaks of 'the Power or the eternal Spirit', he seems to have in mind 'something in which it is man's glory to participate, but nothing as anthropomorphic as the Anglican god'.[45] Klaus Mortensen has gone so far as to argue that God for Wordsworth is 'no longer the Supreme Creator God, raised high above the work of creation, for he is woven together with man's elementary emotional nature and its genesis'.[46] While I agree with all three critics, I would also insist on some qualification here as well. Wordsworth did, in fact, often subvert traditional conceptions of God, but, unlike Whitman, he did not wage full-scale war on the Christian deity. There are enough passages in his verse to bolster either a heterodox or an orthodox version of the poet depending on one's perspective. Romanticism is something of a defensive reaction to the first signs of the disappearance of God, as Leon Waldoff has observed, which means it necessarily should contain a certain degree of nostalgia for traditional religious ideas while also subverting those ideas to meet the needs of an increasingly secularized world.[47]

In 'Wordsworth's Panentheism' Daniel Dombrowski has perceptively noted that Wordsworth typically avoids pantheistic and traditionally theistic extremes in offering a nature-oriented 'panentheistic' vision in which God is *both* immanent and transcendent.[48] I agree with the general thrust of this argument, particularly considering Evelyn Underhill's definition of mystical perception as 'the dual apprehension of the transcendent yet immanent God', which is in accord with Dombrowski's definition of panentheism.[49] But such a reading is also not without its problems, as theism can affirm both God's immanent presence in history and his transcendence, according to David Keubrich.[50] Keubrich also claims it is wrong to state that Christian mysticism denies the senses and the natural world.[51] So there is a considerable measure of indeterminacy in Wordsworth's

---

[43] Keith A. Gould, 'Panentheism in "The Prelude"', in: Donna Fricke & Douglas Fricke (Eds.), *Aeolian Harps*, Bowling Green: Bowling Green University Press, 1976, 120.
[44] Gould, 'Panentheism in "The Prelude"', 120.
[45] Gravil, 'Wordsworth's ontology of love in "The Prelude"', 238.
[46] Mortensen, *The time of unrememberable being*, 30.
[47] Waldoff, 'Wordsworth's healing power', 148.
[48] Dombrowski, 'Wordsworth's panentheism', 138.
[49] Underhill, *Mysticism*, 246.
[50] Keubrich, 'Whitman's new theism', 230.
[51] Idem, 232.

conception of God, which is most accurately called *Wordsworthian* above all else. No doubt, it is significantly informed by the Western tradition in which the poet lived, but it also departs from that tradition enough to render it highly problematic.

In addition to its troubling conceptions of God, Whitman's religion is problematic in its inclusion of sin and immorality, both of which he welcomed with open arms. 'Lusts and wickedness are acceptable to me', he wrote in 'You Felons on Trial in Court'. 'I walk with delinquents with passionate love, / I feel I am of them – I belong to those convicts and prostitutes myself' (12-14). In aligning himself with these social pariahs he is clearly taking a swipe at polite, genteel manners, but he is also challenging exclusionary religious doctrines that would consider such individuals outside of the Christian fold. Whitman is thus 'not the poet of goodness only', as he claims in 'Song of Myself'. 'I do not decline to be the poet of wickedness also' (463). 'What blurt is this about virtue and vice?' he asks in perhaps his most radical tone (464). He did not believe in morality per se, for mindless observance of behavioral codes did little to cosmically expand consciousness. The 'best that can be said for ritualistic legalism', according to Huxley, 'is that it improves conduct [...] A Puritan may practice all virtue and still be thoroughly bad'.[52] Morality for its own sake simply did not serve the poet's brand of religion, which accounts for his attempts to turn the Christian behavioral code on its head.

James Miller has commented that spiritual purification for Whitman is achieved by 'celebrating what has been reviled and degraded'.[53] Whitman's strong and open advocacy of human sexuality and what he believed to be its inherent cleanliness support such an idea. In 'Song of Myself' (among many other poems) he prided himself on being the one to shatter the moral paradigm on sexuality:

> Through me forbidden voices,
> Voices of sex and lusts, voices veil'd and I remove the veil,
> Voices indecent by me clarified and transfigur'd.
> I do not press my fingers across my mouth,
> I keep as delicate around the bowels as around the head and heart,
> Copulation is no more rank to me than death is. (516-521)

He even claims to worship his 'Firm masculine colter' and its 'rich blood', that is, its semen, or what he also calls the 'milky stream pale strippings of my life' (530, 532). 'And sexual organs and acts! do you concentrate in me', he wrote in 'Starting from Paumanok', 'for I am determin'd to tell you with courageous clear voice to prove you illustrious' (166). David Reynolds has demonstrated

---

[52] Huxley, *The Doors of Perception & Heaven and Hell*, 98.
[53] Miller, *A critical guide to Leaves of Grass*, 15.

that such rhetoric participates in the (then) newly emergent discourse of physiology, which captivated the poet with its frank, open, and neutral discussion of the body and its drives.[54] But Whitman infuses this discourse with his own cosmic rhetoric. Copulation becomes a divine act, and sexual energy in general is transmuted into sacred power. Particularly in the 'Children of Adam' sequence, sexuality takes on an otherworldly luster, as it is associated and often commingled with the movement toward transcendence, as Harold Aspiz has observed.[55]

Because of Whitman's candid celebration of sexuality, he was fired from his position as a clerk in the Federal Indian Bureau, which was a sinecure for which he did little work in return for twelve hundred dollars per year.[56] When James Harlan, the Secretary of the Interior and a fanatical Methodist, realized Whitman was the author of the scandalous and indecent *Leaves of Grass*, he promptly terminated the poet's position. If Whitman were as complicit in Christian doctrine as some critics have argued, it is unlikely *Leaves* would have caused such a stir. Even Emerson, who, as Brahma Sharma has argued, significantly subverted Christianity in a variety of ways, was appalled at Whitman's bravura.[57] Before the publication of the 1856 version, which contained the controversial 'Children of Adam' poems, Emerson met with the poet to try to persuade him to expurgate the edition. Whitman, however, was adamant in his refusal to be censored, even by someone whom he genuinely admired such as Emerson. In his response to the Concord philosopher, he claimed that countless 'savans, poets, historians, [and] biographers' before him had by either silence or obedience helped to perpetuate what he calls the 'filthy law' that prevented open discussion about sexuality.[58] He wanted to be the one to rectify the matter.

In his impulse to liberate the 'amativeness of Nature' from its repressive constraints, Whitman claimed 'Nothing is sinful outside of ourselves [...] we are beautiful or sinful in ourselves only' ('By Blue Ontario's Shore' 20, 21). Sin for Whitman resulted from believing that what is natural is sinful; it resulted from subscribing to the general Western attitude towards nature and the body as unclean and thus spiritually impure. Sounding like Blake, he thus claims, 'The pleasures of heaven are with me and the pains of hell are with me, / The first I graft and increase upon myself, the latter I translate into a new tongue' ('Song of Myself' 423-424). Roger Asselineau argued that the Christian notion of sin

---

54 Reynolds, *Walt Whitman's America*, 250.

55 Aspiz, 'Sexuality and the language of transcendence', 1.

56 Asselineau, *The evolution of Walt Whitman*, 178.

57 Brahma Dutt Sharma, 'The echoes of the Bhagavadgita in R.W. Emerson', in: T.R. Sharma (Ed.), *Influence of Bhagavadgita on literature written in English*, Meerut, India: Shalabh, 1988, 52.

58 Qtd. in Bradley & Blodgett, *Leaves of Grass*, 739.

and retribution persisted in Whitman's verse.[59] Such a comment seems unlikely, however, given Whitman's general orientation towards Christianity's repressive morality. What Asselineau calls retribution is more properly situated within the context of the Eastern idea of *karma*, with which the poet was no doubt familiar, as V.K. Chari and other scholars have shown.

Whitman's problematic religion also included evil: His poems, he declares in 'Whoever You Are Holding Me Now in Hand, 'will do just as much evil, perhaps more', as they will do good (36). He is *himself* 'just as much evil as good', as he claims in 'Starting From Paumanok' (100). And yet, he is playing with the word in an attempt to shock the reader's complacency, as Denise Askin has observed.[60] He is also redefining it to be a type of good. He thus says in the same line, 'I say there is in fact no evil, / (Or if there is it is just as important to you, to the land or to me, as anything else)' (100-101). The poet did not naively deny the existence of evil, as Malcolm Cowley observed,[61] for he knew the horrors of the Civil War with its heaps of amputated limbs and many other highly disagreeable sights, the details of which he recounts in *Specimen Days* (26, 35, 78). Evil, rather, 'existed only as part of a universally perfect design'.[62] Underlying the evil in the world is an inherent unity, according to Whitman, the monistic cosmos, which renders everything trivial by comparison.

He may have gotten such an idea from Emerson, who, as Marjorie Elder points out, believed evil was the result of one's perspective and man's disunity with himself.[63] The poet is thus '[v]ery devilish to some, and very divine to some', depending on the reader's relative point of view and state of consciousness, as he claimed in an 'anonymous' review he published in 1855.[64] When pressed on the point of justifying the presence of evil in the world, however, Whitman realized he could put forth no compelling argument to satisfy the skeptics. 'I sit and look out', he says in an eponymous poem, 'upon all the sorrows of the world, and upon all oppression and shame', but he cannot offer a rationalization and can only conclude: 'All these – all the meanness and agony without end I sitting look out upon, / See, hear, and am silent' (1, 9-10). The presence of this underlying good, this unity beyond all division, can only be intuited and never articulated rationally through language.

He may also have gotten such an idea from Wordsworth, who wrote on the question of evil in his 1802 Preface to *Lyrical Ballads*:

---

59 Asselineau, *The evolution of Walt Whitman*, 75.

60 Askin, 'Whitman's theory of evil', 123.

61 Cowley, 'Introduction', 924.

62 Idem, 925-926.

63 Marjorie Elder, *Nathaniel Hawthorne: Transcendental symbolist*, Athens: Ohio University Press, 1969, 20.

64 Qtd. in Bradley & Blodgett, *Leaves of Grass*, 777.

> I should be oppressed with no dishonorable melancholy, had I not a deep impression of certain inherent and indestructible qualities of the human mind, and likewise of certain powers in the great and permanent objects that act upon it, which are equally inherent and indestructible.[65]

Wordsworth, too, believed in an underlying unity behind all things, calling it various names such as 'one life', 'power', 'imagination', and 'God' among others. His idea of 'paradise' includes both good and evil, as Abrams pointed out in *Natural Supernaturalism*.[66] It ranks higher than Milton's paradise, according to Abrams, because it reconciles contraries in its magnitude. Evil as such is merely division or separation from the whole,[67] which is why Wordsworth so frequently collapses opposed categories and transcends philosophical dualism.[68]

Critics generally dislike the sense of joy and unity that pervades Wordsworth's verse, a criticism they often level at Whitman as well, because they feel it denies sociopolitical realities. How could there be inherent unity in the world amidst so much discord, strife, hunger, genocide, racism, and the many other evils? Such critics believe Wordsworth only *met* the harsher realities of life while never *confronting* them, and they find his optimism 'cloying', as Jenny Guest put it.[69] Wordsworthian joy, according to this view, is a naive avoidance of what really matters in life – correcting social ills and combating tyranny. In refuting this criticism Abrams acknowledges that the Romantic poets in general 'were not *complete* poets, in that they represent little of the social dimension of human experience; for although they insist on the importance of the community, they express this matter largely as a profound need of the individual consciousness'.[70] Nevertheless, Romantic poets, particularly Wordsworth and Whitman, 'were almost obsessively occupied with the reality and rationale of the agonies of the human condition'.[71] More important, they acknowledged suffering and evil as playing 'an indispensable role in making the man and the poet more fully, consciously, integrally, and maturely human'.[72] Evil was thus necessary in the soul-making process, but to subsume it into a larger conceptual overview 'is not to annul it, or to lessen the pain of suffering'.[73]

Wordsworth, therefore, did not avoid the treatment of evil and suffering in his verse. Critics level such a charge because of their own pessimism, which is

---

65 Qtd. in Wordsworth, *Selected poems*, 437.
66 Abrams, *Natural supernaturalism*, 116.
67 Huxley, *The Doors of Perception & Heaven and Hell*, 11.
68 Medhusudan, 'Wordsworth', 66.
69 Guest, 'Wordsworth and the music of humanity', 16.
70 Abrams, *Natural supernaturalism*, 443.
71 Ibidem.
72 Idem, 444.
73 Ibidem.

at odds with any profound sense of joy. Wordsworth's decision to privilege joy over despair is by no means an unconscious one made as a result of his conscious distress when faced with overwhelming evil. It is a mature decision to cultivate a psychological sense of healthy-mindedness, which, as William James argued, 'is anything but absurd'.[74] 'I turned away / And walked along my road in happiness', as the Pedlar declares (926-927). Healthy-mindedness allows for the development of a healthy ego amidst adverse situations, and nearly all people practice it to a degree.[75] To fault Wordsworth and other Romantics for not having a better sense of 'realities' is thus to say that psychological health is unimportant; it is to say that if there is evil in the world one must carry its weight at all times and experience no joy until it is eradicated; it is to say that one must commit psychological suicide because other people suffer.

III

If one ignores the materialist dismissal of religion as a detriment to society and acknowledges that it does indeed serve a deep psychological function, then it seems Wordsworth and Whitman are more connected to humanity than some scholars realize, for the poetry of both, however heterodox, serves a religious function. In 'Cosmic Counterfeit: Wordsworth and the Question of Romantic Religion', Nancy Easterlin argues that 'neither Wordsworth's work specifically nor literature as a whole can legitimately function as a substitute for religion'.[76] Easterlin's argument, however, rests upon a too-narrow definition of religion, which she claims implies a 'stabilized conception of reality' and has nothing to do with accessing altered paths of consciousness.[77] When the term 'religion and its appropriate feelings are divorced from a stable form of worship', she adds, 'the believer begins to suspect the veracity of either or both his feelings and his concept of the divine'.[78] Such a comment ignores the immense body of mystical literature, which contains countless examples of religious feelings divorced from stable forms of worship. Mystics are 'aplomb in the midst of irrational things', as Whitman put it. It also overlooks whole religions such as Buddhism and Hinduism, the basis of which is the transformation of consciousness Easterlin says has no place in religion. Easterlin's work insightfully demonstrates the conflicted

---

[74] James, *The varieties of religious experience*, 90.

[75] Ibidem.

[76] Nancy Easterlin, *Cosmic counterfeit: Wordsworth and the question of Romantic religion* (Diss. Temple University, Philadelphia, 1991), viii.

[77] Easterlin, *Cosmic counterfeit*, 20 & 30.

[78] Idem, 28.

religious vision in Wordsworth's verse, but I take exception to her general argument, which imposes a strictly Western understanding of religion on Wordsworth's spirituality.

Religion does not necessarily imply a stabilized conception of reality and stable forms of worship. Such a definition applies to Western *orthodox* religion. Religious *experiences*, in fact, typically upset stabilized conceptions of reality. Although they can bolster traditional forms of worship, such experiences can also undermine orthodoxy. Buddha, Jesus, and Mohammed, for instance, all broke from traditional forms of worship as a result of mystical visions that forever altered their conceptions of reality. Mystics often renew traditions, as Jess Hollenback observes; they do not passively receive their religion.[79] Religious experience, particularly mysticism, is at the heart of religion, as King and others have argued.[80] Although there are clear distinctions between religion and mysticism, as Wayne Teasdale argues, the two are not mutually exclusive.[81] There is, in fact, a direct connection. In *The Varieties of Religious Experience* William James highlighted the experiential aspects of religion:

> Religion, therefore, as I now ask you to arbitrarily to take it, shall mean for us *the feelings, acts, and experiences of individual men in their solitude, so far as they apprehend themselves to stand in relation to whatever they may consider to be the divine.* Since the relation may be either moral, physical, or ritual, it is evident that out of religion in the sense in which we take it, theologies, philosophies, and ecclesiastical organizations may secondarily grow.[82]

Heterodoxy, perhaps equally as much as orthodoxy, thus defines religion. To define religion strictly as orthodox superstructure, to use a Marxist image, is to ignore its heterodox base. It is this heterodox base that traditionalists often elide. T.S. Eliot, for instance, spoke with contempt about a 'psychological mysticism [...] which seeks contact with the sources of supernatural power, divorced from religion and theology'.[83] To dismiss such experiences as 'non-religious', however, is to forget the mystical experiences, which are divorced from religion and theology, lying at the source of all religions. Mystical discourse is generally seen as bordering on blasphemy, as Shira Wolosky has observed, but such heterodoxy is, however paradoxically, the source of orthodoxy.[84]

It is this central paradox that scholars overlook when they dismiss the 'religious' aspects of Romantic verse. In his excellent study, *Romantic Horizons*, James

[79] Jess Byron Hollenback, *Mysticism: Experience, response, and empowerment*, University Park, PA: Penn State University Press, 1996, 119.

[80] King, *Christian mystics*, 8.

[81] Teasdale, *The mystic heart*, 10.

[82] James, *The varieties of religious experience*, xxi.

[83] Qtd. in Spencer, 'Mysticism in T.S. Eliot's four quartets', 232.

[84] Wolosky, 'The metaphysics of language in Emily Dickinson', 26.

Twitchell claims Wordsworth's verse is not religion per se but expanded consciousness, as though the one excluded the other.[85] Although I am heavily indebted to Professor Twitchell's fine research, I disagree with him on this point, for the expansion of consciousness can serve as the basis of a religion. Zen Buddhism is a case in point. Although it is a 'Godless creed', and although the central focus in Zen is not worship or ritualistic observance but the enlightenment of a practitioner's consciousness, it nevertheless qualifies as a religion, according to James.[86]

Religion, according to Donald Marshall, 'is intuition of the universe', a non-rational sense of the cosmos.[87] The religious aspects of *The Prelude*, he thus argues, are found not in the traditional symbols or dogma of Christianity 'but the recovery of the intuition that is itself ramified into those symbols and dogmas and whose omnipresence gives that specific faith its individuality'.[88] In other words Wordsworth takes Christianity back to its origins by not simply 'parrot[ing] its lexicon'.[89] He transforms the tradition instead of blindly adhering to its rituals. In 'Written in London, September, 1802' he lamented the loss of the 'our peace, our fearful innocence, / And pure religion breathing household laws' (13-14). Much of his heterodox cosmic rhetoric was an attempt to restore this 'pure religion' – a vehicle for the transformation of consciousness.

Klaus Mortensen has noted what he calls a 'metaphysical implosion' during the 18th century.[90] Ideas normally associated with orthodoxy are 'moved from the confessional, religious, institutional sphere to an aesthetic-religious sphere [...] Thus during the 18th century art clearly acquires metaphysical functions, not as a servant of an institution, but in its own right and in its own name'.[91] Wordsworth's milieu was one of increasing secularization and antagonism towards traditional religious thought. The Enlightenment program of demystification seriously challenged the fundamental religious concepts that informed many of the assumptions upon which much thinking was based. Wordsworth's religion was heterodox by necessity. Because traditional religious concepts were being demystified by Enlightenment thinkers, he was forced to revise his religion by offering a purer version of Christianity. At least, such an impulse is found in his earlier cosmic rhetoric. Easterlin argues that Wordsworth was not fully conscious of his attempts to recreate religion, claiming he is thus a poet 'of limited self-awareness'

---

[85] Twitchell, *Romantic horizons*, 23.

[86] James, *The varieties of religious experience*, 34.

[87] Marshall, 'Religion and literature after Enlightenment', 56.

[88] Idem, 63.

[89] Idem, 64.

[90] Mortensen, *The time of unrememberable being*, 30.

[91] Ibidem.

– a point to which I vehemently object.[92] As Easterlin herself shows, Wordsworth moved steadily towards orthodoxy as he aged. No doubt, he grew increasingly conscious of the incompatibility of his earlier mysticism and his later adherence to orthodox Anglican dogma. But to say he lacks self-awareness is to elide the intensely subjective mystical experiences of the earlier verse, which Easterlin herself acknowledges. Wordsworth knew all too well what he was doing, as his poetry is too steeped in religious rhetoric to have been an *unconscious* challenge to secularization. Wordsworth made a conscious choice not to become a clergy member, and yet his religious rhetoric equals Blake's in the frequency and intensity with which it appears in his verse. John Mahoney best captures Wordsworth's religious orientation in calling it a 'secular faith' – an oxymoron that poetically reveals the kind of indeterminacy that is characteristic of the English poet's religion.[93]

The question of religion in Whitman is equally fraught with critical disagreement. Perhaps because Whitman claimed to 'inaugurate a religion' and because he positioned himself as a poet of love who offered both solace and a refuge from the cares of the world, overly zealous readers have embraced his verse as an actual religion ('Starting from Paumanok' 102). *The Christian Spiritualist*, a Swedenborgian magazine, for instance, hailed *Leaves of Grass* as a bridge from the 'diseased mentalities of the past' to a new 'Spirit-life'.[94] Whitman himself, the writer claimed, possessed a 'new life flowing down from heaven', which suggested of course that the poet was some sort of prophet or mystic.[95] Many other 'Whitmaniacs', as Roger Asselineau has called them, saw Whitman as the equal of Christ, the founder of a new religion, and took pride in following his doctrine.[96] These early disciples actually formed a loose confederation called 'The Walt Whitman Fellowship', with chapters in New York, Philadelphia, Boston, Chicago, Atlanta, Knoxville, Toronto, and Bolton, England among other places.[97] *The Conservator*, a periodical edited by one of Whitman's most fervent followers, Horace Traubel, was also used as a means to disseminate the poet's new gospel.[98]

George Hutchinson, however, claims the poet does not offer 'full-fledged religion; instead he presents several fundamental religious insights [...] and a form of religious experience that may be found in numerous types of mysticism probably because it provided the foundation for all of them'.[99] While Hutchinson's

92 Easterlin, *Cosmic counterfeit*, 20.
93 Mahoney, 'Critical methodology and writing about religion and literature', 92.
94 Qtd. in Allen, *A reader's guide to Walt Whitman*, 11.
95 Ibidem.
96 Asselineau, *The evolution of Walt Whitman*, 250.
97 Keubrich, 'Whitman's new theism', 1.
98 James, *The varieties of religious experience*, 85.
99 Hutchinson, *The ecstatic Whitman*, xiii.

comment is thoroughly in keeping with my argument, it is important to remember that Whitman did seem to believe he was inaugurating a new religion. In a journal entry from June, 1857 he wrote the following: '*The Great Construction of the New Bible.* Not to be diverted from the principal object – the main life work – the Three Hundred & Sixty five [poems] – it ought to be ready in 1859'.[100] Critics generally agree that this new Bible is nothing other than the 1860 version of *Leaves*, as many of the newer poems seemed to be 'born of the same mood or mystical spirit' as the original twelve untitled poems that appeared in 1855.[101] So Whitman did want to begin a new religion, or he wanted at the least to significantly reform Christianity as to render it compatible with the 19th century.

In *Democratic Vistas* he attempted to name his religious orientation, which he called 'personalism', and which he believed was the backbone of his fledgling American culture: '[T]he vertebration of the manly and womanly personalism of our western world, can only be, and is, indeed, to be, (I hope,) its all penetrating Religiousness. The ripeness of Religion is doubtless to be looked for in this field of individuality, and is a result that no organization or church can ever achieve' (233). He wanted his poetry to serve two functions, as David Keubrich points out: 'to promote the spiritual development of his readers and to provide them with a coherent vision which would integrate their religious experience with the dominant modes of thought and action'.[102] Whitman's greatest ambition, as Gay Wilson Allen observed, 'was to become a moral leader', but the morality he hoped to instill in his readers was thoroughly redefined, unfettered, and serving the interest of consciousness expansion rather than providing a legalistic structure for the promulgation of a new behavioral code.[103]

Roger Asselineau has demonstrated that as a boy Whitman read Volney's *The Ruins*, which portrays religion as consisting of domination by priests and kings.[104] The work profoundly affected the poet, who was also being raised in a Quaker household itself at odds with mainstream Christianity. And yet, as Bruce Allen Bercquist has argued, the Bible exerted a significant, often overlooked, influence on the poet.[105] It is the biblical quality in *Leaves*, in fact, that proved so offensive to many early readers, who viewed the poet's rhetoric as being too audacious, as the authors of *Start with the Sun* observed.[106] Transcendentalism, it should be

---

100 Qtd. in Loving, *Walt Whitman*, 234.
101 Idem, 238.
102 Keubrich, 'Whitman's new theism', 2.
103 Allen, *The solitary singer*, 900.
104 Asselineau, *The evolution of Walt Whitman*, 45.
105 Bercquist, *Walt Whitman and the Bible*, 5.
106 Miller, Shapiro, & Slote, *Start with the Sun*, 61.

remembered, was in part born out of the Unitarian movement, which sought to displace the dominant Calvinist doctrines of Puritan New England.[107] Whitman, moreover, admired the oratory of Edward Taylor and Elias Hicks, as opposed to the more secular figures, Webster and Clay, which prompted Michael Sowder to conclude that the poet's 'new theology replicated many features of the Christian and Evangelical culture it repudiated'.[108] Like Wordsworth's religion, Whitman's occupied the middle ground between orthodoxy and heterodoxy. His, too, was a 'secular faith' – a redefinition according to 19th-century standards.

In her otherwise fine study, Easterlin concludes that Blake was the last Romantic who consciously believed he embodied 'the archaic type, the poet-prophet'.[109] The rest of the Romantics, she argues, wrote late enough in history 'to perceive that this type is an anachronism, and all their glorification of the poet's role is largely metaphorical'.[110] Given Whitman's profound religiosity I must refute such a conclusion, for he, like Blake, believed strongly in the spiritual component of his poetic message. He may not have believed he was in the Christian line of prophets, but he nevertheless seemed highly cognizant of the deeply religious nature of his message, however heterodox it may have been. 'When I commenced years ago, writing my poems', he wrote in his 1872 Preface, 'one deep purpose underlay the others – and that has been the Religious purpose' (80, 84-85). Wordsworth, as well, defies Easterlin's conclusion, as he embraced the rhetoric of the poet-prophet with a zealotry far beyond that of a secular literary figure. In the post-revolution age of demoralization, according to M.H. Abrams, Wordsworth attempted to inaugurate 'a revolutionary mode of imaginative perception which accomplishes nothing less than the "creation" of a new world', which is to say, a new state of consciousness.[111]

He attempted to instill in his reader 'a mystic discovery of meaning in an otherwise meaningless universe of appearances'.[112] According to Coleridge in *Biographia Literaria*, moreover, Wordsworth's specific task in *Lyrical Ballads* was 'to give the charm of novelty to things of every day, and to excite a feeling analogous to the supernatural, by awakening the mind's attention from the lethargy of custom and directing it to the loveliness and the wonders of the world before us; an inexhaustible treasure, but for which, in consequence of the film of familiarity and selfish solicitude, we have eyes yet see not, ears that hear not, and

[107] David Robinson, 'Transcendentalism and its times', in: Laporte & Morris, *The Cambridge companion to Ralph Waldo Emerson*, 14.

[108] Sowder, 'Walt Whitman, the apostle', 204.

[109] Easterlin, *Cosmic counterfeit*, 44.

[110] Ibidem.

[111] Abrams, *Natural supernaturalism*, 338.

[112] Ross, *The ecstatic eye*, 28.

hearts that neither feel nor understand'.[113] No doubt, Wordsworth did not believe he was a prophet in the *Old Testament* tradition, but his poetic mission was inseparable from his spiritual orientation. He believed he was 'divinely' inspired in his own sense of the word.

What governs such an exclusion is one's understanding of religion and its overall function. If by 'religion' one means *Western orthodox* religion, then I would agree with much of Easterlin's argument. But if religion is defined more ecumenically, then Wordsworth and Whitman can be read as deeply religious thinkers who offer a version of spirituality more palatable to the modern world. Their verse was intended to fill the void left by secularization, and on those terms they succeeded tremendously. Admittedly, they may be complicit in the rhetorical practices and ideas they ostensibly reject, just as *all* philosophical positions self-deconstruct. The impulse found in Wordsworth's earlier verse and celebrated throughout *Leaves*, however, is subversive enough to be called heterodox, which means it cannot be associated with mainstream religion. Cosmic rhetoric lies somewhere in the unclaimed middle ground.

[113] Coleridge, *Biographia literaria*, 169.

Chapter XI

THE ROOTS OF COSMIC RHETORIC IN WORDSWORTH AND WHITMAN

Romanticism and Mysticism

As I have argued thus far, what connects Wordsworth and Whitman is a type of mystical rhetoric I have preferred to call 'cosmic' because of its departure from traditional mystical discourse. The parallels are too striking to be ignored or dismissed as being coincidental or irrelevant. Although I have shown the ways in which cosmic rhetoric departs from the mystical tradition, I have focused significantly less attention on the ways in which it does participate in mystical discourse. I have done so because I wanted to avoid reading Wordsworth and Whitman as actual mystics, a mistake some scholars have made. Reading both poets in such a way too often yields an oversimplification of a richly complex subject. It also has prevented scholars from focusing on linguistic concerns – an injustice considering that Wordsworth and Whitman were two of the greatest poets in the anglophone tradition. To elide language in favor of religious and/or philosophical issues is to treat a remarkable body of verse as though the skill with which it was rendered is unimportant. But having focused almost exclusively on linguistic concerns in the preceding chapters, I feel it is necessary to demonstrate the extent to which cosmic rhetoric is indeed a type of mystical language. I would also like to provide a context for the origin of such rhetoric in both poets. As I hope to demonstrate, the seeds of cosmic rhetoric are found in the Romantic *Zeitgeist*, if one can be said to have existed.

Let me begin by discussing mysticism and showing parallels in the rhetoric of Wordsworth and Whitman. One feature of mystical consciousness that both William James and Evelyn Underhill, the two leading thinkers on mysticism in the 20th century, recognize, is its ineffable quality. Mystical consciousness cannot be fully conveyed in words. Although reports of such experiences are considerable, and although mystics themselves are 'notoriously garrulous', as R.A. Gilbert notes, the full import of mystical consciousness remains beyond linguistic utterance. Romantic doctrine, too, stated that mysterious, deeper aspects of the universe and human existence could never be fully captured by language. '[You] can convey only by such means as you have at your command, but you know that this cannot convey the whole of what you are seeking to convey because this whole is literally infinite', as Isaiah Berlin put it.[1]

Mystical states are thus 'more like states of feeling than like states of intellect'.[2] Because it is heart-centered, mystical consciousness can only be suggested. Among mystics, consequently, there is frequently a stated aversion to things of the mind:

> Give up your learnedness!
> Thus you shall become free of sorrows.
> Put away holiness, throw away knowledge,
> Thus the people will profit a hundredfold.[3]
> He comes to the thought of those who know him beyond thought,
> Not to those who imagine he can be attained by thought.
> He is unknown to the learned and known to the simple (*Kena Upanishad*).
> This sacred knowledge is not attained by reasoning (*Katha Upanishad*).

Unlike philosophical thought, which breaks things into parts, mystical insight brings things together into a unified whole. 'Philosophy easily can become a game of conceptual counters', writes F.C. Happold. 'The mystic puts aside this game of conceptual counters, relying not on deductive reason but on an intuitive, unifying vision to pierce to the secret'.[4] The 'knowledge' of mystical consciousness is beyond ordinary awareness and is thus beyond expression. 'Mystical consciousness is *nonconceptual*', according to Teasdale; 'it transcends the need for concepts because it knows all things in its eternal now. It does not perceive successive events and individual objects but rather the totality, in every moment of eternity'.[5]

As I have argued in my discussion of cosmic epistemology, Wordsworth and Whitman both put forth an alternative mode of knowing – an orientation towards Being that transcends normal logic, which is seen as so much mental clutter. Both poets privileged love – the supreme heart-sentiment – over all other feelings. The heart became for both the conduit through which divine energies poured. The resulting wisdom, however, could not be expressed in normal linguistic utterance, which compelled each poet to privilege silence, music, and alternative sounds over language as a means of expression.

However ineffable mystical consciousness is, it carries with it what James called a 'noetic quality', which is to say a special kind of knowledge – a 'state of

---

[1] Isaiah Berlin, *The roots of Romanticism*, Princeton: Princeton University Press, 1999, 101.
[2] James, *The varieties of religious experience*, 390.
[3] *Tao Te Ching* (trans. Richard Wilhelm), New York: Penguin, 1990, 19:1-4.
[4] Happold, *Mysticism*, 42.
[5] Teasdale, *The mystic heart*, 22.

insight into depths of truth unplumbed by the discursive intellect'.[6] As a result, the mystic is often endowed with authority because he has glimpsed something beyond the ken of the average person. This is the fountain from which all of the major religions spring forth. The mystic is seen as the conduit through which divine energy flows.

As 'prophets' both poets certainly had a sense of their authority. Seeing themselves as divine conduits, they claimed to bring the things of spirit to those who need it. Although there is a tremendous egalitarian quality in the verse of each, Wordsworth and Whitman also positioned themselves as savior types who would deliver their divine message. Wordsworth played with the accompanying power of such a role, tempering his rhetoric as he aged. Whitman, however, reveled in the possibilities such freedom and power yielded. Whereas Wordsworth played with the idea of being godlike but then recoiled from such a possibility, Whitman supplanted God altogether. He became God, and he embraced godlike power with a subversive zeal far beyond anything seen in previous literature.

Mystical states are highly transient, seldom lasting for more than an hour or two at best, according to James. And once gone, their quality can but imperfectly be reproduced in memory.[7] Mystical states are like dreams in that they are ephemeral and hard to retain in memory once ordinary consciousness returns. Unlike dreams, however, there is a sense of reality in mystical consciousness – a feeling that the vision is real and the 'real' world is a dream. Wordsworth's recurrent neoplatonic elements equate to a similar kind of world-denying consciousness of 'the real'. Although he celebrated the inherent majesty and beauty of nature, he also frequently wrote of the truth behind appearances, and he was inclined towards depicting moments of 'illumination' in which consciousness would be so altered as to allow for numinous perception. Whitman, as well, celebrated nature – perhaps even more than Wordsworth – while also affirming the 'ultimate' reality. For him there could be no physical world without its suffusing spiritual energy.

Mystical consciousness frequently yields a monistic perspective, which is to say, the myriad things of the world are not only interconnected but of one consciousness. Monism is a bitter pill to swallow for skeptics who point to the world's endless number of oppositions. Mystics assert, however, that duality exists only from the perspective of limited awareness. In mystical consciousness, the dichotomies of the world appear illusory. An insight in which everything appears merged into a cohesive, interdependent whole, the monistic perspective obliterates all oppositions and resolves all contraries. Such perfect harmony exists at a

[6] James, *The varieties of religious experience*, 391.
[7] Ibidem.

level of consciousness that is imperceptible from the perspective of the individualized self, and it is available only to those who wade through the shallows of the ego and plunge to the depths of mystical awareness.

Wordsworth and Whitman both believed in an underlying, unifying good that renders all opposites complimentary and all discrete objects connected. They employed this rhetoric of cosmic unity so much, in fact, that detractors have called it a denial of reality. Romance worlds, according to such critics, are thus a betrayal of the oppressed class, as they deflect attention away from sociopolitical injustices and present the reader with an idealized version of society. But such a view reflects the type of individualized consciousness transcended in oceanic moments. Wordsworth and Whitman may not have been directly involved in political affairs, and their verse may in fact be idealized. But their monism should not be dismissed too readily, as it is central to the poetics of each writer. Both saw themselves as engaging in an attempt at human solidarity that transcended the immediate sociopolitical sphere. Both believed their poetry could alter the reader's consciousness and effect the equivalent of a secular form of religious enlightenment. For both poets the monistic perspective was not only for the privileged elite but for all humanity.

Although mystical states can be prepared for and even induced, mystics are often left with the feeling that the experience was a sacred boon not attained by an exertion of the conscious will. Mystical consciousness is not attained by mystics but bestowed upon them. 'Although the oncoming of mystical states may be facilitated by preliminary voluntary operations [...] the mystic feels as if his own will were in abeyance, and indeed sometimes as if he were grasped and held by a superior power'.[8] Buddhists actually attempt to cultivate what they call *sunyata* (emptiness), which is a state of being in which a person achieves a vacuity of the lower ego-self by extinguishing its desires and cares. Underhill disagrees with James on this point, arguing that 'true mysticism is active and practical, not passive and theoretical. It is an organic life-process, a something which the whole self does...'.[9] The two viewpoints, however, are not irreconcilable. In relinquishing the conscious will, as James claims is necessary, the awareness then expands to encompass the complete Self. As Thomas Merton wrote in *New Seeds of Contemplation*: 'In order to become myself I must cease to be what I always thought I wanted to be; and in order to find myself I must go out of myself; and in order to live I have to die'.[10]

As John Rudy observed in his excellent study, *Wordsworth and the Zen Mind*, Wordsworthian consciousness is often equivalent to the 'wise passiveness' the

---

8 James, *The varieties of religious experience*, 392.

9 Underhill, *Mysticism*, 81.

10 Thomas Merton, *New seeds of contemplation*, New York: New Directions, 1972, 47.

poet puts forth as an ideal in 'Expostulation and Reply'. No doubt, Wordsworth does exercise his imaginative power, celebrating its glory and the freedom and redemption it yields. But in all of the key mystical moments he *receives* otherworldly intimations when he lets go of his hold on rational consciousness. Such receptivity allows for a monistic perception in which subject and object collapse inwardly upon each other. Whitman likewise significantly reveled in the power of self. *Leaves* is sometimes interpreted as an individualistic gospel with little regard for anything outside of its solipsistic world. And yet, the poet's mystical moments are typically bestowed upon him. He is thus raped by his soul in 'Song of Myself', and countless other examples of his mysticism seem to exhibit Wordsworth's 'wise passiveness' in that they loosen the poet's grip on rational awareness and allow him to perceive monistically.

Self-dissolution is thus another characteristic of mystical consciousness. It might be more appropriate to say that the phenomenal ego, or that which is commonly associated with selfhood, is transcended. According to mysticism, the emotions, the personality, and the rational mind do not constitute the real self. The soul, rather, which is a non-individualized nothingness/somethingness connected to all life, is the true reality from the perspective of mystical consciousness. Teasdale, however, refutes this ego/soul dichotomy, arguing that the 'mystical path is [...] psychologically *integrative*: it unites the unconscious, the conscious, and the superconscious'.[11] No doubt, consciousness is retained in mystical experiences, which bolsters Teasdale's assertion.

As I argued in chapter four, both poets portray a mode of consciousness in opposition to the will to will. Self-dissolution occupies a significant position in their cosmic rhetoric. Both poets frequently question the nature of identity, suggesting that self may not be as fixed and determinate as it seems. Wordsworth's countless oceanic moments attest to such self-dissolution, as they fostered in him an immense sense of empathy that allowed for sympathetic merging. The oceanic not only allowed him to see into the life of things and into the souls of others; it also gave him Nature's wisdom – the insight that all things of the physical world are bound together in a unified whole. Wordsworth's sense of the sublime, as well, necessarily entailed the temporary dissolution of self. In perceiving a sublime object the percipient's sense of individuality is threatened because it is forced to acknowledge something significantly greater than itself. Whitman took Wordsworthian sympathy to a new level by merging his identity not only with nature but also with other people. He frequently questions whether his individual sense of self is real, finding in oceanic moments a significantly expanded identity. Self even expands in Whitman to become God. When he

[11] Teasdale, *The mystic heart*, 25.

takes on such a persona he can speak as though there is no separate self, as though there are no universal boundaries whatsoever. He can then transcend space and time, freely moving forward into the future and across the globe.

For the scholars of the purist camp, the mystical experience is incomplete without the element of love. According to Bruno Borchert, the mystical experience can best be described in terms of being in love with another person. 'Replace [the one with the other], and you have a rough and ready description of mysticism in general. As a matter of fact, mystical experience is often felt and described by mystics, themselves, in terms of being in love, and their lives are a love affair with the all-embracing reality that permeates and surpasses mundane existence'.[12] Love is the ultimate truth in mysticism, for it gives meaning to an otherwise strange but valueless experience. Love, according to mystics, is the reason for consciousness itself. As I argued in chapter nine, Wordsworth and Whitman are the supreme poets of love. Their cosmic rhetoric culminates in a mystical vision of love as the great leveler of hierarchies, the equalizer of all things in the cosmos. Love is the highest value in Romantic poetics, and it serves as a kind of spiritual cement connecting not only human to human but mind to matter. Love spans the gulf over the Cartesian schism, allowing both poets the ability to heal fragmented consciousness and to make whole what Enlightenment thought had torn asunder.

The extent to which cosmic rhetoric participates in mystical discourse is thus significant. It is safe to say that despite the many ways in which it departs from mysticism, cosmic rhetoric is sufficiently mystical to be considered an attenuated form of mysticism. The question thus arises: From where did Wordsworth and Whitman get such language? Let me begin to answer this question by stating that mysticism is generally considered to be a transhistorical phenomenon of consciousness occurring in many cultures and eras the world over. Although the experience is undoubtedly conditioned by the cultural milieu in which it occurs, it also seems to be in some ways independent of time and place. While cultural context determines not only the form but often the content of the experience, there do seem to be enough features of mystical consciousness to allow for its recognition among many disparate traditions. I would caution against any kind of polarized definition of the word, however, as mysticism is highly dependant upon the time and place in which it occurs. There is, however, some type of core experience that seems to function as a basis for recognition. In other words mysticism seems to defy both essentialist and historicist modes of categorization.

Wordsworth and Whitman may have gotten their rhetoric as a result of direct perceptual experience. The former's 'wise passiveness' and the latter's spiritual

---

[12] Borchert, *Mysticism*, 40.

musings are no doubt of the same ilk as mystical consciousness. Perhaps it would be safe to say that there is a degree of mysticism in the poets' profound reveries. There are examples in the poetry of both, as I discuss in chapter three, which meet the criteria for *actual* mystical experience. And yet, such moments appear to be more of a literary performance of a mystical experience, as Karl Shapiro has said of Whitman's 'Song of Myself', than any sincere depiction of actual mysticism. Although there are countless moments of legitimate consciousness expansion in Wordsworth and Whitman, their major depictions of mystical consciousness are more dramatic than real. Neither poet, despite some critics who believe otherwise, ever had the kind of earth shattering alteration of consciousness found in so many classic mystical experiences. They were not mystics who happened to write poetry but poets who happened to be mystically inclined. Nevertheless, there could be an experiential component in their cosmic rhetoric, just not the kind found in traditional mysticism. Whitman's notebooks, although they lack the kind of major experience Malcolm Cowley believes the poet had, do reveal many less spectacular moments of consciousness expansion. Wordsworth, as well, reports actually needing to touch something physical as a child to bring him back from what he calls an 'abyss of idealism'.

In addition to the possible experiential source, there are also intellectual influences on both poets. Emerson, to be sure, provided Whitman with a significant portion of his mystical lexicon, and there are other sources as well. In his excellent historicist work on Whitman, David Reynolds traces the influence of several popular movements on the poet's spirituality. Whitman's poetry is thus informed by mesmerism, spiritualism, harmonialism, and Swedenborg, as Reynolds shows.[13] His mystical rhetoric is in part rooted in the 19th-century discourse of popular spirituality. It is also in part rooted in the mystics of Egypt and the Sufis of Persia. As Arthur Ford has argued, Whitman owned a copy of Alger's *Poetry of the East*, a large anthology containing a significant amount of mystical verse. Whitman, according to Ford, read the work over and over, and it thus exerted a considerable influence on his poetry.[14] The sources of influence on Wordsworth are considerably more difficult to trace because they are so indirect. No doubt, much of his rhetoric reverberates with Miltonic overtones. The presence of Milton is ubiquitous in much British Romantic poetry. His mystical language is also highly Coleridgean. His frequent discussions with England's leading metaphysician no doubt influenced his spiritual orientation. Beyond Milton and Coleridge, however, no one, to my knowledge, can be said to have exerted a direct influence on Wordsworth's mystical rhetoric.

---

[13] Reynolds, *Walt Whitman's America*, 258.

[14] Arthur L. Ford, 'The rose garden of the world: Near East imagery in the poetry of Walt Whitman', in: *Walt Whitman Review* 5 (1987) no.1, 13.

Without denying any of the aforementioned scholarship I would like to add the possibility that both poets were also influenced by the spirit of the age – Romanticism and its quasi-mystical discourse. Cosmic rhetoric is highly complicit in such discourse, and, although it is in some ways a departure from it, there is also a considerable amount of common ground. The German sources in particular seem to provide the best support for my assertion. Although Wordsworth knew nothing of the Germans directly, as Abrams points out in *Natural Supernaturalism*,[15] there are many parallels, which are in all probability the result of his almost daily contact with Coleridge. The influence is more apparent in Whitman, who, according to Floyd Stoval, was introduced to German philosophy through the work of Coleridge and Carlyle.[16] Whitman was also familiar with Joseph Gostwick's *German Literature*, according to Karl Walter Malone, from which he gleaned the ideas of Kant, Hegel, Fichte, Schelling, and Liebniz.[17]

In *Natural Supernaturalism* M.H. Abrams lists seven interrelated concepts occurring among German poets, romance writers, and philosophers of the period between 1790-1820: (1) recovered paradise or golden age; (2) journey or quest culminating in self-knowledge; (3) a fall from primal unity which is an indispensable step towards a higher unity; (4) a closure or resolution of contraries; (5) return to an ancestral home; (6) a gradual ascent to a higher consciousness or a sudden breakthrough of imagination or cognition; (7) achievement of the journey's goal signalized by a loving union with a feminine other.[18] All of these concepts participate significantly in mystical discourse, as the Romantic 'journey' is highly spiritual in nature. German Romanticism, as Lovejoy pointed out in his famous essay, was 'a rediscovery of Christian ideas'[19] – the result of which was a reassertion of spirituality under the threat of secularization. But this reemergence was not merely of old ideas in hackneyed language but a significant reworking of such ideas in fresh rhetoric, the parallel of which is found in Wordsworth and Whitman and their cosmic language.

I do not mean to suggest that both poets merely parroted this new lexicon, particularly considering that much of Wordsworth's verse was contemporaneous with the German Romantic movement. Each poet himself reworked this reworking of older ideas. But there were significant thinkers who fathered the Romantic movement who predated Wordsworth's earliest verse. Such ideas circulated

[15] Abrams, *Natural supernaturalism*, 256.

[16] Stoval, *The foreground of Leaves of Grass*, 200.

[17] Malone, *Parallels to Hindu and Taoist thought in Walt Whitman*, 14.

[18] Abrams, *Natural supernaturalism*, 255.

[19] Arthur Lovejoy, 'On the discrimination of Romanticisms' (1948), in: Abrams, *English romantic poets*, 17.

anonymously; they blew in the wind, as it were, and both poet's were thus influenced by them with or without their conscious acceptance of Romantic ideas. Jerome Loving has noted that Whitman's early notebooks 'are awash in Romantic ideas about art and the artist'.[20] To be sure, he may have gotten much of these concepts from Emerson and Wordsworth, but he also owned a copy of Frederick Hedge's *Prose Writers of Germany*, which contained selections by Herder, Goethe, Schiller, Fichte, the Schlegels, and others.[21] Whitman thus read these authors before the first publication of *Leaves of Grass* in 1855. Wordsworth's famous 1802 'Preface' likewise espouses a highly Romantic doctrine concerning art and the artist. His prose work in general, although it contains a considerable 18th-century influence, is often cited as characteristically Romantic, which means he may not have been conscious of the German influence but it informed his poetics nevertheless.

So what are the ideas in Romanticism that have any connection to mysticism. First of all, mysticism and Romanticism are in some ways born of the same impulse. Both wage a kind of ideological war against the same state of consciousness. Romanticism was a reaction to the preceding era's rationalism, materialism, empiricism, determinism, and utilitarianism.[22] It arose at least in part as an alternative to the Enlightenment cult of reason and its corresponding doctrines by privileging non-rational modes of knowing such as intuition, impulse, primal rage, and the like. According to Johann Georg Hamann, the whole of the Enlightenment doctrine killed 'that which was living in human beings, appeared to offer a pale substitute for the creative energies of man, and for the whole rich world of the senses'.[23] Mysticism, too, as I have shown, privileges such non-rational states of consciousness. The end in nearly all forms of mystical thought is an expansion of awareness beyond the confines designated by rationalism, materialism, empiricism, determinism, and utilitarianism. Like Zen masters and Taoist sages, Romantics valued childhood consciousness, which comes 'trailing clouds of glory' from heaven, as Wordsworth put it. The German word for such a state of being is *Ursprunglichkeit* – an archetypal state, which, 'like that of the Noble Savage, could redeem our debased cultural adulthood'.[24]

Whereas the neoclassical thinkers and writers privileged logic, the Romantics valued direct sensory experience.[25] The logician 'attempt[s] to tie things up into

---

[20] Loving, *Walt Whitman*, 162.

[21] Stoval, *The foreground of Leaves of Grass*, 195.

[22] Heath & Boreham, *Introducing Romanticism*, 9.

[23] Berlin, *The roots of Romanticism*, 43.

[24] Heath & Boreham, *Introducing Romanticism*, 46.

[25] W.K. Wimsatt, 'The structure of Romantic nature imagery' (1954), in: Abrams, *English romantic poets*, 35.

neat parcels and arrange them in some beautifully analytic fashion'.[26] Mystics and Romantics, on the other hand, transgress boundaries and explode the myth of order. They are 'aplomb in the midst of irrational things', as Whitman himself put it. The experiential component in each mode of consciousness is one of the primary bonds between Romanticism and mysticism. Just as Romanticism is primarily concerned with perception and its expansion and/or alteration in some way, so is perceptual experience the central ingredient in nearly all forms of mysticism. 'Most men', wrote the poet Novalis, 'possess only a bookish perspective – a fragmentary view of the real world'.[27] Such people lack the mystical perception of cosmic unity – the Romantic version of reason – as they are out of touch with direct experiential knowledge and live not by the dictates of their perception, which has the potential to yield the totality, but of their knowledge, which is highly fragmented and thus limited. 'Reason', according to Hegel, 'had nothing whatever to do with the "reason" of Enlightenment philosophy. Rather, it involved fusion with the World Spirit'.[28] Interestingly, Hegel is often associated with Marx's dialectical materialism. As Paul Strathern points out, however, Marx corrupted Hegel's philosophy, which was highly idealistic and mystical.[29] Marx's philosophy was 'not at all what Hegel had had in mind for the world-spirit'.[30] Hegel himself had a deeply life-altering, mystical experience and spent the rest of his life attempting to articulate it in his philosophy.[31] Hegelian 'reason', as Schelling and other Romantics understood it, could only result from a creative interaction and imaginative involvement with the universe. It is important to point out that Romanticism was not a wholesale rejection of Enlightenment, as Marshall Brown argues, but a transmutation of its doctrines.[32] Romanticism's rejection of reason, in fact, was made possible largely by the cult of reason itself and its project of demystification, which was so thorough that it could only end, as Max Horkheimer believed, 'by discrediting the entire project of objective reason itself'.[33]

---

[26] Berlin, *The roots of Romanticism*, 49.

[27] Novalis, 'Aphorisms and fragments' (1798; trans. Alexander Gelley), in: A. Leslie Wilson (Ed.), *German Romantic criticism*, New York: Continuum, 1982, 74.

[28] Peter Thorsley, 'German romantic idealism', in: Curran, *The Cambridge companion to British Romanticism*, 79.

[29] Strathern, *Derrida*, 54.

[30] Ibidem.

[31] Idem, 20.

[32] Marshall Brown, 'Romanticism and Enlightenment', in: Curran, *The Cambridge companion to British Romanticism*, 31 & 38.

[33] David Simpson, 'Romanticism, criticism, and theory', in: Curran, *The Cambridge companion to British Romanticism*, 21.

The primary aim of such consciousness expansion in both modes is to bridge the gap between mind and universe, subject and object. The mystic tries to transcend self (or self-dissolution passively occurs) to commune with the whole, the One, God, oversoul, or whatever other labels the concept has been given. Monistic vision and perceptions of oneness are thus highly characteristic of mystical experiences. For the Romantics, the sublime was similarly used as a way to bridge the gap between mind and universe.[34] As James Twitchell puts it, 'the sublime was a way to span the abyss between inner and outer, and outer and "the Beyond"'.[35] The imagination, in particular, was the key Romantic vehicle for achieving such a conjoining of self and other. For many Romantics, as Twitchell adds, the imaginative faculty was synonymous with what the Neoplatonic mystic, Plotinus, called 'the One' – the supreme connecting power whose ultimate identity is 'imageless and unfathomable'.[36] Romantics often lamented the loss of this sense of unity and called for a reunification with it. As Friedrich Hölderlin claimed, 'Blissful unity, being in the true sense of the word, has been lost to us, and we were obliged to lose it if we were to strive for it and to conquer it [...] To put an end to this eternal conflict between ourselves and the world, to unite ourselves with nature into one boundless whole, that is the object of our endeavor'.[37]

For both mystics and Romantics, the resulting 'enlightenment' that occurs as a result of the acquisition of monistic truth is often described in terms of an awakening. 'Many Romantic writers', as M.H. Abrams observed, 'testified to a deeply significant experience in which an instant of consciousness, or else an ordinary object or event, suddenly blazes into revelation; the unsustainable moment seems to arrest what is passing, and is often described as an intersection of eternity with time'.[38] The Wordsworthian 'moment' in particular, which Abrams claims influenced many 19th-century writers and even informs Joyce's epiphanies, has a very clear parallel in the Zen concept of *satori* – a sudden moment of illumination in which a percipient experiences the totality of all things, internal and external. The Zen comparison, incidentally, is more than a mere simile for comparison's sake, for Paulino Lim argues that the German thinkers played a key role in disseminating Zen ideas to the West.[39] The Zen element in Wordsworth's

---

34 Heath & Boreham, *Introducing Romanticism*, 19.

35 Twitchell, *Romantic horizons*, 11.

36 Idem, 34.

37 Hölderlin, Friedrich, 'On the process of the poetic mind' (trans. Ralph R. Read), in: A. Leslie Wilson (Ed.), *German Romantic criticism*, New York: Continuum, 1982 (orig. published 1826), 219.

38 Abrams, *Natural supernaturalism*, 385.

39 Lim, 'Zen and Wordsworth', 129.

verse, which scholars such as Lim and Rudy have noted, is in all likelihood the result of this indirect influence. The moment of awakening 'is ubiquitous in Romanticism', and it served the function of nonpolitical revolution, that is, it was not fundamentally a 'rebellion against its predecessors' but a 'revolution that gathers up and collects, as it sweeps all with it toward the future'.[40] Romanticism's praxis was consciousness change rather than direct sociopolitical involvement. Instead of toppling governments, the Romantics heralded a new era of spiritual awareness, and their writings signaled the call for a transformed state of being.

This revolution was Promethean in that it attributed divine power to human beings. Johann Georg Hamann, one of 'true fathers' of Romanticism, according to Berlin, believed in a kind of 'mystical vitalism' in which God could be perceived in both nature and human history.[41] History, he believed, is one of the methods whereby the divine is actualized.[42] Human beings were thus given a significantly greater degree of agency by the Romantics. God, according to Friedrich Wilhelm Schelling, is a kind of self-developing principle that realized and expanded its own consciousness through human affairs.[43] By expanding our own consciousness we thus contribute to the betterment of the divine. In liberating ourselves from the tyranny of reason, we become divine. Such a doctrine borders on heresy, depending on how it is interpreted, which renders problematic the notion of Romanticism as merely a displaced form of Protestantism. The godlike perspective accompanying such divine power, which Whitman celebrates on an unprecedented scale, is also found in much mysticism. Meister Eckhart, for instance, believed in a similar doctrine, which accounts in part for the many problems he had with church authorities. Sufi mystics have been tortured and murdered for such a belief, whereas in Vedanta the concept *tat tvam asi*, which translates as 'thou art that', has been much more favorably received perhaps because Hinduism is highly tolerant of all religious perspectives.

Both mystics and Romantics thus declare subjectivity as a principle truth. Both believe human beings can shape reality, that to be human is to be in some way divine, which by necessity entails a belief in 'the transubstantiation into the divine' of all corporeality.[44] Nature, matter, mind, the self – all exist in God, indeed are God, according to Romantic doctrine and, incidentally, mysticism. No one knows this better than the Romantic poet, whose central truth is that

[40] Brown, 'Romanticism and Enlightenment', 45.

[41] Berlin, *The roots of Romanticism*, 49.

[42] Ibidem, 49.

[43] Qtd. in idem, 98.

[44] Jean Paul Friedrich Richter, 'School for Aesthetics' (1813; trans. Margaret R. Hale), in: Wilson, *German Romantic criticism*, 42.

'by liberating ourselves from the tyranny of logic consciousness we can become as a god'.[45] Romantic poets blur the boundaries between nature and human artifacts, imposing an 'aesthetic model upon reality'.[46] Through the operation of the creative imagination all things become different aspects of the same 'Creative Will, of the World Soul', as Schelling believed.[47]

The Romantic poet is a member of the secular clergy. His re-enchantment of consciousness unifies human awareness with the divine. In doing so he eliminates orthodox priests. The poet and the priest are one. 'They were so conjoined in ancient times', according to Novalis, and 'the future will restore this state of affairs'.[48] The Romantic poet is a kind of 'transcendental physician', and poetry 'is the great art of the construction of transcendental well-being'.[49] His verse heals what has been diseased – the human psyche. The Fall, according to Romanticism, is the Cartesian separation of mind and matter – the gulf estranging human from the divine. Romantic poetry bridges this gulf by instilling in the reader a sense of wonder, by re-enchanting a disenchanted state of consciousness. Whereas the philosopher attempts to create order with his logic consciousness, the Romantic poet 'dissolves all ties. His words are tones – terms of enchantment'.[50] And yet, the poet has to delve deep to achieve this reconciliation. He must plunge himself into 'the dark and unconscious forces which move within him, and to bring these to consciousness by the most agonizing and violent internal struggle', as Schelling's doctrine dictated.[51]

Romantics yearned for the golden age, and their poetry, with its great 'sense of wonder, even of reverential awe',[52] was an attempt to recapture what had been lost through the dominant modes of thought in Western culture. Whereas the 'exegetical theologian' destroys this accompanying sense of wonder, the poet 'locates it in the soul, the only place where it can dwell next to God', as Richter put it.[53] Poetry, for the Romantics, had its origins 'in ecstasy and is a manifestation of the universal creative urge'.[54] Romantic poetics is thus highly steeped in mystical thought, so much so that Richter called Romanticism a 'poetic mysticism' whose spirit could never be understood by the rationalist.[55] Friedrich

---

45 Berlin, *The roots of Romanticism*, 106.
46 Idem, 145.
47 Thorsley, 'German romantic idealism', 79.
48 Novalis, 'Aphorisms and fragments', 66.
49 Idem, 69.
50 Idem, 68.
51 Berlin, *The roots of Romanticism*, 98.
52 Thorsley, 'German romantic idealism', 94.
53 Richter, 'School for Aesthetics', 43.
54 Aspiz, 'Sexuality and the language of transcendence', 1.
55 Richter, 'School for Aesthetics', 61.

Hölderlin went so far as to call for an actual *Volksreligion* – a pantheistic people's religion that would reunite human beings with their natural roots.[56] Friedrich Schlegel similarly called for a new mythology to be formed 'out of the outermost depths of the spirit, which will serve as the unifying ground of all poetry'.[57] In so establishing a new faith, Romantic poetry could serve its purpose of metaphysical reconnection, and it could also liberate humankind from its 'fallen', disconnected condition.[58]

Just as mystics proclaim 'all is God', Romantics see the divine in all things. A common feature of many Romantics, according to Wimsatt, was 'to read meanings into the landscape'.[59] Romantics often summoned deep spiritual significance out of surfaces, and the finite was, consequently, often viewed as a symbol of the infinite.[60] Because the physical was thus a metaphor for the spiritual, and the body a metonym for the soul, Romantics often attempted to render the material world in a strange, supernatural light. Such a feature is central to Romantic poetics, and it is arguably the heart of Romantic doctrine. As Friedrich Schlegel put it in his definition of *romantische* literature, 'By endowing the commonplace with a lofty significance, the ordinary with a mysterious aspect, the familiar with the merit of the unfamiliar, the finite with the appearance with infinity, I am romanticizing'.[61] Romanticism is thus a secularized version of being at one with God. And yet, what informs such an idea is mysticism from a variety of sources – Plato, Plotinus, and several other mystics and mystical thinkers from Eckhart to Boehme.[62]

As I have attempted to show, Romanticism is informed by mysticism to a considerable extent. Perhaps the reason why so many Romantic writers embraced mystical rhetoric is because, as Arthur Clements points out, 'to convey mystical experiences it is necessary to use the language of imagination and love', which makes mysticism and Romanticism a very suitable combination.[63] Regardless of whether we embrace Romanticism or believe it is essentially the 'illusion of beholding the infinite within the stream of nature, instead of apart from that stream', as Paul Elmer More put it in his dismissal of the school of thought, it is important to understand the school of thought on its own terms.[64] The notion of an 'inspired' artist may indeed be an illusion, as intertextual theories today

---

56 Heath & Boreham, *Introducing Romanticism*, 74.
57 Abrams, *Natural supernaturalism*, 67.
58 Bloom, *The visionary company*, xxiv.
59 Wimsatt, 'The structure of Romantic nature imagery', 31.
60 Berlin, *The roots of Romanticism*, 101.
61 Heath & Boreham, *Introducing Romanticism*, 68.
62 Berlin, *The roots of Romanticism*, 105.
63 Clements, 'Mysticism, science, and the task of poetry', 55.
64 Qtd. in Lovejoy, 'On the discrimination of Romanticisms', 4.

indicate, and there may be only people whose art is determined by a given social context. But considering that Romanticism represents the single greatest shift in Western consciousness, as Berlin believed, I think the mystical component warrants significant attention beyond the patronizing nod with which many scholars often acknowledge it. I have tried to bring this aspect of Romantic doctrine to light as fully as this short chapter allows. Significant attention to each particular writer's own use of mystical rhetoric is needed. There is some scholarship out there, but there should be considerably more. I hope this study will contribute to the body of scholarship and stimulate further explorations into such an important topic in Romantic studies.

CHAPTER XII

COSMIC RAMIFICATIONS

The Larger Context

In a famous lecture in 1976, Michel Foucault discussed what he called 'totalitarian theories' of knowledge in scholarship, which suppress other forms of knowing. These other modes of ideation he called 'subjugated knowledges':

> [B]y subjugated knowledges one should understand [...] a whole set of knowledges that have been disqualified as inadequate to their task or insufficiently elaborated: naive knowledges, located low down on the hierarchy, beneath the required level of cognition or scientificity. I also believe that it is through the reemergence of these low ranking knowledges, these unqualified, even directly disqualified knowledges (such as that of the psychiatric patient, of the ill person, of the nurse [...] that it is through the reappearance of his knowledge, that criticism performs its work.[1]

Although Foucault does not mention mysticism, I would argue that it, too, is a subjugated knowledge, that it has been repressed by the Western hierarchy of knowledges, and that the radical component in the verse of Wordsworth and Whitman, the strangeness of both poets, is attributable to the fact that they led what Foucault called an 'insurrection of subjugated knowledges'.[2] My study is an attempt to elucidate this insurrection, and in doing so I hope it also furthers the cause of altering perceptions in the West of modes of being traditionally associated with the East – ways of perceiving and being often seen as nonsensical, fanciful, and imaginative.

Many western scholars have a bias against expressions of mystical perception and frequently dismiss it as nonsense, irrationality, or outright madness. In his discussion of T.S. Eliot's mysticism, Donald Childs bemoans this Western prejudice: 'Mysticism is often used in a semi-contemptuous way to denote vaguely any kind of occultism or spiritualism, or any specially curious or fantastic

[1] Foucault, *Madness and civilization*, 130.
[2] Ibidem.

view about God and the universe'.[3] As an example, Childs cites Irving Babbitt's discussion of mysticism in Romanticism, which Babbitt called 'a revulsion from the rational that masquerades as a quest for a heavenly idealism'.[4] Mysticism is a slippery subject, and the 'truths' mystics utter are equally elusive to many Western scholars, exposing as they do what Theodor Adorno has called 'the conceptual fetishism of philosophy'.[5] Such prejudice against mysticism is rooted in the Greek legacy, which permeates Euro-American thought. Stanislav Grof decries the 'western tendency to marginalize all states of consciousness besides rationality and logic'. He claims that this 'is actually an anomaly in history since many previous cultures valued altered states'.[6] Interestingly, Graham Parkes argues that the philosophical standards of the West are inapplicable to most kinds of thinking in languages unrelated to the Indo-European family,[7] which is to say, Western rationalism is just as unintelligible to many Easterners as mysticism is to Westerners.

In his discussion of Heidegger's 'planetary thinking', which is itself often likened to a form of mysticism, J.L. Mehta calls for 'a rethinking of the meaning, and the negative value, assigned by metaphysical thinking to the notions of the irrational, the magical, the mythic, the symbolic, the merely poetic and fanciful and so forth'.[8] He also claims it is necessary 'to rethink the concept of mysticism as a legitimate type of religious or philosophical view or position' if one is to break the fetters of the Greek rationalist legacy.[9] Wordsworth and Whitman were among those who, although deeply influenced by Greek modes of ideation, were among the first to break the fetters of Hellenic epistemology. In his famous work *Of Grammatology* Derrida claims that 'between rationalism and mysticism there is [...] a certain complicity'.[10] I would argue, however, that rather than complicity it is more appropriate to acknowledge rationalism's debt to mysticism, for in defining itself reason must have an 'other' – an unreason, which is precisely what one finds in mysticism.

As I have attempted to show, mysticism typically runs against the grain of orthodoxy. In his introduction to *Trajectories of Mysticism in Theory and Literature*, Philip Leonard raises the 'possibility that orthodox forms of identity and knowledge are disturbed by concepts and practices at the margins of Western

3 Childs, 'T.S. Eliot', 99.
4 Idem, 104.
5 Qtd. in Winchell, 'Semantics of the unspeakable', 81.
6 Grof, *The holotropic mind*, 13.
7 Parkes, 'Introduction', 6.
8 Qtd. in Parkes, 'Introduction', 28.
9 Ibidem.
10 Philip Leonard, 'Divine horizons: Levinas, Derrida, transcendence', in: idem (Ed.), *Trajectories of mysticism in theory and literature*, 227.

theology'.[11] Leonard discusses the work of several theorists as an example of the use of mystical discourse to subvert the Western tradition. 'There seem to be definite parallels', he argues, 'between [Walter Benjamin's] conception of literary works of art as hieroglyphs of redeemed life and the Kabbalistic idea of a state of redemption whose nature can be intuited through a linguistic analysis of sacred texts'.[12] Leonard claims Harold Bloom likewise draws extensively upon the Kabbalistic tradition in his work, *A Map of Misreading*, in the idea of poetic agonism. 'Theresa of Avila's encounters with God through raptures and bodily experiences', he claims, 'are echoed in Luce Irigarary's claim that God and woman are both a "Mystery, me-hysteria, without determinable end or beginning..."'.[13] Emmanuel Levinas, in 'seeking a passage out of the violence of rationality', develops a 'transgressive and transcendental criticism which attempts to escape from the notion of being pervading Western thought'. In spite of Levinas's 'onslaught against metaphysical and positive theology', Leonard sees in him 'a return to the divine'.[14] Leonard also views Julia Kristeva's post-Freudian description of melancholy as an alternative condition of despondency and exaltation in terms of 'mystical ascesis [...] where sadness became essential as a means towards paradoxical knowledge of divine truth and constituted a major touchstone for faith'.[15]

Leonard concludes his introduction with the observation that 'mystical and negative theologies challenge the primacy that has been given to the way that self and other are conceptualized by Western theology'. 'Mysticism and apophaticism', he adds, '[not only] disturb the foundations of religious belief in the west [...] These counter-hegemonic theologies follow a radical trajectory away from rationalism and throw into crisis the violently repressive structures of knowledge and identity which prevail in Western culture'.[16]

Other thinkers have also embraced mystical discourse as a means to subvert Western philosophical imperialism. In an essay on Hélène Cixous, Elena Carrera discusses the ways in which Cixous reclaims a 'feminine space' by utilizing mystical discourse – by following 'an age-long but long-forgotten tradition characterized by its search of the beyond and its inscription of love as the way to know the unknown, the ineffable'.[17] Carrera acknowledges that the label mystic, 'traditionally used to name various trends within religion which have

[11] Philip Leonard, 'Introduction', in: idem (Ed.), *Trajectories of mysticism in theory and literature*, xv.

[12] Leonard, 'Introduction', xvi.

[13] Idem, xvi.

[14] Leonard, 'Divine horizons', 234.

[15] Leonard, 'Introduction', xvi.

[16] Idem, xvi-xvii.

[17] Elena Carrera, 'The fertile mystical maze: Derrida's dry theological gorge to Cixous's dialogic disgorging', in: Leonard, *Trajectories of mysticism in theory and literature*, 95.

been kept marginal, at bay and even 'repressed', may not be what Cixous wants for herself'.[18] But she does positively assert that what Cixous calls 'feminine economy' and 'feminine writing' have 'a lot in common with the mystics' way of knowing through love and through desire, and with their way of writing through metaphors, through displacement'.[19]

In 'Power, Gender and Ecstasy: Mysticism in Post/Modernity' Grace Jantzen argues that 'modernity has built itself upon a valorization of rationality construed as objective and opposed to emotion, passion, and ecstasy'.[20] Consequently, such things as mysticism, God, female sexuality, and ignorance are constructed by Western scholars as the other of masculinity, rationality, and the scientific gaze.[21] Academic disciplines, she argues, 'behave like Lacanian subjects, constituting themselves by a violent abjection of that of which they must at all costs remain unconscious, the threatening other which, once admitted, would subvert the carefully erected edifice'.[22] Mysticism, therefore, is presented in much Western thinking 'not in its own right but as "the other of the same", the binary opposite of philosophical rationality'. It is portrayed as 'ecstatic, irrational, ineffable, subjective and private, rather than as genuine alterity'.[23] Nevertheless, she celebrates 'mystical ecstasy as a place of excess, a place where the constricting categories of modernity are displaced and it becomes possible to think otherwise'.[24]

Roland Barthes turns to Zen mysticism in his work *Empire of Signs* to illustrate his theory of the emptiness of language: 'The text does not gloss the images, which do not illustrate the text. For me, each has been no more than the onset of a kind of visual uncertainty, analogous perhaps to that loss of meaning Zen calls Satori'.[25] Barthes contrasts the West's attempts to 'pierce meaning, i.e., to get into it by breaking and entering' with the Japanese haiku – the 'literary branch' of Zen:

> The West moistens everything with meaning, like an authoritarian religion which imposes baptism on entire peoples [...] We have two ways of sparing discourse the infamy of non-meaning (non-sense), and we systematically subject utterance (in a desperate filling-in of any nullity which might reveal the emptiness of language) to one or the other of these *significations* (or active fabrications of signs): symbol and reasoning, metaphor and syllogism.[26]

---

[18] Carrera, 'The fertile mystical maze', 95.
[19] Ibidem.
[20] Jantzen, 'Power, gender, and ecstasy', 388.
[21] Idem, 386.
[22] Idem, 389.
[23] Idem, 390.
[24] Idem, 387.
[25] Roland Barthes, *Empire of signs* (trans. R. Howard), New York: Farrar, 1982 (orig. publ. 1970), xi.
[26] Idem, 70.

The haiku, on the other hand, is 'an enormous praxis destined to *halt language*, to jam that kind of internal radiophony continually *sending* in us [...] to empty out, to stupefy, to dry up the souls incoercible babble'.[27] Mystical illumination is for him 'a moment when language ceases' and one realizes the emptiness, the essencelessness, of reality.[28]

Mysticism, or more properly one of the many languages of mystical discourse, has in part made possible the work of Jacques Derrida. In one of his foundational concepts – 'differance' – Derrida is forced to resort to the *via negativa* of the mystics. *Differance* is 'neither a word nor a concept', and it is 'beyond the order of understanding'. There is no realm of difference, just as there is no name for it.[29] Consequently, Derrida acknowledges that 'the detours, phrases, and syntax that I shall often have to resort to will resemble – will sometimes be practically indiscernible from – those of negative theology'.[30] To avoid the charge of 'logocentrism' he levels at everyone else, Derrida is quick to point out that

> *differance* is not theological, not even in the most negative order of negative theology. The latter, as we know, is always occupied with letting a supraessential reality go beyond the finite categories of essence and existence, that is, of presence, and always hastens to remind us that, if we denying the predicate of existence to God, it is in order to recognize him as a superior, inconceivable, and ineffable mode of being.[31]

This homogenization of all negative theology into an essentialist category, however, is unfounded. It is true that *some* forms of Western, negative theology negate the existence of God in order to assert the presence of God, but other forms of negative theology are employed by mystical traditions to demonstrate the 'essencelessness' of existence. It is no coincidence, therefore, that Madhyamika (Middle-Way) Buddhism employs some of the same arguments deconstructors do, 'often angering and confusing both Hindus and other Buddhists with its deconstructive logic'.[32]

So it seems mysticism as a topic is quite relevant in literary and philosophical studies, as it provides a way to shatter paradigms and to escape dominant modes of thought. Mysticism is also relevant in other fields as well. Just as modern theory is beginning to embrace mystical discourse, so is science – particularly the 'new' physics. In *The Quantum Self* Danah Zohar characterizes the older Cartesian/Newtonian worldview against which the new physics defines itself:

---

[27] Idem, 74.

[28] Ibidem.

[29] Jacques Derrida, 'Differance', in: Kearney & Rainwater, *The continental philosophy reader*, 463.

[30] Derrida, 'Differance', 444.

[31] Ibidem.

[32] Jim Powell, *Derrida*, New York: Writers & Readers, 1997, 162.

> In Cartesian philosophy, which has so deeply influenced the individualist strain of modern thought about the self and its relationships, there are no intimate personal relations. Everything in Descartes' thinking takes place from the first person point of view of the isolated *cogito*, the 'I' who thinks and is nothing but his thinking. Any relationships this *cogito* may have to anything or anyone else it has indirectly, mediated through Newtonian matter or through the mind of God. 'I' and 'you' never meet.
> Cartesian isolation was further underpinned by Newton's physics, or the concept of matter as consisting of so many separate and indivisible billiard balls complemented Descartes' separate and indivisible minds. The notion of a relationship as a set of *external* influences enacted between strangers became the paradigm for all relationships.[33]

But this mindset is now the subject of considerable revision. Employing the same mystical rhetoric I have discussed in this study, quantum theorists are now averring the new myth of wholeness. 'Inconceivable as it seems to ordinary reason', writes Ken Wilber, 'you – and all other conscious beings as such – are all in all. Hence this life of yours which you are living is not merely a piece of the entire existence, but is, in a certain sense, the *whole*; only this whole is not so constituted that it can be surveyed in one single glance'.[34] The perspective of individualized ego-consciousness, therefore, is an illusion both to mystics and quantum theorists. The individual self is akin to a hologram, whose constituent parts contain an image of the whole. Such concepts baffle the rational mind, but as Wilber also points out, 'logical thinking brings us up to a certain point and then leaves us in the lurch'.[35] Physicists, like mystics, are concluding that 'nonsense is merely that which does not fit into the prearranged patterns which we have superimposed on reality. There is no such thing as nonsense', in fact, 'apart from judgmental intellects which calls it that'.[36]

The new physics has begun to blur the lines of distinction between science and theology, as Russell Stannard points out.[37] The findings of quantum theory, too complex deal with adequately in this conclusion, have yielded the 'mystical' insight that there is an essential unity and interrelation of all phenomena, as Arthur Clements observes in his essay 'Mysticism, Science, and the Task of Poetry': 'it is now an ecological truism that everything is alternately connected to everything else, that organism and environment are indivisibly interrelated, define each other, can only be understood and, indeed, are only real in terms of

---

[33] Zohar, *The quantum self*, 129.

[34] Ken Wilber (Ed.), *Quantum questions: Mystical writings of the world's greatest physicists*, Boston: Shambhala, 2001, 98.

[35] Wilber (Ed.), *Quantum questions*, 96.

[36] Zukav, *The dancing Wu Li masters*, 131.

[37] Russell Stannard (Ed.), *God for the 21st century*, Philadelphia: Templeton, 2000, 150.

each other'.[38] This new notion of wholeness denies the classical ideal of analyzability, or breaking the world down into its constituent parts, (which was, incidentally, the cornerstone of Enlightenment thinking and the bane of Romanticism):

> Quantum theory has thus demolished the classical concepts of solid objects and of strictly deterministic laws of nature. At the subatomic level, the solid material objects of classical physics dissolved into wave-like patterns of probabilities, and these patterns, ultimately, do not represent probabilities of things, but rather probabilities of interconnections. A careful analysis of the process of observation in atomic physics has shown that the subatomic particles have no meaning as isolated entities, but can only be understood as interconnections between the preparation of an experiment and the subsequent measurement. Quantum theory thus reveals a basic oneness of the universe. It shows that we cannot decompose the world into independently existing smallest units. As we penetrate into matter, nature does not show us any isolated 'basic building blocks', but rather appears as a complicated web of relations between the various parts of the whole.[39]

Lloyd Davies observes that 'the truth now seems to be more allied with mysticism than with materialism'.[40] Although quantum theorists have shattered the notion that matter is real and solid, however, they have not confirmed the philosophy of idealism, which ultimately asserts that the physical world does not exist, that it is an illusion. 'Recent physics', writes Daniel Dombrowski, 'has made materialism and dualism problematic and has made Wordsworth's view of nature more plausible than ever'.[41] Matter does not exist in the sense of being composed of individual constituent parts, according to quantum theory; rather, matter exists because we perceive its existence. In some strange sense, according to John Wheeler, 'the universe is a participatory universe'.[42] Quantum physicists have thus shattered the illusion of absolute objectivity. 'The distinction between objective and subjective vanishes in the quantum realm', writes Gary Zukav. 'If the new physics has led us anywhere it is back to ourselves'.[43] Stanislav Grof goes so far as to argue that all perceptions and knowledge are not objective reconstructions of reality but 'creative activities comparable to artistic expressions'.[44] Subjectivity, incidentally, according to Isaiah Berlin, is one of the two unifying

---

[38] Clements, 'Mysticism, science, and the task of poetry', 51.

[39] Fritjof Capra, *The Tao of physics*, Boston: Shambala, 2000 (orig. publ. 1975), 68.

[40] Lloyd Davies, 'Prenatal life and the idea of loss in Wordsworth's "Immortality Ode": Toward remembrance', in: *Journal of Evolutionary Psychology* 19 (1998) no.3-4, 262.

[41] Dombrowski, 'Panpsychism', 41.

[42] Qtd. in Capra, *The Tao of physics*, 141.

[43] Zukav, *The dancing Wu Li masters*, 127.

[44] Grof, *The holotropic mind*, 10.

elements in all of the various Romanticisms (the other one being *will*), and it is also a cornerstone of the cosmic rhetoric in Wordsworth and Whitman.

Gregg Easterbrook proclaims that 'at the dawn of the new millennium, the concept of meaning is poised for a major comeback':

> Cosmologists, expected by now to possess proof that the genesis of the universe was just an aimless technical event, instead are uncovering ever more evidence that existence is shrouded in mystery, and maybe both infinite and eternal. Biologists, expected by now to possess proof that life is just a weird chemical accident, instead are uncovering ever more indications that the natural world is somehow pre-wired to make life probable. And literary thinkers, who would have expected that by now postmodern ennui would have routed all other schools of thought, instead are finding a striking revival of interest in religion, ethics, and the difference between right and wrong – ideas associated with meaning.[45]

Stannard also claims that 'as science comes to embrace more buoyant views of the human prospect, literature and philosophy may turn in this direction as well', a process which, as I have suggested, has already begun. Many contemporary literary thinkers have espoused despondent views of life because they too often assume, as Easterbrook points out, that 'since science is busy proving existence to be meaningless, intellectuals must do the same'.[46] But 'to think that science already knows enough to be certain there are no mystical forces', he argues, quoting Nobel prize-winning physicist Charles Townes, 'is illogical. As the course of science shifts away from dispirited views of a senseless cosmos, toward a new vision of creation as poignantly favorable to life, then philosophy and literature will have to adjust'.[47]

Quantum theorists have reached such conclusions as a result of the wave/particle paradox, which says that subatomic elements can have either a particle or a wave aspect but never both. The wave aspect of an electron, for instance, represents the probability of its orbit. Prior to changing its orbit, an electron will appear as a wave and thus appear to occupy all potential orbits at once. When it becomes a particle, the electron collapses its wave function and inhabits only one of the many possible orbits. Depending on how a scientist structures an experiment, particles can appear as waves and vice versa, which leads physicists such as Werner Heisenberg to conclude that the linguistic problems involved in articulating the findings of quantum theory are 'really serious. We wish to speak in some way about the structure of the atoms [...] But we cannot speak about atoms in ordinary language'.[48] Quantum theorists, consequently, turn to paradox

---

[45] Qtd. in Stannard, *God for the 21st century*, 32.
[46] Idem, 34.
[47] Ibidem.
[48] Qtd. in Capra, *The Tao of physics*, 45.

(an instrument of both poetry and mysticism) to express the seeming contradictions of reality at the subatomic level. In *Healing Our Worldview* John Hitchcock celebrates the paradoxical language of quantum theory, claiming it 'liberates us from the prison of intellectualism and returns us to our humanity' (xii). 'Disciplined paradoxical thinking', he adds, 'has definite structure. It is not at all a failure of effort, but requires rather an intensification of effort'.[49]

Physicists, like mystics, are also saying some very strange things about time, which, they argue, is actually unified with space to form space-time – a continuum whose unity 'takes place on a higher plane beyond normal perception'.[50] There are also saying strange things about sound as a result of the new 'superstring theory', which says that beyond the wave/particle mystery is 'a vibrating, oscillating, dancing filament that physicists have named a string'.[51] Everything in the universe consists of string, which is the underlying unity of all. Particles are different not in kind but merely in the resonance of their string.[52] Just as poets and mystics have told us that sound/vibration permeates all life, so are physicists claiming that 'the winds of change [...] gust through an aeolian universe'.[53]

Modern physics has given us the notions that matter is energy, that the universe is alive, that rudimentary consciousness may well be a property of all living systems, and that contradiction (or complementarity as it is called) is the only essential truth. Most important, however, quantum theory has begun to heal our worldview:

> Ever since Plato, the West has stressed the rational and the analytic, the rules by which we form thoughts and make decisions, the 'component parts' of our conscious life. The logic of this has led naturally to the computational, or computer, model of the brain. The cost of this model, however, has been the overlooking of another side to human knowing and experience, what might be called the intuitive side, the side that draws on wisdom, imagination, and creativity. In modern neuropsychological terms, these two sides of our mental life have been spoken of as the right-brain/left-brain split, and our culture as a left brain culture. Using an equally good metaphor from quantum physics, we might speak of this situation as a particle/wave split and say that our culture has emphasized the particle aspect of the mind.[54]

Nobel prize-winning physicist Max Planck argues that 'every serious and reflective person realizes [...] that the religious element in his nature must be recognized

[49] Hitchcock, *Healing our worldview*, x.
[50] Capra, *The Tao of physics*, 150.
[51] Brian Greene, *The elegant universe*, New York: Random House, 1999, 14.
[52] Greene, *The elegant universe*, 136.
[53] Idem, 135.
[54] Zohar, *The quantum self*, 72.

and cultivated if all the powers of the human soul are to act together in perfect balance and harmony. And, indeed, it was not by any accident that the greatest thinkers of all ages were also deeply religious souls, even though they made no public show of their religious feeling'.[55] Even Albert Einstein, who epitomized left-brain intelligence, argued that the most important function of art and science is to awaken what he called the 'cosmic religious feeling', which he believed is 'the strongest and noblest motive for scientific research'.[56]

Wordsworth and Whitman are two great poets in whom this cosmic religious feeling was fully awakened, and in whom the powers of human soul are unified to produce an alternate mode of human knowing and experience through the avenues of wisdom, imagination, and creativity. The relevance of their mystical rhetoric to modern philosophy, literary scholarship, and science cannot be overstated. Critics, nevertheless, dismiss this rhetoric in both poets, claiming it denies sociopolitical realities and transmutes historical energies into an ahistorical aesthetic. Christopher Caudwell claims that romance worlds are a betrayal of the class for whom the poet speaks.[57] Romantic poets, according to such thinking, thus labor under the 'bourgeois illusion' of offering revolution by creating alternative worlds, but unwittingly they revolt against the oppressed class by deflecting attention away from unjust conditions.[58]

In such a vein Allen Trachtenberg sees Whitman's 'revolution' as a turning away from realities. His visionary politics veer 'dangerously toward an inevitablist idealism, a buoyancy in spite of all, a cheerful theodicy in the face of swine and spiders'.[59] Similarly, Wynn Thomas has argued that Whitman does not embody the essential spirit of America in his verse. Contrary to the view of him as the poet of democracy, Whitman changed his 19th-century world into a *kosmos* 'by displacing social materials from the relatively uncongenial historical milieu of his own time into the preferred realm of a supposedly eternal and universal natural process. His poetry was the means whereby the alchemy of displacement took place'.[60] Thomas goes on to say that the creation of a kosmos is merely Whitman's unconscious need to revolutionize or at least reform his social world.[61] But according to such an argument, Whitman's idealized nation is a distraction from the social ills that plagued 19th-century America.

---

[55] Qtd. in Wilber, *Quantum questions*, 161.

[56] Idem, 105.

[57] Christopher Caudwell, 'English poetics: The decline of capitalism' (1946), in: Newton, *Twentieth-century literary theory*, 161.

[58] Caudwell, 'English poetics', 160.

[59] Allen Trachtenberg, 'Whitman's visionary politics', in: Sill, *Walt Whitman of Mickle Street*, 104.

[60] Wynn M. Thomas, *The lunar light of Whitman's poetry*, Cambridge: Harvard University Press, 1987, 78.

[61] Thomas, *The lunar light of Whitman's poetry*, 87.

Jerome McGann has likewise criticized Wordsworth's Romanticism, whose 'grand illusion' is an idealized urge to break 'free of the ruins of history'.[62] According to McGann, buried in the poet's verse is an ideology that seeks to displace and conceal the realities of the social and political worlds in its celebration of the imagination.[63] Wordsworth's cosmic rhetoric and his celestial light, moreover, are merely transmutations of his disappointment over the French counter-revolution and the Terror under Robespierre.[64] Perhaps not willing to consciously face the disillusionment of the revolution's failure, Wordsworth turned to the creation of his own cosmos – his romance world in which the ideals of the revolution prevail (or so the argument goes).

Alan Liu has gone so far as to argue that the lyric form in general denies sociopolitical realities in privileging the individual over the social in its bourgeois subjectivity.[65] The Romantics thus embraced a genre that particularly lends itself to denial, to the concealment of truth, according to this argument. Mikhail Bahktin, whose work is currently in vogue among many theorists, has contributed largely to such a view. According to Bahktin, the lyric is 'inadequate to writing towards truth because the process closes itself off to the palimpsest of the external; it denies history and its heteroglossic superfluity of meaning'.[66] The poetic process is a forgetting, 'an active refusal to allow the whole to be seen'.[67]

Regarding the issue of time, critics have been equally unfair to Wordsworth and Whitman. Paul de Man in his essay, 'The Rhetoric of Temporality' argues that 19th-century Romantics longed for a transcendental source or ground of being, and there was a resulting tendency for the self to borrow the temporal stability it lacked from nature. Romantic poets, consequently, spiritualized the symbol and thus fled from 'an authentically human destiny', which caused them to become trapped 'in the contradiction of a pseudo-dialectic between subject and object'.[68]

The foregoing discussion, I hope, will serve as a refutation of such views. As I have attempted to show, romance worlds are by no means a betrayal of the oppressed classes. They are, in fact, intimately concerned with human life. Admittedly, they do not promote a Marxist agenda, but they do depict the highest

---

62 Qtd. in Nicola Zoe Trott, 'Wordsworth, Milton and the inward light', in: Lisa Low & Anthony John Harding (Eds.), *Milton, the Metaphysicals, and Romanticism*, New York: Cambridge University Press, 1994, 114.

63 Trott, 'Wordsworth, Milton and the inward light', 115.

64 Idem, 122.

65 Qtd. in Oerlemans, *The dynamics of lyric and narrative in the poetry of Wordsworth and Whitman*, 10.

66 Qtd. in idem, 17-18.

67 Qtd. in idem, 18.

68 Qtd. in McSweeney, *The language of the senses*, 25.

human value – love, which is offered as a form of psychic/spiritual healing. The accompanying expressions of cheer and joy are no doubt in contrast to 'real' world evils, but they are by no means intended to elide such problems. Consciousness, contrary to a common corruption of Marx's ideas, is not exclusively determined by society, as David Hawkes argues in *Ideology*.[69] Both consciousness and society determine each other, which means that there is some value in offering through poetry or any other medium a means by which consciousness can be transformed.

Marxists decry the Romantic retreat into nature, and yet it is important to remember that human civilization is a relative newcomer if considered within the context of the earth's four-billion-year history. Human concerns are, to be sure, of immense importance, particularly to human beings. It is important to remember, however, that we are merely part of the natural order, not its master. Romanticism in general and Wordsworth and Whitman in particular have given us a picture of human existence in touch with nature. Overcoming the fragmentation and isolation of Cartesian consciousness, theirs is a vision of nature not as a mere resource to be exploited but as a connecting, unifying, and thus healing force. This orientation towards the natural world leads to an apprehension of a holistic perception of unity that does not ignore sociopolitical affairs; it encompasses and thus transcends them. To say the lyric as a genre is a forgetting, a refusal to allow the whole to be seen, is thus a misreading. This dismissal is itself an elision of cosmic rhetoric and the tremendous sense of unity at its core.

To insist that Romantic poetry be in the service of depicting sociopolitical oppression is to insist that it not be Romantic poetry. To claim it flees from an authentic human destiny is to say that the 'inner' life does not matter. It is to subscribe to the determinist's position, which says that consciousness is merely the effect of some outward cause, that there is no value in the immense power of the human imagination, that the cosmic religious emotion, which so many great mind's have claimed is necessary if the human race is to genuinely advance forward without destroying itself, is unimportant. I believe exactly the opposite – that these matters are immensely important – and I hope this study in some way furthers the discussion.

I also hope this study contributes to Wordsworth and Whitman scholarship and to comparative studies in several other respects. Too often critics misunderstand statements made from the perspective of mystical consciousness. Wordsworth and Whitman both have been charged with narcissism and solipsism, which, as I have argued, is a gross misreading of a central aspect of their work. I have also attempted to explode the myth that Wordsworth and Whitman were

[69] David Hawkes, *Ideology*, New York: Routledge, 2000, 88-89.

nature mystics, as many critics have claimed in passing remarks. This is simply a misunderstanding of the type of rhetoric they employ. I have frequently extended the work of Wordsworthian scholarship to Whitman's verse, and vice versa. In demonstrating trajectories of mysticism in both writers I have tried to further the work of East/West comparitivists. Perhaps most important, I have attempted to make contact with the imagination of both writers, since this is such a central concern in their verse and since modern theory can do little to account for such matters of the human soul. N.D. O'Donoghue has argued that all true poetry is receptive – a listening rather than the speaking. The same is true of criticism. I have tried to present not only a reading, therefore, but also a listening of Wordsworth and Whitman – an appropriate endeavor since both were such highly auditory poets. There is music in them, and I hope this study has served to amplify it.

BIBLIOGRAPHY

Abhayananda, S., *History of mysticism: The unchanging testament*, Naples, FL: Atma, 1987.

Abrams, M.H., *Natural supernaturalism*, New York: Norton, 1971.

Adams, Stephen, 'The luminist Walt Whitman', in: *American Poetry* 2 (1985) no.2, 2-16.

Allen, Gay Wilson, *The solitary singer: A critical biography of Walt Whitman*, Chicago: University of Chicago Press, 1955.

Allen, Gay Wilson, *A reader's guide to Walt Whitman*, Syracuse: Syracuse University Press, 1970.

Allen, Gay Wilson, 'Walt Whitman and Stoicism', in: Duane MacMillan (Ed.), *The Stoic strain in American literature: Essays in honour of Marston LaFrance*, Toronto: University of Toronto Press, 1979, 43-60.

Ashton, Rosemary, *The life of Samuel Taylor Coleridge*, Oxford: Blackwell, 1997.

Askin, Denise T., 'Whitman's theory of evil: A clue to his use of paradox', in: *ESQ* 28 (1982), 121-132.

Aspiz, Harold, 'Sexuality and the language of transcendence', in: *Walt Whitman Review* 5 (1987) no.2, 1-7.

Asselineau, Roger, *The evolution of Walt Whitman*, Iowa City: University of Iowa Press, 1999 (orig. publ. 1954).

Bailey, John, *Walt Whitman*, New York: Macmillan, 1926.

Barnstone, Willis, *The poetics of ecstasy: Varieties of* ekstasis *from Sappho to Borges*, New York: Holmes, 1983.

Barry, Peter, *Beginning theory*, New York: Manchester University Press, 1995.

Barth, Robert, 'Wordsworth and Hopkins: In pursuit of transcendence', in: *Renascence: Essays on Value in Literature* 48 (1996), no.3, 174-189.

Barthes, Roland, 'The Death of the Author' (1977, trans. S. Heath), in: K.M. Newton (Ed.), *Twentieth-century literary theory*, New York: St. Martin's, 1997, 120-123.

Barthes, Roland, *Empire of signs* (trans. R. Howard), New York: Farrar, 1982 (orig. publ. 1970).

Bercquist, Bruce Allen, *Walt Whitman and the Bible: Language echoes, images, allusions, and ideas* (Diss. University of Nebraska, Lincoln, 1979).

Berlin, Isaiah, *The roots of Romanticism*, Princeton: Princeton University Press, 1999.

Bevis, William, 'Emerson: Ecstasy and aphorism', in: *Studia Mystica* 5 (1982) no.3, 44-59.

The Bhagavad-Gita (trans. Barbara Stoler Miller), New York: Bantam, 1986.

Bialostosky, Don, *Wordsworth, dialogics, and the practice of criticism*, New York: Cambridge University Press, 1992.

Bloom, Harold, *The visionary company*, Ithaca, NY: Cornell University Press, 1961.

Bloom, Harold, *The Western canon*, New York: Riverhead, 1994.

Borchert, Bruno, *Mysticism: Its history and challenge*, York Beach, ME: Weiser, 1994 (orig. publ. 1989).

Bradley, Sculley, & Harold W. Blodgett (Eds.), *Leaves of Grass: A Norton critical edition*, New York: Norton, 1973.

Brooks, Cleanth, 'The language of paradox', in: Arthur Clements (Ed.), *John Donne's poetry*, New York: Norton, 1992, 195-202 (orig. publ. 1942).

Brown, Marshall, 'Romanticism and Enlightenment', in: Stuart Curran (Ed.), *The Cambridge companion to British Romanticism*, New York: Cambridge University Press, 2000, 25-47.

Bucke, Richard Maurice, *Cosmic consciousness*, New York: Penguin, 1991 (orig. publ. 1901).

Bugliari, Jeanne, 'Whitman and Wordsworth: The janus of nineteenth century idealism', in: *Walt Whitman Review* 19 (1973), 63-67.

Burgess, Anthony, 'The answerer', in: Sculley Bradley & Harold W. Blodgett (Eds.), *Leaves of grass*, New York: Norton, 1973, 972-975 (orig. publ. 1968).

Callow, Philip, *From noon to starry night: A life of Walt Whitman*, Chicago: Elephant, 1992.

Capra, Fritjof, *The Tao of physics*, Boston: Shambala, 2000 (orig. publ. 1975).

Carrera, Elena, 'The fertile mystical maze: Derrida's dry theological gorge to Cixous's dialogic disgorging', in: Philip Leonard (Ed.), *Trajectories of mysticism in theory and literature*, London: Macmillan, 2000, 94-112.

Carter, Steve, 'Emily Dickinson and mysticism', in: *ESQ: A Journal of the American Renaissance* 241 (1978) no.1, 83-95.

Caudwell, Christopher, 'English poetics: The decline of capitalism (1946)', in: K.M. Newton (Ed.), *Twentieth-century literary theory*, New York: St. Martin's, 1997, 160-163.

Chari, V.K., *Whitman in the light of Vedantic mysticism*, Lincoln, NE: University of Nebraska Press, 1964.

Chari, V.K., 'Whitman criticism in the light of Indian poetics', in: Ed Folsom (Ed.), *Walt Whitman: The Centennial essays*, Iowa City: University of Iowa Press, 1994, 240-250.

Chase, Richard Volney, 'Oneself I sing (1955)', in: Sculley Bradley & Harold W. Blodgett (Eds.), *Leaves of Grass*, New York: Norton, 1973, 889-894.

Childs, Donald, 'T.S. Eliot: From varieties of mysticism to pragmatic poesis', in: *Mosaic* 22 (1989) no.4, 99-116.

Cixous, Hélène, 'Conversations (1988)', in: K.M. Newton (Ed.), *Twentieth-century literary theory*, New York: St. Martin's, 1997, 225-233.

Clements, Arthur, 'Mysticism, science, and the task of poetry', in: *Studia Mystica* 9 (1986) no.4, 46-59.

Coleridge, Samuel Taylor, *Biographia Literaria*, London: Dent, 1993.

Cook, Albert, 'The transformation of "point": Amplitude in Wordsworth, Whitman, and Rimbaud', in: *Studies in Romanticism* 30 (1991) no.2, 169-188.

Cooke, Michael, 'Romanticism and the paradox of wholeness', in: *Studies in Romanticism* 23 (1984) no.4, 435-453.

Cowley, Malcolm, 'Introduction', in: idem (Ed.), *Leaves of Grass: The first (1855) edition*, New York: Viking, 1959, vii-xxxvii.

Critchley, Simon, *Continental philosophy*, New York: Oxford University Press, 2001.

Cummings, Glenn, 'Placing the impalpable: Walt Whitman and Elias Hicks', in: *Modern Language Studies* 28 (1998) no.2, 69-86.

Curran, Stuart (Ed.), *The Cambridge companion to British Romanticism*, New York: Cambridge University Press, 1993.

Davies, Lloyd, 'Prenatal life and the idea of loss in Wordsworth's "Immortality Ode": Toward remembrance', in: *Journal of Evolutionary Psychology* 19 (1998) no.3-4, 262-269.

Davis, Helen Benigni, 'The cosmic solution in Walt Whitman's *Leaves of Grass*', in: *The Cloverdale Review* (1992-93), 89-100.

Dawson, P.M.S., 'Poetry in an age of revolution', in: Stuart Curran (Ed.), *The Cambridge companion to British Romanticism*, New York: Cambridge University Press, 2000, 48-73.

Delancey, Mark, 'Texts, interpretations, and Whitman's "Song of Myself"', in: *American Literature* 61 (1989) no.3, 359-381.

Deleuze, Giles, 'What is philosophy?', in: Richard Kearney & Mara Rainwater (Eds.), *The continental philosophy reader*, New York: Routledge, 1996, 404-410.

Derrida, Jacques, 'Differance', in: Richard Kearney & Mara Rainwater (Eds.), *The continental philosophy reader*, New York: Routledge, 1996, 441-464.

De Selincourt, Basil, 'The form: Constructive principles (1965)', in: Sculley Bradley & Harold W. Blodgett (Eds.), *Leaves of Grass*, New York: Norton, 1973, 821-833.

Dombrowski, Daniel, 'Wordsworth's panentheism', in: *The Wordsworth Circle* 16 (1985) no.3, 136-142.

Dombrowski, Daniel, 'Panpsychism', in: *The Wordsworth Circle* 19 (1988) no.1, 38-45.

Easterlin, Nancy, *Cosmic counterfeit: Wordsworth and the question of Romantic religion* (Diss. Temple University, Philadelphia, 1991).

Elder, Marjorie, *Nathaniel Hawthorne: Transcendental symbolist*, Athens: Ohio University Press, 1969.

Eliade, Mircea, *Shamanism: Archaic techniques of ecstasy* (trans. Willard R. Trask), Princeton: Princeton University Press, 1974 (orig. publ. 1951).

Elmessiri, Abdelwahab, *The critical writings of Wordsworth and Whitman: A study of the historical and anti-historical imaginations* (Diss. Rutgers, Camden, New Jersey, 1969).

Empson, William, 'Sense in *The Prelude*', in: Jonathan Wordsworth, M.H. Abrams, & Stephen Gill (Eds.), *The Prelude 1799, 1805, 1850: Authoritative texts, context and reception, recent critical essays*, New York: Norton, 1979, 625-641.

Engell, James, 'The soul, highest cast of consciousness', in: Beverly Taylor & Robert Bain (Eds.), *The cast of consciousness: Concepts of the mind in British and American Romanticism*, Westport, CT: Greenwood, 3-19.

Fayez, Ghulam Muhammad, *Mystic ideas and images in Jalal al-Din Rumi and Walt Whitman* (Diss. University of Arizona, Phoenix, 1978).

Ferguson, Frances, *Wordsworth: Language as counter-spirit*, New Haven: Yale University Press, 1977.

Ferlazzo, Paul, 'Dylan Thomas and Walt Whitman: Birth, death, and time', in: *Walt Whitman Review* 23 (1977), 136-141.

Ferry, David, *The limits of mortality: An essay on Wordworth's major poems*, Middletown, CT: Wesleyan University Press, 1959.

Fish, Stanley, 'Rhetoric', in: Frank Lentricchia & Thomas McLaughlin (Eds.), *Critical terms for literary study*, Chicago: University of Chicago Press, 1995, 203-222.

Ford, Arthur L., 'The rose garden of the world: Near East imagery in the poetry of Walt Whitman', in: *Walt Whitman Review* 5 (1987) no.1, 12-20.

Foucault, Michel, *Madness and civilization* (trans. Richard Howard), New York: Random House, 1965 (orig. publ. 1961).

Foucault, Michel, 'Lecture: 7 January 1976', in: K.M. Newton (Ed.), *Twentieth-century literary theory*, New York: St. Martin's, 1997, 129-134.

Freke, Timothy, & Peter Gandy, *The complete guide to world mysticism*, London: Piatkus, 1997.

Fromm, Erich, *The art of loving*, New York: Continuum, 1956.

Frye, Northrop, *The educated imagination*, Bloomington, IN: Indiana University Press, 1967.

Gallie, W.B., 'Is The Prelude a philosophical poem?', in: Jonathan Wordsworth, M.H. Abrams, & Stephen Gill (Eds.), *The Prelude 1799, 1805, 1850:*

Authoritative texts, context and reception, recent critical essays, New York: Norton, 1979, 663-678.
Garber, Frederick, 'Point of view and the egotistical sublime', in: *English Studies* 49 (1968), 409-418.
Garber, Marjorie, *Academic instincts*, Princeton: Princeton University Press, 2001.
Gatta, John, 'Whitman's re-vision of Emersonian ecstasy in "Song of Myself"', in: Joann P. Krieg, (Ed.), *Walt Whitman: Here and now*, Westport, CT: Greenwood, 173-183.
Gellert, Michael, *Modern mysticism: Jung, Zen, and the still good hand of God*, York, ME: Nicholas-Hays, 1994.
Gilbert, R.A., *The elements of mysticism*, Rockport, MA: Element, 1991.
Glimm, James, *Five essays on mystical experience in the works of Wordsworth, Coleridge, and Shelley* (Diss. University of Texas, Austin, 1968).
Gould, Keith A., 'Panentheism in "The Prelude"', in: Donna Fricke & Douglas Fricke (Eds.), *Aeolian Harps*, Bowling Green: Bowling Green University Press, 1976. 111-131.
Gravil, Richard, 'Wordsworth's ontology of love in "The Prelude"', in: *Critical Quarterly* 16 (1974), 231-249.
Gravil, Richard, '"The Discharged Soldier" and the "Runaway Slave": Wordsworth and the definition of Walt Whitman', in: *Symbiosis* 1 (1997) no.1, 48-68.
Green, Keith, & Jill LeBihan, *Critical theory and practice*, New York: Routledge, 1999.
Greene, Brian, *The elegant universe*, New York: Random House, 1999.
Grof, Stanislav, *The holotropic mind*, New York: HarperCollins, 1990.
Guest, Jenny, 'Wordsworth and the music of humanity', in: *The Critical Review* 20 (1978), 15-30.
Hafiz, *The gift* (trans. Daniel Ladinsky), New York: Penguin, 1999.
Hallisey, Joan Frances, *Walt Whitman, Hart Crane, and Denise Levertov: Poet/prophets in the tradition of Ralph Waldo Emerson* (Diss. Brown University, Providence, Rhode Island, 1978).
Happold, F.C., *Mysticism: A study and an anthology*, New York: Penguin, 1990 (orig. publ. 1963).
Hartman, Geoffrey, '"Was it for this...?": Wordsworth and the birth of the gods', in: Karen Hanson & Herbert Marks (Eds.), *Romantic revolutions*, Bloomington: Indiana University Press, 1990, 8-25.
Hartman, Geoffrey, *The unremarkable Wordsworth*, Minneapolis: University of Minnesota Press, 1989.
Hartman, Geoffrey, 'The poetics of prophesy', in: Lawrence Lipking (Ed.), *High romantic argument: Essays for M.H. Abrams*, Ithaca: Cornell University Press, 1981, 15-40.

Hartman, Geoffrey, 'Nature and the humanization of the self in Wordsworth' (1970), in: M.H. Abrams (Ed.), *English romantic poets*, New York: Oxford University Press, 1975, 123-132.

Hartman, Geoffrey, 'A poet's progress: Wordsworth and the *via naturaliter negativa*' (1962), in: Jonathan Wordsworth, M.H. Abrams, & Stephen Gill (Eds.), *The Prelude 1799, 1805, 1850: Authoritative texts, context and reception, recent critical essays*, New York: Norton, 1979, 598-612.

Hawkes, David, *Ideology*, New York: Routledge, 2000.

Heath, Duncan, & Judy Boreham, *Introducing Romanticism*, New York: Totem, 1999.

Heidegger, Martin, *Basic writings* (trans. Joan Stambaugh; ed. David Farrell Krell), New York: HarperCollins, 1993 (orig. publ. 1962).

Heitner, John, *At the edge of consciousness*, Edina, MN: Alpha, 1986.

Herman, Barbara, *The pleasure of heaven, pains of hell, intimations of immortality: Remembrance, repression, and reconciliation in Wordsworth and Whitman* (Diss. Texas Christian University, Fort Worth, Texas, 1991).

Hitchcock, John, *Healing our worldview*, West Chester, Penn: Chrysalis, 1999.

Hobbs, John, 'Theodore Roethke: The poet as mystic', in: *Studies in Mystical Literature* 3 (1983) no.1, 18-42.

Hoffman, Daniel, 'Hankering, gross, mystical, nude: Whitman's "self" and the American tradition', in: Geoffrey M. Sill (Ed.), *Walt Whitman of Mickle Street*, Knoxville: University of Tennessee Press, 1994, 1-17.

Hölderlin, Friedrich, 'On the process of the poetic mind' (trans. Ralph R. Read), in: A. Leslie Wilson (Ed.), *German Romantic criticism*, New York: Continuum, 1982, 219-237 (orig. published 1826).

Hollander, John, 'The music of silence', in: *Prose* 7 (1973), 79-91.

Hollenback, Jess Byron, *Mysticism: Experience, response, and empowerment*, University Park, PA: Penn State University Press, 1996.

Holmes, John, *William Blake's place in the mystical tradition* (Diss. Kent State University, Kent, Ohio, 1985).

Hopkins, Brooke. 'The mystical dimensions of Wordsworth's poetry', in: *Studia Mystica* 4 (1981) no.2, 49-62.

Horkheimer, Max, & Theodor Adorno, 'The concept of Enlightenment', in: Richard Kearney & Mara Rainwater (Eds.), *The Continental philosophy reader*, New York: Routledge, 1996, 199-211 (orig. published 1947).

Husserl, Edmund, 'The Vienna lecture and phenomenology', in: Richard Kearney & Mara Rainwater (Eds.), *The Continental philosophy reader*, New York: Routledge, 1996, 3-22 (orig. published 1935).

Hutchinson, George B., *The ecstatic Whitman*, Columbus, OH: Ohio State University Press, 1986.

Huxley, Aldous, *The perennial philosophy*, New York: Harper, 1944.

Huxley, Aldous, *The Doors of Perception & Heaven and Hell*, New York: Harper, 1963.

Jackson, Joe Kenneth, Wonder and defamiliarization in Wordsworth (Diss. Syracuse University, Syracuse, New York, 1978).

James, William, *The varieties of religious experience*, New York: Penguin, 1985 (orig. publ. 1902).

Jantzen, Grace M., 'Power, gender, and ecstasy: Mysticism and post/modernity', in: *Literature and Theology* 11 (1997) no.4, 385-402.

Jaspers, Karl, *Philosophy of existence*, Philadelphia: Pennsylvania University Press, 1971.

Johnson, Don, 'The grief behind the spots of time', in: *America Imago* 45 (1988) no.3, 287-307.

Kabir, *Songs of Kabir* (trans. Rabindranath Tagore), York, ME: Weiser, 1998 (orig. publ. 1915).

Kalita, Dwight, 'Walt Whitman: Ecstatic sea-voyager', in: *Walt Whitman Review* 21 (1975), 14-22.

Kaplan, Justin, *Walt Whitman: A life*, New York: Simon & Schuster, 1980.

Katz, Steven T., *Mysticism and language*, New York: Oxford University Press, 1992.

Keller, Joseph, 'The function of paradox in mystical discourse', in: *Studia Mystica* 6 (1983) no.3, 3-19.

Kelly, Erna, 'Whitman and Wordsworth: Childhood experiences and the future poet', in: *Walt Whitman Review* 23 (1977), 59-68.

Keubrich, David, 'Whitman's new theism', in: *ESQ* 24 (1978), 229-241.

Keubrich, David, *Minor prophesy: Walt Whitman's new American religion*, Indianapolis: Indiana University Press, 1989.

Khan, Hazrat Inayat, *The mysticism of sound and music*, Boston: Shambala, 1991.

Kidney, Jennifer, *An American prelude: Nostalgia and the sense of death in American poetry* (Diss. Yale, New Haven, Connecticut, 1974).

Kiefer, Daniel Reynard, *Figurations of poetic voice in Whitman and Wordsworth* (Diss. Yale University, 1985).

King, Francis, 'Love and landscape in Wordsworth', in: *The Wordsworth Circle* 18 (1987) no.1, 12-18.

King, Ursula, *Christian mystics*, New York: Simon & Schuster, 1998.

Kotoh, Tetsuaki, 'Language and silence: Self-inquiry in Heidegger and Zen', in: Graham Parkes (Ed.), *Heidegger and Asian thought*, Honolulu: University of Hawaii Press, 1990, 201-212.

Kramer, Lawrence, 'Ocean and vision: Imaginative dilemma in Wordsworth, Whitman, and Stevens', in: *Journal of English and Germanic Philology* 79 (1980), 210-230.

Laski, Marghanita, *Ecstasy in secular and religious experiences*, Los Angeles: Tarcher, 1961.

Lawrence, D.H., 'Whitman' (1921), in: Sculley Bradley & Harold W. Blodgett (Eds.), *Leaves of Grass*, New York: Norton, 1973, 842-850.

Lemay, Eric, & Jennifer Pitts, *Heidegger*, New York: Writers & Readers, 1994.

Leonard, Philip, 'Divine horizons: Levinas, Derrida, transcendence', in: idem (Ed.), *Trajectories of mysticism in theory and literature*, London: Macmillan, 2000, 219-235.

Leonard, Philip, 'Introduction', in: idem (Ed.), *Trajectories of mysticism in theory and literature*, London: Macmillan, 2000, x-xviii.

Lewitt, Fil, 'Wordless words and the evolution of poetry', in: *Kyoto Journal* 29 (1995), 143-149.

Lim, Paulino, 'Zen and Wordsworth', in: *The Wordsworth Circle* 7 (1976), 129-132.

Lindenberger, Herbert, 'Images of interaction in The Prelude' (1963), in: Jonathan Wordsworth, M.H. Abrams, & Stephen Gill (Eds.), *The Prelude 1799, 1805, 1850: Authoritative texts, context and reception, recent critical essays*, New York: Norton, 1979, 642-662.

Lovejoy, Arthur, 'On the discrimination of Romanticisms' (1948), in: M.H. Abrams (Ed.), *English romantic poets*, New York: Oxford University Press, 1975, 3-24.

Loving, Jerome, *Walt Whitman: The song of himself*, Los Angeles: University Press of California, 1999.

Mack, Stephen John, *Walt Whitman and the struggle for a pragmatic vision of spiritual democracy* (Diss. University of Southern California, Los Angeles, California, 1997).

Mahoney, John, 'Critical methodology and writing about religion and literature', in: *Religion and the Arts* 1 (1997) no.4, 89-95.

Mahoney, John L., *William Wordsworth: A poetic life*, New York: Fordham University Press, 1997.

Malone, Walter Karl, *Parallels to Hindu and Taoist thought in Walt Whitman* (Diss. Temple University, Philadelphia, Pennsylvania, 1964).

Marshall, Donald, 'Religion and literature after Enlightenment: Schleiermacher and Wordsworth', in: *Christianity and Literature* 50 (2000) no.1, 53-68.

Massey, Lance, 'Tintern Abbey's "Tranquil Restoration": Toward a methodology of healing in an age of anxiety', in: *Publications of the Missouri Philological Association* 21 (1996), 45-61.

Matthiessen, F.O., *American Renaissance*, New York: Oxford University Press, 1941.

McSweeney, Kerry, *The language of the senses: Sensory-perceptual dynamics in Wordsworth, Coleridge, Thoreau, Whitman, and Dickinson*, Buffalo: McGill-Queen's University Press, 1998.

Meher, William, 'Whitman vs. Wordsworth: The fundamental aesthetic difference', in: *Journal of American Culture* 20 (1997) no.1, 75-87.

Mehta, J.L., 'Heidegger and Vedanta: Reflections on a questionable theme', in: Graham Parkes (Ed.), *Heidegger and Asian thought*, Honolulu: Hawaii University Press, 1990, 15-46.

Meltzer, Françoise, 'Unconscious', in: Frank Lentricchia & Thomas McLaughlin (Eds.), *Critical terms for literary study*, Chicago: University of Chicago Press, 1995, 147-162.

Merleau-Ponty, Maurice, 'Preface to "Phenomenology of Perception"', in: Richard Kearney & Mara Rainwater (Eds.), *The Continental philosophy reader*, New York: Routledge, 1996, 79-93 (orig. published 1962).

Merton, Thomas, *Mystics and Zen masters*, New York: Farrar, 1967.

Merton, Thomas, *New seeds of contemplation*, New York: New Directions, 1972.

Miller, James E., *A critical guide to Leaves of Grass*, Chicago: University of Chicago Press, 1957.

Miller, James E., Karl Shapiro, & Bernice Slote, *Start with the Sun: Studies in the Whitman tradition*, Lincoln, NE: University Press of Nebraska, 1960.

Mitchell, W.J.T., 'Representation', in: Frank Lentricchia & Thomas McLaughlin (Eds.), *Critical terms for literary study*, Chicago: University of Chicago Press, 1995, 11-22.

Monroe, Robert A., *Far journeys*, New York: Doubleday, 1985.

Morris, Brian, 'Mr. Wordsworth's ear', in: *Wordsworth Circle* 10 (1979), 113-121.

Mortensen, Klaus Peter, *The time of unrememberable being: Wordsworth and the sublime, 1787-1805*, Copenhagen: Museum Tusculanum, 1998.

Neihardt, John G., *Black Elk speaks*, Lincoln, NE: University Press of Nebraska, 1979 (orig. publ. 1932).

Nichols, Ashton, 'The epiphanic trance: Why Tennyson is not a mystic', in: *Victorian Poetry* 24 (1986) no.2, 131-148.

Novalis, 'Aphorisms and fragments' (trans. Alexander Gelley), in: A. Leslie Wilson (Ed.), *German Romantic criticism*, New York: Continuum, 1982, 62-83 (orig. published 1798).

O'Donoghue, N.D., 'Mystical imagination', in: James Mackey (Ed.), *Religious imagination*, Edinburgh: Edinburgh University Press, 1986, 186-205.

Oerlemans, Onno Dag, *The dynamics of lyric and narrative in the poetry of Wordsworth and Whitman* (Diss. Yale University, New Haven, Connecticut, 1992).

O'Neil, Michael, '"Wholly incommunicable by words": Romantic expressions of the inexpressible', in: *Wordsworth Circle* 31 (2000) no.1, 13-20.

Otto, Rudolph, *Mysticism east and west*, New York: Macmillan, 1932 (orig. publ. 1926).

Palmer, Donald, *Structuralism and poststructuralism*, New York: Writers & Readers, 1999.

Parkes, Graham, 'Introduction', in: idem (Ed.), *Heidegger and Asian thought*, Honolulu: Hawaii University Press, 1990, 1-14.

Parrington, Vernon Louis, 'Afterglow of the Enlightenment', in: Sculley Bradley & Harold W. Blodgett (Eds.), *Leaves of Grass*, New York: Norton, 1973, 854-865.

Pati, Medhusudan, 'Wordsworth: An Indian view', in: Visvanath Chatterjee (Ed.), *The Romantic tradition*, Calcutta: Jadavpur University Press, 1984, 64-73.

Plato, 'The Republic', in: Allan Gilbert (Ed.), *Literary criticism: Plato to Dryden*, Detroit: Wayne State, 1962, 24-54.

Poggeler, Otto, 'West-East dialogue: Heidegger and Lau-tzu', in: Graham Parkes (Ed.), *Heidegger and Asian thought*, Honolulu: Hawaii University Press, 1987, 47-78.

Powell, Jim, *Derrida*, New York: Writers & Readers, 1997.

Powers, Luke A., 'The poem "That Print Cannot Touch": Interweavings in the poetry of Walt Whitman and William Blake', in: *The Cloverdale Review* (1992-93), 50-62.

Purkis, John, *A preface to Wordsworth*, New York: Longman, 1970.

Restak, Richard, *The brain*, New York: Bantam, 1984.

Reynolds, David S., *Walt Whitman's America: A cultural biography*, New York: Vintage, 1996.

Richter, Jean Paul Friedrich, 'School for Aesthetics' (trans. Margaret R. Hale), in: A. Leslie Wilson (Ed.), *German Romantic criticism*, New York: Continuum, 1982, 31-61 (orig. published 1813).

Robinson, David, 'Transcendentalism and its times', in: Joel Laporte & Saundra Morris (Eds.), *The Cambridge companion to Ralph Waldo Emerson*, New York: Cambridge University Press, 1999, 13-26.

Roche, John, 'Democratic space: The ecstatic geography of Walt Whitman and Frank Lloyd Wright', in: *Walt Whitman Quarterly Review* 6 (1988) no.1, 16-32.

Rogers, David, 'God and pre-existence in Wordsworth's immortality ode', in: *Durham University Journal* 30 (1969), 143-146.

Ross, Robert, *The ecstatic eye: Wordsworth and eighteenth-century modes of seeing* (Diss. Cornell University, Ithaca, New York, 1969).

Rudy, John G., *Wordsworth and the Zen mind: The poetry of self-emptying*, Albany: SUNY, 1996.

Rule, Philip, 'The gendered imagination in religion and literature', in: John Mahoney (Ed.), *Seeing into the life of things: Essays on literature and religious experience*, New York: Fordham University Press, 1998, 59-72.

Saintsbury, George, 'Leaves of Grass' (1874), in: Sculley Bradley & Harold W. Blodgett (Eds.), *Leaves of Grass*, New York: Norton, 1973, 782-789.

Salvesen, Christopher, 'Aspects of the Romantic sublime', in: *Charles Lamb Bulletin* 50 (1985), 37-51.

Sampson, David, 'Wordsworth and the "Deficiencies of Language"', in: *ELH: A Journal of English Literary History* 51 (1984) no.1, 53-68.
Schimmel, Annemarie, *The mystical dimensions of Islam*, Chapel Hill, NC: University of North Carolina, 1975.
Sharma, Brahma Dutt, 'The echoes of the Bhagavadgita in R.W. Emerson, in: T.R. Sharma (Ed.), *Influence of Bhagavadgita on literature written in English*, Meerut, India: Shalabh, 1988, 49-60.
Shklovsky, Victor, 'Art as technique', in: K.M. Newton (Ed.), *Twentieth-century literary theory*, New York: St. Martin's, 1997, 3-6, (orig. published 1965).
Showalter, Elaine. 'Towards a feminist poetics' (1979), in: K.M. Newton (Ed.), *Twentieth-century literary theory*, New York: St. Martin's, 1997, 216-220.
Simon, Gary, 'Craft, theory and the artist's milieu: The myth-maker and Wordsworth', in: *Walt Whitman Review* 22 (1976), 58-66.
Simpson, David, 'Romanticism, criticism, and theory', in: Stuart Curran (Ed.), *The Cambridge companion to British Romanticism*, New York: Cambridge University Press, 2000, 1-24.
Smith, Huston, *The world's religions*, San Francisco: Harper, 1991.
Sowder, Michael, 'Walt Whitman, the apostle', in: *Walt Whitman Quarterly Review* 16 (1999) no.3-4, 202-210.
Spencer, Michael D., 'Mysticism in T.S. Eliot's four quartets', in: *Studies in Spirituality* 9 (1999), 230-266.
Sperry, Stuart, 'Wordsworth and the grounds of human consciousness', in: Beverly Taylor & Robert Bain (Eds.), *The cast of consciousness: Concepts of the mind in British and American Romanticism*, Westport, CT: Greenwood, 1987, 59-76.
Stambaugh, Joan, 'Heidegger, Taoism, and the Question of Metaphysics', in: Graham Parkes (Ed.), *Heidegger and Asian thought*, Honolulu: Hawaii University Press, 1987, 79-92.
Stannard, Russell (Ed.), *God for the 21st century*, Philadelphia: Templeton, 2000.
Stein, William, 'Emerson's "History": The rhetoric of cosmic consciousness', in: *ESQ* 69 (1972), 199-206.
Stovall, Floyd, *The foreground of Leaves of Grass*, Charlottesville: University Press of Virginia, 1974.
Strathern, Paul, *Hegel*, Chicago: Dee, 1997.
Strathern, Paul, *Derrida*, Chicago: Dee, 2000.
Suzuki, D.T., *Swedenborg: Buddha of the North* (trans. Andrew Bernstein), West Chester, PA: Swedenborg Foundation, 1996.
Takeichi, Akihiro, 'On the origin of Nihilism: In view of the problem of technology and karma', in: Graham Parkes (Ed.), *Heidegger and Asian thought*, Honolulu: Hawaii University Press, 1990, 175-186.
Tao Te Ching (trans. Richard Wilhelm), New York: Penguin, 1990.

Taylor, Dennis, 'The need for a religious literary criticism', in: John L. Mahoney (Ed.), *Seeing into the life of things*, New York: Fordham University Press, 1998, 3-30.

Teasdale, Wayne, *The mystic heart*, Novato, CA: New World, 1999.

Terrell, Carroll, 'The reenchantment of the word', in: *Rendezvous* 22 (1986) no.1, 65-73.

Thomas, M. Wynn, *The lunar light of Whitman's poetry*, Cambridge: Harvard University Press, 1987.

Thorsley, Peter, 'German romantic idealism', in: Stuart Curran (Ed.), *The Cambridge companion to British Romanticism*, New York: Cambridge University Press, 2000, 74-94.

Trachtenberg, Alan, 'Whitman's visionary politics', in: Geoffrey M. Sill (Ed.), *Walt Whitman of Mickle Street*, Knoxville: University of Tennessee Press, 1994, 94-108.

Trilling, Lionel, 'The immortality ode' (1942), in: M.H. Abrams (Ed.), *English romantic poets*, New York: Oxford University Press, 1975, 149-169.

Trott, Nicola Zoe, 'Wordsworth, Milton and the inward light', in: Lisa Low & Anthony John Harding (Eds.), *Milton, the Metaphysicals, and Romanticism*, New York: Cambridge University Press, 1994, 114-135.

Tseng, Ming-yu, 'Symbolic discourse: Mystical writing as anti-language', in: *Language and Literature* 6 (1997) no.3, 181-195.

Tufariello, Catherine, 'The remembering wine: Emerson's influence on Whitman and Dickinson', in: Joel Laporte & Saundra Morris (Eds.), *The Cambridge companion to Ralph Waldo Emerson*, New York: Cambridge University Press, 1999, 162-191.

Twitchell, James B., *Romantic horizons: Aspects of the sublime in English poetry and painting, 1770-1850*, Columbia: University of Missouri Press, 1983.

Tyson, Lois, *Critical theory today*, New York: Garland, 1999.

Underhill, Evelyn, *Mysticism: The nature and development of spiritual consciousness*, Oxford: Oneworld, 1994 (orig. publ. 1911).

The Upanishads (trans. Juan Mascaro), New York: Penguin, 1965.

Waldoff, Leon, 'Wordsworth's healing power: Basic trust in "Tintern Abbey"', in: *University of Hartford Studies in Literature* 4 (1972), 147-166.

Wankhade, Manohar Namdeo, *Walt Whitman and Tantrism: A comparative study* (Diss. University of Florida, Gainesville, Florida, 1965).

Wedd, Mary R., 'Wordsworth's "Spots of Time"', in: *Literature and Belief* 10 (1990), 43-65.

Wedd, Mary, 'The conjunction of the matter-of-fact and the visionary in the 1805 Prelude', in: *Charles Lamb Bulletin* 104 (1998), 159-172.

Weisbuch, Robert, *Atlantic double-cross: American literature and British influence in the age of Emerson*, Chicago: University of Chicago Press, 1986.

Welty, Ward Paul, *Walt Whitman, Kosmos: A study of the Persona of 'Song of Myself'* (Diss. Drake University, Des Moines, Iowa, 1980).
Whitman, Walt, *Leaves of Grass: The first (1855) edition* (Ed. Malcolm Cowley), New York: Viking, 1959.
Whitman, Walt, *Leaves of Grass* (Ed. Sculley Bradley & Harold W. Blodgett), New York: Norton, 1973.
Whitman, Walt, *Specimen Days & Collect*, New York: Dover, 1995 (orig. publ. 1883).
Wilber, Ken (Ed.), *Quantum questions: Mystical writings of the world's greatest physicists*, Boston: Shambhala, 2001.
Willey, Basil, 'On Wordsworth and the Locke tradition, in: M.H. Abrams (Ed.), *English romantic poets*, New York: Oxford University Press, 1975, 112-122.
Wilson, Harry, *Psychological projection in six Romantic poems* (Diss. University of California, Davis, CA, 1976).
Wilson, Norma, 'Heartbeat: Within the visionary tradition', in: Geoffrey M. Sill (Ed.), *Walt Whitman of Mickle Street*, Knoxville: University of Tennessee Press, 1994, 224-235.
Wimsatt, W.K., 'The structure of Romantic nature imagery' (1954), in: M.H. Abrams (Ed.), *English romantic poets*, New York: Oxford University Press, 1975, 25-36.
Winchell, James, 'Semantics of the unspeakable: Six sentences by Simone Weil', in: Philip Leonard (Ed.), *Trajectories of mysticism in theory and literature*, London: Macmillan, 2000, 72-93.
Wolosky, Shira, 'The metaphysics of language in Emily Dickinson', in: Philip Leonard (Ed.), *Trajectories of mysticism in theory and literature*, London: Macmillan, 2000, 25-44.
Wordsworth, Jonathan, M.H. Abrams, & Stephen Gill (Eds.), *The Prelude 1799, 1805, 1850: authoritative texts, context and reception, recent critical essays*, New York: Norton, 1979.
Wordsworth, William, *Selected poems* (Ed. John O. Hayden), New York: Penguin, 1994.
Wordsworth, William, *Selected poetry of William Wordsworth* (Ed. Mark Van Doren), New York: Modern Library, 2002.
Wordsworth, William, *The Prelude 1799, 1805, 1850: Authoritative texts, context and reception, recent critical essays* (Ed. Jonathan Wordsworth, M.H. Abrams, and Stephen Gill), New York: Norton, 1979.
Wu, Qian-zhi, *The Wordsworthian imagination: Seeing nature as it is. A Taoist reading of Wordsworth* (Diss. Cornell University, Ithaca, New York, 1988).
Yoshizaki, Kuniko, 'The Oriental sources of Walt Whitman', in: *Kyushu American Literature* 20 (1979), 14-20.
Zohar, Danah, *The quantum self*, New York: Quill, 1990.

Zukav, Gary, *The dancing Wu Li masters*, New York: HarperCollins, 2001 (orig. publ. 1979).

PRINTED ON PERMANENT PAPER • IMPRIME SUR PAPIER PERMANENT • GEDRUKT OP DUURZAAM PAPIER - ISO 9706
N.V. PEETERS S.A., WAROTSTRAAT 50, B-3020 HERENT